SoulMates

SOUL MATES

Honoring the Mysteries

of Love and Relationship

Thomas Moore

HarperCollins*Publishers*

Grateful acknowledgment is made for permission to reproduce the following material: Excerpts from "The Kama Sutra of Kindness" from *Dear Dance of Eros* by Mary Mackey. Copyright © 1987 by Mary Mackey. Reprinted by permission of the author. "The Wild Horse" by Rabi'ah bent Ka'b from *The Drunken Universe*, translated by Peter Lamborn Wilson and Nasrollah Pourjavady. Copyright © 1987 by Peter Lamborn Wilson and Nasrollah Pourjavady. Reprinted by permission of Phanes Press. Poem number 303 from *The Poems of Emily Dickinson*, Thomas H. Johnson, editor, Cambridge, Mass.: The Belknap Press of Harvard University Press, Copyright © 1951, 1955, 1979, 1983 by the President and Fellows of Harvard College. Reprinted by permission of the publishers and the Trustees of Amherst College.

HarperCollins books may be purchased for educational, business, or sales promotional use. For information please write International Sales Department, HarperCollins Publishers, 10 East 53rd Street, New York, NY 10022.

FIRST INTERNATIONAL EDITION

Designed by David Bullen
Typeset by Wilsted & Taylor
ISBN 0-06-092496-9

94 95 96 97 RRD 10 9 8 7 6 5 4 3 2 1

Contents

CONTENTS

Shadows of Intimacy

Pleasures of Soul Mates

Preface

*T*HE ONLY thing as challenging as getting tangled in the underbrush of relationship is trying to write about it. My own experiences with relationship, the good and the bad, weigh heavy as I try to write for others. And so I write in faith, focusing on the soul, without many judgments and without prescriptions for success. I present relationship here not as a psychological problem or issue, but as a mystery in the religious and theological sense, knowing that it is always a mistake to talk authoritatively about mysteries.

I'm also aware that I write as a white, male, heterosexual American with a classical European education, and that many who will read these words do not share that background. While writing, I've tried to maintain some consciousness of these potential differences, but to do so at every turn is to become so self-conscious and contorted as to lose touch with my own experience, which is an important source of my reflections. So I ask the reader to allow me to speak from my own context. I hope that what I say from my experience will apply, with reservations and sometimes with substantive changes, to various other arrangements and other cultural and educational backgrounds.

I might give a small warning at the start about my methods and purposes here. It's my conviction that slight shifts in imagination have more impact on living than major efforts at change. I will try very hard to offer some key shifts in ways of imagining relationship, but I won't give many concrete, direct suggestions of what to do, because of my conviction that deep changes in life follow movements in imagination. The very idea of soul underscores the importance of being individuals, and every relationship calls for a unique response. The point of this book is to free ourselves of longstanding and rigid ideas and images of what it means to love, to be married, to be a friend, or to live in community.

I also speak here about religion and spirituality. In case there is any doubt, I am not advocating any particular church, tradition, practice, or teaching. The Renaissance theologians, my primary teachers, advocated "natural religion"—not in the eighteenth-century sense of a rational religion, but as a sensitivity to the sacred in everyday life. Relationships, I believe, are truly sacred, not in the superficial meaning of simply being high in value, but in that they call upon infinite and mysterious depths in ourselves, in our communities, and in the very nature of things.

This book follows my previous book, *Care of the Soul*, and it develops ideas expressed many times in that book: The soul has a strong desire and need for intimacy, and it loves vernacular life—the particular place, family, friends, and neighborhood that are part of our daily lives. The soul doesn't thrive on grand schemes of salvation or on smooth, uncluttered principles, nor does it thrive on theories and creeds, and so I don't offer a way out of the inevitable messes relationships bring, or present yet another theory about how relationships work or should work. Soul does love imagination, though, and so my emphasis throughout this book is on deepening and enriching our imagination.

Although the book is called *Soul Mates*, it takes that notion broadly, to include the soul in all kinds of relationships. A soulful connection can be found in families, on the job, in the neighborhood, with colleagues, and among friends, among longstanding acquaintances and in fleeting encounters, in socially sanctioned matings and in murky rendezvous. This book extends the idea of soul mate in order to suggest ways of being in any relationship soulfully, and it also celebrates those rare and profoundly satisfying bonds we feel with certain people who in the strictest sense are soul mates.

I'd like to acknowledge the help of a few people who have taught me about relationship and soul, and have made special contributions to this book: in Dallas, Pat Toomay; in the Berkshires, Christopher Bamford and Laura Chester; in Florence, Carmelo Mezzasalma and his students; in Brussels, Léonard Appel and Marie Milis; in London, Noel Cobb and Eva Loewe; in Chicago, Ben Sells; in Michigan, the many aunts, uncles, and cousins of a warm and always supportive family, my brother Jim and his family, and my parents. I also want to acknowledge the extraordinary wisdom and generous friendship of my editor at HarperCollins, Hugh Van Dusen, as well as the friendly and effective support of William Shinker, the publisher of HarperCollins trade books. I have been gifted with an agent of exceptional intuition, insight, and capacity for mating souls and guiding books to the light of day, Michael Katz. I have also been graced to have a fine poet as an editor, Jane Hirshfield, who elicits potential poetry and elusive clarity from my occasionally rough thoughts. Finally, I ask a blessing on this book from my true soul mate, Joan Hanley, to whom, with Abraham and Siobhán, this book is dedicated.

Introduction

THE HEART has its own reasons. When we try to understand why relationships come into being and fall apart, why some families are nurturing and others devastating, why some friendships endure long absences and bitter arguments while others fade, we come face to face with the unknown core of the human heart. Of course, we spend a great deal of time coming up with all kinds of explanations for unexpected turns in emotion and feeling, but these "reasons" are more rationalizations and simplifications than understanding. We are left with Plato's solution, that relationship is based on a form of madness, erotic madness. Rather than finding solutions for understanding and controlling this heart, we may have no recourse but to honor its mysteries.

The heart is a mystery—not a puzzle that can't be solved, but a mystery in the religious sense: unfathomable, beyond manipulation, showing traces of the finger of God at work. Like the resurrection of Jesus or the mission of Moses, the angelic visitation to Mohammed or the enlightenment of the Buddha, the heart has its own mysteries every bit as profound as the mysteries we encounter in the religions of the world. Everything associated with the heart—relationship, emotion, passion—can only be grasped and appreciated with the tools of religion and poetry.

Yet, in our time we have tried to apply to the heart the same kind of mechanical and structural thinking that has made an astounding technological world. We regard marriages and families and speak of systems, we analyze whole societies according to grids and charts, and we try to help people "relate" to each other by organizing groups and developing exercises for communication and intimacy.

When we focus our attention on the *soul* of relationship, instead of on its interpersonal mechanics, a different set of values comes to the foreground. We are now interested in fantasy and imagination. We begin to see relationship as the place where soul works out its destiny. We are not so concerned with how to make relationship "work," because the soul point of view isn't ambitious in that way. It doesn't make love a life project. Instead, it recognizes the truth in a line from John Donne, that great poet of soul and relationship: "Love's mysteries in soules doe grow."

Concerned about the soul, we don't ask *why* something has happened in a relationship, or *how* to make it better. Rather, we wonder about the soul's own purposes: "What is happening in the soul when we fall madly in love? What is the soul wanting in its fantasies of separation? What is this longing for deeper love, and why does it never seem to be satisfied?" With our focus on the soul, we won't feel the impossible burden of "doing" relationship right, as though we had full control over the intimacies that develop between people, and so we need not become so discouraged as we make our way through our emotional dilemmas. Instead, we may live through the mystery of endings, crises, and turning points in love, marriage, friendship, and family, and submit to the life that is always germinating in them.

In the modern world we also tend to see everything as if it were a machine, including our most precious relationships. Notice how quickly the metaphors of computer language have infiltrated everyday speech, how nonchalantly people say they are "programmed" to act the way they do. As a result of this kind of mechanization in our thinking, we've lost an appreciation for the mysterious factors that bring people together and force them apart. In the face of difficulties that have profound roots, we bring to relationship a fix-it attitude, assuming that all failures need to be corrected. When our focus is on the surfaces of life, we seek out mechanical causes and solutions to problems, but if our attention were on the soul, we would explore instead its dreams and fantasies, its own unpredictable intentions.

Jung pointed out that even though we experience the soul intimately, still it has an objective quality. We can look at soul without identifying with it. If I ask, What is wrong with me that I can't have a long-lasting relationship? the question borders on narcissism—the focus is on "me." To get to the soul, we might direct our questions more outward: "What does fate want in its demands on me? What is the meaning of this continuing failure to find love? What am I made of that my heart moves in directions different from my intentions?" This shift from self-reflexive, narcissistic questions to a more open, objective point of view is in itself a fundamental move toward soul.

The soul is a wide, spacious area in which fate plays a great role, and in which family, society, and history—personal and cultural—are major influences. Much of this material is beyond an individual's power either to invent or to control. As the Greek mystical philosopher Heraclitus taught, "The soul is its own source of unfolding." It has its own reasons, which may be only dimly apparent to consciousness. If we want to see the soul in a relationship, we have to look beyond our intentions and expectations.

Another advantage of regarding relationships from the soul's viewpoint is that it offers us a more tolerant attitude toward the down side, the shadows and gaps that will inevitably present themselves at times. Ordinarily we assume that a relationship should be smooth and complete, and when trouble arrives, we think the relationship itself is open to doubt. But matters of soul lie beyond simple judgments of good and bad, or smooth and rough. In initiation rites around the world, the neophyte is profoundly stirred by some kind of pain, perhaps from ritual incisions or sleeplessness and fasting, and out of that experience a new level of awareness dawns. Religion recognizes pain and failure as important in the soul's deepening and sophistication. We can apply this insight to relationships as well: pain and difficulty can sometimes serve as the pathway to a new level of involvement. They do not necessarily mean that there is something inherently wrong with the relationship; on the contrary, relationship troubles may be a challenging initiation into intimacy.

When we look at the soul of relationship, we may find positive value in failures, endings, complexities, doubts, distancing, the desire for separation and freedom, and other troubling aspects. We can see these as initiatory opportunities rather than simply as threats. Soul often hides in the darkest corners, in the very places we would rather avoid, and in the very problems that tempt us into disillusionment; and so, we have to be intrepid when we look for it in our lives.

Yet another special quality of soul is the way that it expresses itself in enigmatic images. The soul lives in the realm of imagination, and influences the direction and quality of life through a kind of poetics, a language of image and symbol. When a couple comes to me for therapy, I usually ask one to sit quietly and listen as the other talks to us about her memories, her dreams, her fantasies and images of her life, and of marriage and intimacy, sex and closeness. In this way we glimpse the soul, which is really the deep seat of relationship, and which would be ignored if we emphasized instead only the mechanics of communication and interaction.

Although I always recommend that we take time simply to observe, to look at relationship with tolerance and a quiet mind until we begin to see the deeper layers of soul, this does not mean that we should not "work on" our relationships. There is a place for such work, especially if we understand work alchemically rather than heroically. Just as the alchemist watches the processes of nature so that he or she can play an artful role in them, so we can enter the deep processes of a relationship by closely observing its chemistries. This kind of work, however, is ninety percent observation and ten percent action. As we watch the soul without heroic interventions, our attitudes may change, allowing alchemical transformations to take place on their own accord—changes in the coloring of our moods, the weight of our thoughts, and the textures of our feelings.

Soul-centered effort on behalf of relationship has yet another quality that makes it different from more familiar modern schools of love and intimacy: the soul is not dedicated to perfection. Work with the soul is not at all aimed at achieving an unblemished, unruffled relationship; on the contrary, it has an appreciation for human limitation and folly. The alchemical view of the soul's progress makes room for the putrefaction of decay, and *melanosis*, or blackening—shadow aspects highly valued in traditional alchemy. Relationships have a way of rubbing our noses in the slime of life—an experience we would rather forego, but one that offers an important exposure to our own depth.

One of the aims of this book is to sketch out a handbook for ensouling our most ordinary and our most treasured relationships. At times, this unusual primer of intimacy may contradict the assumptions and values of a more sociological or psychological approach, but that is the way of the soul—at times it seems to be at odds with the desires and rules of surface life. When we devote ourselves to soul, other attachments may have to be loosened, and when we grant soul its own intentionality and purposes, we may have to ease our attachment to long-held values and expectations.

The ways of the soul are filled with paradox. One day we are sad about losing a job, and a year later we see that this loss was the best thing that ever happened to us. We wish we could feel more at ease in a marriage, but years later we realize that this discomfort was urging us to move on to something much more deeply satisfying.

If we are going to look with respect at the soul in relationship, we may have to change our views on many central issues, including our ideas of morality. For morality certainly enters into our relationships and must be both subtle and deeply rooted if it is to be adequate to the demanding paradoxes of the soul. We may also have to change our ideas about goals in a relationship. For the soul, it isn't enough to endure just for the sake of enduring. Everyone knows that a relationship can go on for years after its soul has disappeared. In order to care for the soul, it may be important to honor endings and radical changes. Ideas about togetherness and separateness within a relationship may also shift as the years go by.

Working on the soul of a relationship requires, in addition to sensitive observation, certain "technologies of intimacy." In this book I want to examine in particular the ways we establish closeness and maintain attachment. These technologies I propose here may seem extremely simple, but they are also fragile. For example, letter-writing and conversation are common ways to tend relationships; still, doing them well calls for care and thoughtfulness. Fortunately, attention to soul is not a new idea. We have centuries of experience and development behind us, and many sources in which we can find guidance. At certain times in our history, writing letters and engaging in conversation were carefully studied arts. Obviously, one can become trite and precious about such things, but it is useful to consider, in the light of past masters of these technologies, ways of talking and writing to each other that foster soulfulness. This examination might be especially important in our own day when communication is technologically sophisticated and speedy, but not necessarily more soulful.

Technologies of the soul tend to be simple, bodily, slow, and related to the heart as much as the mind. Everything around us tells us we should be mechanically sophisticated, electronic, quick, and informational in our expressiveness—an exact antipode to the virtues of the soul. It is no wonder, then, that in an age of telecommunications—which, by the way, literally means "distant connections"—we suffer symptoms of the loss of soul. We are being urged from every side to become efficient rather than intimate.

A soul mate is someone to whom we feel profoundly connected, as though the communicating and communing that take place between us were not the product of intentional efforts, but rather a divine grace. This kind of relationship is so important to the soul that many have said there is nothing more precious in life. We may find a soul partner in many different forms of relationship—in friendship, marriage, work, play, and family. It is a rare form of intimacy, but is not limited to one person or to one form.

This book is a manual for fostering many kinds of soulful relationships, first by becoming aware of the nature of the soul, and especially its role in intimacy, and then by discovering concrete ways in which such relationships can be tended. All of our relationships can have soul, not only those that are specifically in the soul mate category.

If it seems strange to talk about soul in relation to intimacy, that perception is only a sign of the times. It was once a matter of course for specialists in the soul to explore minutely the nature of such relationships. One reason why we have so much trouble with relationship today may be our neglect of its study. We expect to find intimacy naturally, without education or initiation. When we fail in this area, we assume that we must have some inborn lack. But the fact is, we can do nothing well in life, and that includes intimacy, unless we have the schooled imagination for it.

When I call this book a "manual," therefore, I mean that word literally. It tells how to "handle" something, how to take it into "hand." Or you can think of it as akin to a book of style, a little volume that tells you how to write well and expressively. It intends to offer some reflection on how to talk intimately, how to nurture friendships, and how to deepen marriage; how to write letters that waken souls, and how to care for another person in a way that stirs the soul's affection.

I don't pretend to know all these things, and certainly I don't claim to do them all well myself. In fact, certain things I write about I know first hand from outrageous failures and follies of my own. I do have a strong feeling for our traditions, which over centuries of discussion and experimentation have refined these special skills and attitudes, and I have a strong desire in all my work to be a translator for these traditions, rephrasing these antique writings about soulful style so that they speak to us directly today.

As you read, think about all of your relationships, past and present. Think about family ties and alienations. Think about old loves and present affections. Think about hopes and dreams, and don't overlook the disasters and tragedies. Think about all of these in relation to your soul. Try to avoid familiar judgments about them. Above all, try to wash away some of the narcissism that makes you think more about your own success and failure rather than the large mysteries held in these tales and memories.

Take up this book not as a collection of specific suggestions, but as a guide for meditation. The only thing keeping you from deep, satisfying, soulful relationships is your imagination. Is it rich enough? Is it too pragmatic, too modern, too plain? Allow this reading to give your thoughts about relationship branches, shoots, and blossoms. The more fertile your imagination about intimacy, the more likely you will be to find this alchemical gold in your heart.

THE SOUL
IN LOVE

The Soul selects her own Society—
Then—shuts the Door—
To her divine Majority—
Present no more—

Unmoved—she notes the Chariots—pausing—
At her low Gate—
Unmoved—an Emperor be kneeling
Upon her Mat—

I've known her—from an ample nation—
Choose One—
Then—close the Valves of her attention—
Like Stone—

EMILY DICKINSON

Chapter One

ATTACHMENT AND FLIGHT

WHEN WE consider the soul of relationship, unexpected factors come into view. In its deepest nature, for example, the soul involves itself in the stuff of this world, both people and objects. It loves attachments of all kinds—to places, ideas, times, historical figures and periods, things, words, sounds, and settings—and if we are going to examine relationship in the soul, we have to take into account the wide range of its loves and inclinations. Yet even though the soul sinks luxuriantly into its attachments, something in it also moves in a different direction. Something valid and necessary takes flight when it senses deep attachment, and this flight also seems so deeply rooted as to be an honest expression of soul. Our ultimate goal is to find ways to embrace both attachment and resistance to attachment, and the only way to that reconciliation of opposites is to dig deeply into the nature of each. As with all matters of soul, it is in honoring its impulses that we find our way best into its mysteries.

Attachment

THE SOUL manifests its innate tendency toward attachment in many ways. One way is a penchant for the past and a resistance to change. A particularly soulful person might turn down a good job offer, for example, because he doesn't want to move from his home town. The soulfulness of this decision is fairly clear: ties to friends, family, buildings, and a familiar landscape come from the heart, and honoring them may be more important for a soulful life than following exciting ideas and possibilities that are rooted in some other part of our nature.

A radically attached person may lead a sedate life because he seldom likes to leave home; he may even decide not to buy an automobile for that very reason. Many writers and artists have exhibited this soulful orientation away from worldly activity. Emily Dickinson, for example, spent her entire mature life at her family's homestead in Amherst, Massachusetts. In a letter of 1851 to her brother Austin she wrote, "Home is a holy thing— nothing of doubt or distrust can enter its blessed portals. . . . Here seems indeed to be a bit of Eden which not the sin of any can utterly destroy."[1] Samuel Beckett was notorious for his love of his sparse apartment and for his resistance to the world. "All I want to do," he once said early in his career, "is sit on my ass and fart and think of Dante."[2]

C. G. Jung said that the soul itself is fundamentally oriented toward life—the soul, he said, is the archetype of life—while the search for meaning or the quest for higher consciousness has some other root. The soul finds its home in the ordinary details of everyday life and does not in itself have an urgent need for understanding or achievement. James Hillman, Jung's unorthodox follower, picks up on Jung's distinction between soul and spirit, saying that soul resides in the valleys of life and not on the peaks of intellectual, spiritual, or technological efforts. In his essay on this theme, "Peaks and Vales," Hillman writes that the soul is the psyche's actual life, including "the present mess it is in, its discontent, dishonesties, and thrilling illusions."[3] Something in us—tradition calls it spirit[4]—wants to transcend these messy conditions of actual life to find some blissful or at least brighter experience, or an expression of meaning that will take us away intellectually from the quagmire of actual existence. When the soul does rise above the conditions of ordinary life into meaning and healing, it hovers closely and floats; it doesn't soar. Its mode of reflection is reverie rather than intellectual analysis, and its process of healing takes place amid the everyday flux of mood, the ups and downs of emotions, and the certain knowledge that there is no ultimate healing: death is an eternal presence for the soul.

By definition, the soul is attached to life in all its particulars. It prefers relatedness to distancing. From the point of view of the soul, meaningfulness and value rise directly out of experience, or from the images and memories that issue modestly and immediately out of ordinary life. The soul's intelligence may not arrive through rational analysis but through a long period of rumination, and its goal may not be brilliant understanding and unassailable truth, but rather profound insight and abiding wisdom.

This penchant of the soul for the complications of life plays a role in personal relationships, our ultimate theme in this book. Relatedness means staying in life, even when it becomes complicated and when meaning and clarity are elusive. It means living with the particular individuals who come into our lives, and not only with our ideals and images of the perfect mate or the perfect family. On the other hand, honoring the particular in our lives also means making the separations, divorces, and endings that the soul requires. The soul is always attached to what is actually happening, not necessarily to what could be or will be.

Dreams, which have much to teach us about the nature of the soul, sometimes portray our many ways of being attached to the past. They may take us back to places we once visited or where we lived long ago. A dreamer may begin telling his dream by saying,

"I was in the bedroom of the house where I grew up, and some of my favorite dolls were gathered around me." People will sometimes say, "I've tried to put this divorce behind me, but in spite of my wishes I find myself dreaming of my former husband." The soul is inclined toward the past rather than the future, toward attachment to people, places, and events rather than detachment, and so it is not quick to move on. In outer life, we may leave a person or a place, but in memory and dream the soul clings to these former attachments.

Care of the soul requires that we respect these apparently natural, if paradoxical, tendencies. If our dreams keep us attached to people we'd rather let go of, then we could take the lead of these dreams and ease up on our spirited desire for change, giving a place to our sometimes painful and disturbing memories. If we run singlemindedly counter to these attachments, then we are in danger of losing a degree of soulfulness. Liberation acquired at the cost of soul's desire may prove to be a questionable achievement.

Rather than come up with new understandings and new and improved ways of doing things, the soul prefers to get what it can gradually, taking its nourishment from what already is present. Like a cow chewing its cud, like grapes slowly fermenting into wine, like tobacco ripening into flavor, the past gives the soul its fodder, its stuff, the source of its particular kind of understanding and progress. Insight and change blossom from the soul like a flower coming into bloom after a long period of incubation. The soul's fertility is slow and organic, in comparison to the more spirited ways in which we pursue insight and transformation. Ralph Waldo Emerson said that the soul does not advance in a straight line, but by an "ascension of state," like the movement "from egg to worm to fly."

Soul-work, therefore, demands patience and loyalty, virtues not in vogue in our fast-changing times. The soul asks that we *live through* our attachments, rather than try to make swift, clean breaks. It may seem wise, at the end of a divorce or when we've been fired from a job, to "get the past behind us" and "start a new life." But the soul may need more reflection on that painful past, and there may be untouched fertile material in past events. Anyway, the soul may keep us tied to yesterday's traumas through tenacious memories and recurring dreams.

I myself have had a recurring dream for about fifteen years now that I think touches on our theme. I'm usually in an airplane, sometimes a jumbo jet, sometimes a small two-seater. The plane has trouble taking off or achieving altitude. Once, the plane was on busy State Street in Chicago, in the middle of a traffic jam, and had trouble getting into the air because there wasn't enough "runway." Another time, the plane was filled with passengers and was flying over a city. More accurately, it was flying *through* a city, trying to find its way through the tall skyscrapers, which towered higher than the plane could fly. In the most recent version, I was being ferried across the country by the pilot of a small single-engine plane, but on the last leg of the trip, the last ten miles or so, unable to get into the air, the plane was taxiing along on a highway in the direction of the airport. I, the dreamer, was angry at the pilot for not being able to fly better.

These dreams could be seen negatively as a failure of spirit, adventure, or imagination—some kind of inability to get up and take off. On the other hand, especially for a high-flying, ungrounded person like me, they can also be seen as a useful wounding of my typical airy spirit, a way of forcing me to become more attached to earth. Often we are healed by interference with our strengths and proven abilities. My anger at the pilot in the last dream is a further hint that consciously I don't understand the point of keeping the plane on the ground. I might even see the writing of this book on finding soul in relationship as a reflection of my dream, as a way for me to get grounded by meditating on difficult lessons in attachment.

It is possible to see our complaints about feeling stuck, or of

7

not being able to get past the latest trauma, as the work of the soul *binding* us to our given existence. We tend to suffer soul's movements and feel its inferiority. It doesn't propel, like spirit; rather, it feels the impact of events. It is easily stung and disturbed. The spirited side enjoys power, strength, well-being, and superiority. The soul, given to the pleasures of actual earthly existence, suffers its intimacies, to the extent that attachment often feels like bondage. Parents may like the emotional closeness they feel with their children, but they are also, sometimes frustratingly, *tied to* them. We may go to great extremes in order to have a solid romantic relationship with another person, but then we are also caught in an emotional bond and may begin to feel a contrary desire for freedom to relate to others.

Again, because we live in a world that prizes freedom, uncomfortable feelings of bondage could be seen as an invitation to deeper attachment. A psychological symptom always points in the direction of both what the soul needs and what we are defending against.[5] Our discomfort may come in part from our resistance. If we feel negative about attachment and about being tied to the past, to our lives, and to our own particular fate, then we probably haven't refined our ways of being attached. They may need education and instruction so that they can be more subtle and better articulated and realized.

The emotion of melancholy sometimes accompanies attachment. For centuries, melancholy has been seen as a characteristic mood of the soul. Again, from our devotion to more spirited feelings such as joy and excitement, we may undervalue this emotion and may even try to find ways of banishing it. Alternatively, however, we might sense the downward tug of melancholy as appropriate to the soul that resides in the valleys of experience. Melancholy is a toning down of the upward rush of emotion, and therefore it may feel uncomfortable, or even like a disease, but from the soul point of view, it is simply the motion of settling down into the folds of actual life. The past, too, often lies shrouded in a cloud of melancholy, an emotion that is appropriate to memory as the musty odor of decay is to old furniture and buildings. We may not like the smell and patina of an antique, but without them a precious old object would seem incomplete and maybe even false. So it is with melancholy: we can learn to appreciate it as an emotional mustiness that signals the presence of soul.

Attachment, of course, is not always problematic. There may be profound pleasure in longing for the past and in indulging in memories. When the soul stirs in us, we may be pulled to visit an old, familiar neighborhood or friends of another time in life. Writer Horton Foote's soulful 1985 film *The Trip to Bountiful* paints the emotions of attachment with beautiful impressionistic colors. In it, Mrs. Watts, a sensitive old woman living in the city with her son and his wife, develops a yearning to visit her family home, now long abandoned, in Bountiful, Texas. Her daughter-in-law interprets this wish as sentimental senility, and she convinces her husband to thwart the old lady's attempts to take a train or bus to visit her long-abandoned homestead. Mrs. Watts expresses the elemental nature of her longing plainly: "I haven't had my hands in dirt in twenty years. My hands feel the need of dirt."

Finally, Mrs. Watts finds her way, picking up an understanding friend and losing her purse, which contains the pension check she had planned on using as a stake for setting up a new life back home. To her daughter-in-law, this check represents money needed to pay the rent in the city; to Mrs. Watts the check's loss is an opportunity to be free of the future. A sheriff finally drives her to her home, where the land has gone to weed and the people of her childhood have all died. Still, having made this brief visit, she is content. She is well aware that her home is truly bountiful. Thinking about her loveless marriage and the problems of her friends, she says, "Well, I don't think about these things now.

But they're all part of Bountiful." For all of us, the past to which
the soul is attached, even when our intentions are to be liberated
from it, and even though it is teeming with failures, is bountiful:
rich, full, and, in its own way, necessary.

Horton Foote said he hoped to write this story in a way that
would avoid sentimentality; yet there is a kind of sentimentality
that is appropriate to the soul. The longing for a bountiful home
is an archetypal theme, a mood and a fantasy that can visit us at
any time, but perhaps especially as we get older. There is also, of
course, a pragmatic, forward thinking Daughter-in-Law in most
of us, who sees this soul-longing as a nuisance and a distraction,
but if we give in to the Old Woman, we may find an important
nutrient for the soul in her sentimentality.

The feeling of longing, the ache of desire for a familiar place or
thing, the urgency to visit old friends and places, are all expressions of the soul. The soul wants these things fiercely, as though
its well-being required them, even if the demands of life make
fulfilling these needs seem impractical. Like the visit to Bountiful, Texas, the trip may not be easy, but even for only a moment of
memory, it may be worth the effort.

Attachment to people, things, and places can feel like a burden. It's a nuisance to carry useless things around with us as we
move from state to state and house to house. It takes care, attention, and time to write the letters and make the phone calls that
sustain attachments. Care of the soul can be demanding, requir-
ing a decision that the needs of the soul are as important as the
more future-oriented things that claim our attention.

Every day we feel the soul's minor or major discomforts, but
because we habitually overlook these signals of soul pain, we may
fail to respond. Just as some people can't perceive colors or musical tones, so we may be soul-blind and soul-deaf. The soul's
yearnings simply don't get through to consciousness; or if they
do, we try to numb ourselves to them with medications, frenzied
activities, or other palliatives. From the higher, transcendent,

and progressive place of our aims and desires, the soul may appear regressive. The resulting alienation within our very hearts bears its own painful melancholic loneliness.

A first step, then, in tending to the soul in regard to our relationships is to understand and honor the soul's particular mode of being. It may help to realize, as tradition has taught for centuries, that there are two pulls in us, one upward toward transcendence, ambition, success, progress, intellectual clarity, and cosmic consciousness, and another downward, into individual, vernacular life. The first is obviously magnetically inspiring, while the latter is much more quietly and subtly satisfying, its challenges pedestrian and its opportunities less than inspiring. Yet soul lives in this pregnant ordinariness. It is always attached to life in an involving, complicating way, unlike the upward movement, which aims toward a streamlined, unfettered route toward some imagined goal.

As we work through difficult family relationships, struggle with the demands of marriage, apply ourselves to the job we're doing, become settled into the geographic region fate has chosen for us, and continually sort through the personality issues that never seem to change or improve—in all these areas we are gathering the stuff of the soul. The soul wants to be attached, involved, and even stuck, because it is through such intimacy that it is nourished, initiated, and deepened.

The Flight from Attachment

THE SOUL is a complicated field of paradoxes and contradictions, and so we need now to examine the other side of what we have been saying. It would be a mistake to honor attachment as the only inclination of the soul in relationships. As strong as the yearning for attachment is, there is obviously something else in us that yearns for solitude, freedom, and detachment. Our examination of relationship must include both sides of this spectrum and embrace the tension that may exist as we try to give attention to each.

One of the most beautiful of classic myths, the story of Daphne and Apollo, speaks to this theme. I'd like to use this captivating tale as the primary text in our meditations on this unlikely aspect of relationship: the desire for distance.

In the myth, Daphne is a lovely young woman who likes to run through the woods hunting. As Ovid tells the tale, she is a true daughter of Diana (Artemis in Greek)—she has no desire for relationship. But she attracts the attention of the great god Apollo, who immediately falls in love with her. He pursues her, but she runs away. This *flight* of the young nymphlike woman away from the great Apollo is the key image in the story, and may help us gain insight into dreams of flight and those times in our lives when we find ourselves anxiously running away from attachment.

Apollo tries to seduce Daphne away from her flight, telling her that he is not her enemy, that he has accomplished great things and that he is no dunce: he can speak oracles, he invented music, and he is the archetypal physician. But she is unresponsive to his appeal, and continues to run. An interesting detail is that Daphne in flight becomes even more alluring to Apollo. There is something attractive about running away from intimacy, not only to the person doing the running but also to the pursuer.

When it looks as though Apollo might finally catch up with her, just as he is literally breathing down her neck, she calls out to her father, the river god Peneus, for help. Then, as her prayer is answered, she is gradually transformed into a tree. In the laconic poetic translation by Charles Boer: "Heavy numbness seizes limbs, soft breasts enclose in bark, hair in leaf, arms branch, feet (so swift) root; head, a tree-top."

Many artists have depicted this wondrous image, the girl becoming a tree. In marble, Bernini shows the leaves delicately growing from her arms and hands. In Perugino's *Allegorical Combat between Chastity and Voluptuousness*, Daphne is woman from her neck down, but from her head and arms grows a tall branching tree. In a Magrittelike modern painting by Jan Balet, Apollo wears a bowler hat and black suit, while Daphne, naked, her hair flaming red, her arms having become brilliant green branches, runs among tall dark trees just out of reach.

Daphne, as we have said, is one of the faces of Diana, usually identified with the Greek virgin goddess Artemis, who lives deep in the woods, away from civilized life. As a hymn to the goddess by the Greek poet Callimachus puts it, "Seldom it is that Artemis goes to town." Daphne shares the great goddess's mobility, spirit of adventure, solitary ways, exclusive femininity and virginity, chaste beauty, and tendency to retreat from human contact. In fact, we could see Daphne as one particular facet of Artemis's remoteness, namely, the flight from Apollonic claims on the soul.

The story speaks to many dimensions of life. One way to look at it is to see Daphne as the virgin soul fleeing from the spirit of cultural, Apollonic achievements of intellect, art, and even healing. Often we may feel that something in us doesn't want to be understood or healed. We don't want to go to the doctor. We decide against taking a class. We're tired of the friend who always tries to change us, give us advice, or figure us out. These feelings, sometimes dismissed as resistance or defense, may be Daphne sensitivities, honest emotions keeping the soul intact.

In a more general sense, Daphne is the virginal in flight from the marital. She is the solitary trying to evade the relational. She is nature protected from culture. She is the untouched preferring to be transformed backward into nature, rather than forward into human culture.

Several modern writers have offered different readings of Daphne's story. Norman O. Brown interprets the metamorphosis of Daphne into a tree as the resurrection of ordinary life into poetry.[6] He compares her to Orpheus, who is traditionally seen as nature speaking or singing through the poet's art. Daphne, he says, represents a sublimation of nature. When Apollo finally caught up with her, he still loved her bark skin and her leafy limbs, and decided to use her laurel leaves as a symbol of high achievement. This artistic Apollonic move, saying that this tree's branch is now an emblem of purification and celebration after struggle, is, in Brown's view, the crucial image of the story. At the end of a life struggle, we may end up with meaningfulness, insight, maybe even a poem or a letter or a painting epitomizing the initiation that has taken place.

Brown's reading of the story favors the side of Apollo and makes of Daphne a spiritual figure, and in fact there is a high degree of spirituality in all of Artemis's manifestations. Daphne actually fosters the work of Apollo—making life pure, whole, meaningful, and poetic—by leading him into her uncontaminated woods, and by inspiring him to transform nature into art. In Greek stories, Apollo and Artemis were twins. The story also contains, as Brown points out, an allusion to sublimation in the Freudian sense: a changing of the sexual impulse into the artistic. Apollo's lust is fulfilled in symbol rather than in body. Our desires for literal experience may be fulfilled unexpectedly at a more refined level.

To turn to yet another point of view, Daphne's resistance can also be seen as a flight from soul. It is precisely her lovely spiritual posture that can make the turbulent tendencies of attachment appear unattractive. People sometimes flock to personal growth groups to find their way out of entangled relationships, instead of deeper into them. Something virginal and Daphnelike runs away from engagement and begs to be preserved from it. We may be caught up in Daphne's myth: calling on a father figure to keep us in a regressive state, like a tree instead of a person, safely insulated with bark, and unattached to the world that sees our beauty and our potential, that desires us and quite naturally seeks out intimacy with us.

Our resistance to attachment might come from that place in us that wants our lives to be clear and ordered, morally clean, and unfettered. Our thoughts, like the branches of Daphne in her self-preserved state, might reach heavenward, indicating our desire to avoid the entanglements of life. Daphne's becoming a sky-ward branching tree reveals her inherent spirituality, which in the case of Artemis is seen in her tall stature. Daphne's branches share the same spirit that places spires and steeples on churches, though these *point* heavenward rather than branch—a significant difference. The figure of Daphne is a particularly subtle blend of spirit and soul: her branching arms stretch upward in the direction of purity and transcendence, while the many points of her branches and leaves suggest the multiple perspectives of the soul, softening and deflecting her rising spirit.

This is a gentle resistance to the soul and its attachments, the Daphne reach toward the uncluttered sky; nevertheless, it is an effective defense against the soul's labyrinthine nature. Life spoils our innocence and our psychological virginity. Relationship and attachment hold down that spirit that would like to roam the woods of this world in playful hunting. Taking the role of Apollo, people sometimes say that they enjoy the pursuit in a relationship more than the relationship itself, while others, following Daphne, seem to indulge in the flight.

Daphne's story also reveals that relationship may be more than the effort of two individuals to blend their lives together. On a far deeper level, it may also be the eternal struggle to reconcile nothing less than heaven and earth—the upward yearning for simplicity, order, meaning, and freedom, with the downward need for complexity, change, moodiness, rootedness, and attachment. Daphne may escape Apollo, but she still gives up her free life, becoming a creature rooted in the earth and subject to its climate.

There is no need to take sides in this contest between worldly life and self-preservation. Yet we always speak from one place at a time, so it is precisely in the paradoxes and contradictions that arise when we include both dimensions sympathetically that the deepest insights of the story come to the surface, and our theme gathers some necessary complexity. The same is true in our most concrete relationships: there is always a tension and a dialectic—a shifting back and forth—between concrete life and mental work on it, between living our loves and understanding them, between the desire for intimacy and the wish for solitude, between the soul of attachment and the spirit of detachment.

Spirituality and Detachment

NOT SURPRISINGLY, the literature of spirituality usually counsels a life of detachment. The Christian mystic Teresa of Avila, counseling her nuns, who have "abandoned all worldly things and possessions" in order to live the contemplative life, says, "There is no doubt that if a person perseveres in this nakedness and detachment from all worldly things he will reach his goal."[7] The spirit of detachment makes sense from a spiritual point of view. It's important to clear the decks and to be free of everyday worldly concerns in order to explore fully the realm of the spirit. The world can easily distract from this higher endeavor. But the soul has an equal task and commitment, to find the treasures and explore the ins and outs of life by being attached. Just as there is spiritual practice in search of the highest and most refined reaches of human potential, so there is soul practice in pursuit of the juices and nutriments of life's entanglements.

When its own necessary practices are neglected, the soul may react by presenting difficult problems tuned exactly to what has been slighted. If a person decides to forego an ordinary sexual life on behalf of spiritual dedication, it is possible that sex will become a preoccupation and may find modes of expression that are unusually compulsive and perhaps in some way distorted. I once led a retreat for priests. I told them at the beginning that I'd like to set aside two hours on the third day of the retreat to discuss sex. There were many other issues to discuss, including ritual and a deepening of the very idea of priesthood, that I thought were central in the retreat. To my surprise, during a break on the first day several priests came to me and asked that we discuss sex for a whole day, or maybe for the whole retreat, they considered it such a grave problem.

In my seminary days I also had occasion to discover how sex can take some odd shapes in the lives of those who for spiritual reasons have chosen to live without it. Not in my own community, but in a religious order I once visited, I spoke with a man soon to be ordained as a priest who had created a following among a group of nuns. He was their "shepherd," and they his "sheep." Among other similar devotions, the nuns, at a certain predetermined time each day, would think of their "shepherd" and kneel facing whatever direction they knew him to be in, praying for him, picturing him in their minds, and offering themselves to him completely. The obvious, if spiritually gilded, sexuality in this arrangement gave the whole enterprise an odd flavor.

I knew a minister, too, who prided himself on his collection of photographs of automobile accidents. He had a box filled with bloody scenes, pictures he had gathered during his days as a police chaplain. He treated them like "dirty" pictures, showing them to friends as though they were pornography.

The first case appears to be an acting out of the Daphne myth: a flight from sex, a reaching heavenward, and a compelling Apollo. But acting out a myth is a way of avoiding it, not fulfilling it. It is a form of defense, and usually in these cases one sees the myth perverted in some way. The subtle interplay between the virginal and the Apollonic is lost in this acting out, to be replaced by absurd literalizations of the characters and situations. Fleeing sex, these nuns found themselves snared in a profoundly distorted sexual arrangement glossed over by a strange form of spiritual community. In the second case, the flight from sex led to a gruesome, lurid fascination with the body.

On the other hand, a solid spiritual life, including an attitude of detachment, can be extremely soulful. Daphne's escape can make a great deal of sense and even can be seen as leading to a fully realized life. Many people find fulfillment in the single life, and some feel drawn to a life of dedication to special causes, to social action, or to a spiritual vision. Some callings in life demand a degree of detachment, whether for travel or for reasons of time, or the necessary solitariness of the job.

I sometimes thought of Daphne's wisdom when as a professor I stood in front of dozens of fresh young students in a college classroom. I was filled with Apollo as I tried to sharpen their minds and rope them into the traditions of knowledge I knew. For their part, they squirmed in their seats and tried in every way to avoid being touched. They preferred their naive, untutored ways of thinking and living to the honored traditions of the establishment. Clearly, there is some wisdom in that retreat from intellectual conquest, something self-preserving and honest. Education is one arena in which the story of Daphne and Apollo gets played out every day.

Closeness and Distance in Relationship

WE CAN apply these principles of attachment and freedom to our relationships, discovering that our involvement with people may be most soulful when we can live fully amid the tension of these two inclinations. If we have strong desires to have a family, live with another person, or join a community, but find, after these desires have been satisfied, that we are drawn in exactly the opposite direction, then we might remember that this complexity is simply the way of the soul. We may have to look for concrete ways to give life to both sides of the spectrum, enjoying both our intimacies and our solitude.

Sometimes the matter presents itself as a questioning of our own natures: Am I the kind of person who should get married, or do I need to live alone? Should I get a job in a large corporation, or should I be self-employed? Should I attach myself to some school of thought, or should I find my own way intellectually?

The best answer to questions like these is intellectually and emotionally to hold both sides at once. Out of the tension may come a unique solution, a way of being attached and separate at the same time. Just as it is difficult in reading the story of Daphne and Apollo not to side with one or the other, so in life it is not easy to give assent to attractions of both intimacy and solitude. The poet Rainer Maria Rilke's famous solution to relationship is for each person to protect the solitude of the other. His emphasis is clearly on solitude; yet two people in a relationship might just as well protect the other's capacity for intimacy.

In everyday life there are always opportunities to honor both separateness and togetherness. Often one person in a relationship feels one emotion more than the other. In his essay on marriage Jung describes one partner as the "contained" and the other as the "container." Maybe the best way to tend these two needs is to notice where the anxiety is. In matters of soul it is advisable never to compensate or to try to escape but instead to tend better the very thing that is causing trouble. A person in a marriage who is longing for freedom, finding marriage too limiting and confining, might best avoid the temptation to flee and instead work at reimagining marriage and partnership. His notion of marriage is likely too limited and therefore painful in the living of it.

Many people seem to live the pain of togetherness and fantasize the joys of separateness; or, vice versa, they live a life of solitude and fill their heads with alluring images of intimacy. Bouncing back and forth between these two valid claims on the heart can be a frustrating, endless struggle that never bears fruit and never settles down. In the end, the only answer, as in all matters of soul, is a polytheistic one. Honor both gods, Daphne and Apollo. Pursue and run away. Be lustful and chaste. Wholeheartedly link up with someone else, but just as passionately find your own way. It's too bad that our language doesn't have more words, like *bitter-*

sweet, that convey the oxymorons and contradictions not only of language but of life itself. We need help in imagining these complexities that invite soul and that offer a way out of the divisions and dualisms that keep life anxious and unsettled.

I'm not suggesting, by the way, a *balance* of individuality and togetherness. Balance is a perfectionist ideal, never to be found in actual life. Therefore, it is not a good image to keep in mind. Rather, the soul's complexity is achieved over time, through error and extreme. There may be only rare moments, quickly fading, in which the desired amalgam appears to be within reach. Most of the time we feel the unwelcome tug of one side or the other. That, I believe, is as it should be. We are guided by our emotions, by pain, by the feeling of going wrong. The point is to enter the mysterious complexity of the soul's polytheistic structures, and not to arrive at some static point of perfect balance.

Another clue is to follow the advice of the Renaissance magus Marsilio Ficino, who taught that it is essential to find your own daimon, that "other" within you and in your fate who bears the seeds of your unfolding nature, your uniqueness. Don't contradict this daimon, who sometimes guides in a negative way, warning through intuition and through subtle signs in life against taking certain directions; or who at other times is like a protective guardian angel; or who might even occasionally lead the way. W. B. Yeats, who wrote passionately about daimonic living, emphasized the struggle that may characterize contact between the individual person and his daimon: "The Daimon comes not as like to like but seeking its own opposite, for man and Daimon feed the hunger in one another's hearts."[8]

For some people Daphne is not only a presence to be dealt with, she is a defining figure, setting the tone of a life and personality. Such a person, who is both graced and challenged to live a life dominated by the Daphne style, may have to struggle with many Apollo figures within and without, and may discover that flight is a way of life. For this person the struggle against attachment and being civilized can be a unique way of establishing soulfulness, of working out profound and competing demands on the heart. A flight from the world, from civilization, or from marriage may be seen superficially as a failure to be social or normal. But, having a sympathetic appreciation for the myth, we could understand that such flights and struggles can be manifestations of a soul's passionate response to its own nature and destiny. The same struggle may be lived out in the effort to be both intimately connected with another, and at the same time preserve one's integrity and individuality.

For the rest of us, a strong dose of individuality can be the best quality to bring to a relationship. That nymph in your heart who runs away at the first sign of love, sex, and commitment might be doing an important service to the soul, which needs flight as much as it needs embrace. On the other hand, the proud spirit that rushes into relationship at the first twitch of eros is also important to the soul. Without Apollo's impetuous desire, there may be no intimacy. In a relationship all we can do is follow the lead of our emotions and images. An abstract comprehensive understanding is both impossible and undesirable. In matters of the heart, we may have no choice but to allow other forces and factors beyond our intentional selves to work out the debates, the incongruities, and the contradictions, as we bring hope and desire to new love and affection.

Chapter Two

THE MYSTERY OF INTIMACY

THE WORD *intimacy* means "profoundly interior." It comes from the superlative form of the Latin word *inter*, meaning "within." It could be translated "within-est," or "most within." In our intimate relationships, the "most within" dimensions of ourselves and the other are engaged.

Within doesn't necessarily mean introspective, self-absorbed, confessional, inactive, self-conscious, or narcissistic. People can be engaged intimately while playing a game of tennis or cards, holding a conversation, taking a trip together, arguing heatedly, or sitting in a room, each quietly reading a book. The deep interiority of a person may be revealed in her transparent life: allowing her emotions to show, letting her thoughts out, being familiar with her deeper soul. It is the controlled, tightly lidded individual who finds intimacy difficult, because she is disconnected from her interiority, and therefore it has no place in her relationships. The unintimate person hovers nervously in air, separated both from her own depth and from the souls of others.

Intimacy begins at home, with oneself. It does no good to try to find intimacy with friends, lovers and family if you are starting out from alienation and division within yourself. I'm not suggesting that all psychological experience is interior, but it's clear that the dynamics, dramas, and characters of the individual soul play themselves out in the external world, so that relationship is always a dialectic between inner and outer, a dance between actual people and one's own life of soul.

If we do not take into account our own relationship to soul, then the inner and the outer may become confused. Being a friend to yourself is no mere metaphor or purely sentimental idea. It is the basis of all relationship, because it is a fundamental recognition of soul. We may feel tension in our lives and assume it is due to problems in a relationship with someone, but that seemingly outer tension may be an echo of inner conflict.

For example, we may think we're lonely because we have no friends, when the fact is we have no relationship to ourselves, and for that reason feel lonely and friendless. Something is always stirring in the soul that will have an impact on our relationships. Since we Americans are such an externally directed people, it's easy to think that anything troubling to the heart has its roots in the world, particularly in an intimate relationship, but the reverse can also be true: a current emotional disturbance can be rooted deep in the far reaches of the soul, where it may affect what happens in the world. And certain people, certain kinds of relationship, and certain events can evoke familiar, longstanding patterns set deep in the soul, so that although the relationship is in a sense the "cause" of the disturbance, it is not the ultimate source.

"Intimacy with oneself" is an odd phrase. It assumes a differentiation between "I" and "self." But as Jungian and archetypal psychology have made abundantly clear, the relationship is even more complicated. Soul is made up of a multitude of sub-personalities. Jung called them the "little people" of the psyche, complexes that have a consciousness and will of their own. If we take the figures who appear in dreams as representations of these soul-persons, then we see that they, too, enjoy relationships among themselves. The mother of my soul has a relationship to the children of my soul, for instance. A thief figure steals from me and is pursued by the police of my soul.

If I am unaware that I am made up of these many personalities, or if I think that what we call ego is the whole of what I am, then my life will become an arena in which these relationships are lived out blindly. I will be unconscious of my own rich inner life, and of the crowded inner lives of the people with whom I am in relationship as well. The result can be a simplistic view of relationship and a narcissistic style, since the attention remains on a narrow conception of self instead of on the soul.

In his essay "Marriage as a Psychological Relationship," Jung explores these notions in an interesting way, including the limitations of a narcissistic approach to relationship. He notes that one of the most basic problems in relationship is unconsciousness on the part of the people involved. Two people in an intimate relationship may be completely unaware of the themes that give their life together its meaningfulness and its tensions. People whose marriages are in danger of collapse often provide superficial reflections on their problems. Sometimes, apparently to avoid stirring the waters too much, people will restate truisms that have little to do with their particular situation, or they will offer sincere comments on their relationship that are so general and vague that they provide no insight and foster no movement.

Another narcissistic problem Jung points to is the tendency of people in a relationship to assume that psychological life is simple. One person may not realize how complicated the other is, and assume that she is as transparent as she appears. One person may be psychologically naive, expecting his partner to be like himself;

in Jung's words, "One person presupposes in the other a psychological structure similar to his own."[1] In a soulful relationship, in contrast, the partners know that we are all individuals, with our own kind of richness that may not be fully and plainly revealed in daily life, and that an intimate relationship demands a courageous and openhearted acknowledgment of differences.

An unconscious relationship begins in unconscious individuals. Naturally, no person and no relationship is going to be perfectly free of unconsciousness. To be completely conscious, were such a condition possible, is not even desirable, since "unconsciousness" is a negative word for what could be described more positively as the richness that lies beneath the surface of awareness. Much of what goes on in a relationship, and even much of what accounts for its pleasures and rewards, is unconscious. Still, conflicts and difficulties can arise from faulty connections to that richness of personality and soul.

"Becoming conscious" may not necessarily entail an analytical understanding of what is going on in the relationship, but rather a sophisticated, thoughtful, not so literal attitude toward people in general and relationships in particular. A person who is familiar with the soul knows that it is extremely complicated and rarely conforms to the norms and expectations of rational thought. The psychologically conscious person is savvy about the multidimensional ways of the soul and so is able to *read* the expressions and experiences of an intimate friend, a family member, or a partner, knowing that things are not always as they appear to be.

I am reminded of a couple who came to me to discuss their marriage and who demonstrated the two poles of psychological consciousness and its avoidance. They were suffering from a rather common malady. If I were inclined to multisyllabic jargon, I might call it "asymmetrical revitalization." The wife was going through a remarkable period of renewal. She was waking up to possibilities for herself that she had never considered before. Her husband, however, was still asleep, going through the rote motions of a career and marriage. It was his habit to blame the external world for everything negative that was happening to him. His wife, her mother, his boss, the town in which they lived—all these things were at fault. He never said anything of substance about his own thoughts, feelings, or experiences. From the outside, at least, it appeared that he had no relationship to his soul.

One sign of soul is reflection. The soul doesn't have to know what is going on in life. It doesn't need interpretations, explanations, or conclusions, but it does require musing, reverie, consideration, wonder, and exploration. This man's wife couldn't say exactly what was happening in her life at the moment, and she didn't know when or why it began in the first place, yet she wondered what it all meant and where it was headed. Her husband wanted to ignore the upheaval she was experiencing, and his own reactions to it as well.

Maybe the husband was protecting himself from opening up issues he knew would be painful and would reveal the bad condition of his marriage, certainly threatening the status quo and maybe even signaling separation or divorce. But he also seemed to suffer the common malady of indifference to the life of the soul. Many people imagine relationship fundamentally as a simple structure of being together. They may have never considered that a whole world of thoughts, images, and memories lies just beneath the surface, often giving a powerful emotional charge to the simplest interactions.

In this case, the wife decided after a while to go her own way. She felt that her husband would never be a real partner, that he would never be able to appreciate the intense experiences she was having or to be there himself as a person, alive with fresh thoughts and reflections. Even the separation that his wife eventually insisted upon didn't seem to stir him to look at his life with open eyes.

It's difficult for a relationship to have soul if the people involved don't wonder about what is happening to them, especially in times of ferment. I am not referring to endless analysis and introspection, which can dry out a relationship with the drive toward understanding. Wonder and open discussion are more moist. They keep people close to their experience, while at the same time they offer a degree of imagination, an element sorely needed in every intimate relationship.

A soulful relationship offers two difficult challenges: one, to come to know oneself—the ancient oracle of Apollo; and two, to get to know the deep, often subtle richness in the soul of the other. Giving attention to one side usually helps the other. As you get to know the other deeply, you will discover much about yourself. Especially in moments of conflict and maybe even despair, being open to the demands of a relationship can provide an extraordinary opportunity for self-knowledge. It provides an occasion to glimpse your own soul and notice its longings and its fears. And as you get to know yourself, you can be more accepting and understanding of the other's depth of soul.

If I am aware that I occasionally fall into a deep, illusory period of paranoia, for example, then I may be better able to accept moments of irrationality in my partner and in others. Recently I had just such an experience. One morning I received a magazine article in the mail about one of my books that tore my writing to shreds. The reviewer had no sympathy whatsoever for what I was doing, and in many pages devoted to my book the magazine attacked me personally and questioned my honesty and veracity. I knew the attack was coming from an ideological position contrary to my own, yet the anger and hatred in the attack stung me.

That same day the head of an organization called to tell me they were taking back an invitation to give a lecture at their annual meeting. Immediately paranoid thoughts began pouring into my head: "Did they read the negative review? Were people now coming out of the shadows and launching their attacks on me? Did this person represent a group within the organization who were fighting it out with others who valued my point of view?"

Later I learned that the problem was only a matter of scheduling, and was soon resolved. I could then see the paranoid nature of my thoughts and the effect one strong emotional experience had on another.

Sometimes, of course, our paranoid fantasies have a solid basis in reality. Maybe even now I don't know all that was going on behind the scenes in the decision to rescind the invitation to speak. The point is, on that day my imagination was more affected by criticism than I was willing to admit, and my soul, reeling from the attack, was ready to look through paranoid eyes at anything that came along.

Something similar may happen in our relationships. We may be deeply affected by something that happens in another part of our life, and not realize how deep the effect is. Then we may interpret some interaction in a relationship from within a soul condition that is not clean, that has been so affected that it colors our perception. Only sophistication about the ways of the soul can save us from acting on such irrational thoughts and feelings.

Sometimes popular psychology lays down impossible rules and expectations for a relationship. We are told to be clear and forthright in the expression of our feelings. We are supposed to *communicate* to our partners. We are expected to be good listeners and to be full of patience and empathy. We are given the illusion that it's possible to understand ourselves and others. But it seems to me that these expectations ignore soul. The soul is always complicated. Most of its thoughts and emotions could never be expressed in plain language. You could have the patience of Job and still never understand your partner, because the soul by nature doesn't lend itself to understanding or to clarity of expression.

If we are going to be soulful in our relationships, then we will have to give up these expectations that are foreign to soul. We may have to enter the confusion of another's soul, with no hope of ever finding clarity, without demanding that the other be clear in expressing her feelings, and without the hope that one day this person will finally grow up or get better or express herself more plainly.

There are many aspects of the soul that change very little over time. There are many things that will always be located in a thick, tangled skein of memories, fears, confusions, and intricacies. Soulful intimacy demands that we enter this thick soup, this multicolored kaleidoscope of personality, with an appreciation for its richness, and without unrealistic expectations that are psychologically moralistic. We may think that "it's only right and proper" that a person change her ways and that her soul be something other than what it is, but this kind of thinking moves us away from the person's own nature. Sometimes it appears that there is more moralism in the field of psychology than there is in religion.

It isn't easy to expose your soul to another, to risk such vulnerability, hoping that the other person will be able to tolerate your own irrationality. It may also be difficult, no matter how openminded you are, to be receptive as another reveals her soul to you. Yet this mutual vulnerability is one of the great gifts of love: giving the other sufficient emotional space in which to live and express her soul, with its reasonable and unreasonable ways, and then to risk revealing your own soul, complete with its own absurdities.

The idea of a soulful relationship is not a sentimental one, nor is it easy to put into practice. The courage required to open one's soul to express itself or to receive another is infinitely more demanding than the effort we put into avoidance of intimacy. The stretching of the soul is like the painful opening of the body in birth. It is so painful in the doing that we often will attempt to avoid it, even though such opening is ultimately full of pleasure and reward.

What I am suggesting about intimacy in relationship here is a particular aspect of the general need to respect the soul's wide range of mood, fantasy, emotion, and behavior. Most of us contain ourselves fairly well, but eventually some type of irrationality may come to the surface. We all have skeletons in our closets and monsters in our hearts. It can be taken as an axiom: the person who displays his or her sanity and morality most dramatically is likely to be the very person who finds it difficult to be sane and moral.

Being in a soulful relationship is to some extent frightening because by nature such a relationship asks that we show our soul, complete with its fears and follies. In *In Praise of Folly*, the Renaissance humanist Erasmus says that it is precisely in their foolishness that people can become friends and intimates. "For that the greatest part of mankind are fools, . . . and friendship, you know, is seldom made but amongst equals." The soul, as our dreams reveal, is not terribly lofty. We may present a high-minded image to the world, but the soul finds its fertility in its irrationalities. Maybe this is a hint as to why great artists appear mad, or at least eccentric, and why, in times of strong emotion and difficult decision-making, we so often act foolishly. More than one person in therapy has confessed to me that the most difficult part of an intense episode of jealousy was the fear of being made a fool by their partner—a sign to me that soul was trying hard to enter their lives in the dress of the fool.

Oddly, then, the most intimate relationships may be the very ones that appear foolish. The couple madly in love are "fools for love." The most unpredictable couplings sometimes make the best marriages. A person who appears quite ordered and logical at work may engage in outrageously irrational behavior at home. Some of the most tightly knit families don't hide their battles and jealousies. In short, when a relationship is soulful, the soul's irrationality will be revealed for all to see.

Within an individual, too, intimacy calls for love and acceptance of the soul's less rational outposts. Soulfulness is not so much a matter of knowledge and awareness, as of our relationship to the love and hatred that exist within our own heart. The "unconscious," that which we don't know, is too often also the "unloved," that which we do not accept. The trouble with defining therapy as "becoming conscious" is that it sounds like a purely intellectual operation, but the condition of unconsciousness, in the negative sense, is also a state of detachment. We not only need to know more about ourselves, we also need to love more of ourselves in an unsentimental way. We need to be close to the movements of soul that run deep and yet have everything to do with the way we act and feel in life.

Such love of the soul, sometimes felt as nothing more than tolerance of its unreasonable demands, is the basis for intimacy among people. Honoring that aspect of the soul that is irrational and extreme, we have far fewer expectations of perfection, in ourselves and in others—one of the most corrosive elements in any relationship. This kind of self-love also spills over into the kind of love of another that is tolerant, that knows the soul's tendency to move into new, positive areas through odd and apparently negative behavior. The truly soulful person may be surprised, but is not completely undone by unexpected developments in those he loves.

Our Personal Mythologies of Intimacy

ALL OF US have strong ideas about intimacy, and we may have been influenced by stories and creeds that affect our relationships. We could examine some of these beliefs and values, axioms and rules, and gradually discover our own mythology of love. How do I believe relationships work? Who are my models of success or failure? Who are my teachers?

The sources of this personal mythology can be subtle or obvious, and they are probably legion. Movies, books, magazine articles, a church sermon, popular songs, the experience of a friend, a class in school—all of these may contribute to a vast and intricate imagination of love and intimacy that may account in good measure for the patterns our relationships take. We may be completely unaware of these influences, and yet they can still have a profound effect on us.

An example would be the mythologies of love we have gathered from our parents. When people talk about their relationships, frequently the conversation shifts to parents. "My mother is a very emotional person," someone will say, "and I have that tendency from her." Talk about parents often takes a cause-and-effect tone, but from a deeper perspective, the *images* we have of our parents may be more important than any observable direct influence. These parents of the imagination are parental figures who provide nurturing, guidance, inhibition—all the things that actual parents might do—at the soul level. Stories about our parents are not only actual memories, but also stories that tell the myths we live by and that account for our feelings.

By reflecting on the way our parents love each other, we can gain insight into our current mythology of love. To imagine our own parents is not unlike thinking about Adam and Eve, for our own parents are to a large extent figures bigger than life, for good or ill, who live in the imagination less as memories and more as myths. Thinking about our parents and their way of loving, therefore, serves as an entry into our own mythology of love.

A man once complained to me that he found it difficult to maintain a satisfying, enduring relationship. His explanation was that his father had been emotionally distant. My sense—I felt this man's coldness quite clearly—was that his story *allowed* him to be emotionally cool. It was an excuse, not an insightful reflection on his own feelings. As I talked to him, I tried to elicit a fuller story, including his more complicated feelings about his father. He was angry at him for not giving him enough love as a child, and as long as he kept his anger directed against his father he was also angry at love itself. When I confronted him with my feeling that he was emotionally cool, his anger immediately flared up, hot and aggressive. Over the next several weeks we tried to keep both qualities, the hot and the cold, in our conversations, so that gradually they became less divided from each other. Over time, he was able, through the heat of his anger, to mitigate his former coldness.

Another source of a personal mythology of love is a basic philosophy of life. This philosophy doesn't have to be terribly complicated or formal, and it may be largely unconscious. Nevertheless, it is useful to reflect on the way we see things, the manner in which we give order to experience, and the basis of our hierarchy of values. We are all philosophers—not in a professional sense, of course, but as we imagine the way things are, the way we should behave, and the reasons why things turn out the way they do.

Often when I'm sitting with someone who is in deep despair about a relationship, he or she will make philosophical pronouncements about love. "Love is always doomed to failure," one person told me. "Men and women are not meant to be together," a young man said, "so it's not wise to have great expectations from a relationship." "Love is only for the young," an elderly man sighed to me over and over.

These statements of personal, vernacular philosophy have considerable impact on a person's relationships. Our ideas about life inevitably shape its structure, and, because they are usually too simple, it is wise to reflect on them. In the statements I just quoted you can sense tones of pessimism, paranoia, and depression, but all these emotions are reduced to simplistic rules of life. Just as a great deal of mythology lies hidden in professional and academic philosophy, so, too, do many stories and experiences, laden with complicated emotions, lie within these apparently simple life axioms.

Pronouncements of this kind also betray fear. They sound like defenses against love. The first is afraid of failure, yet it is surely impossible to have love in your life at all without the possibility of its loss. The second is afraid of self-revelation and vulnerability, and yet how can there be love without an opening of the heart and considerable emotional risk? The third is afraid of mortal love—the knowledge that although love itself may be eternal, the people who love are faced with the inevitable separation of death. This last is no remote factor in love; love is always laced with death, and death plays a more significant role in our loves than we might imagine.

Our simplistic philosophies can be transformed into more sophisticated reflection by honoring the soul's complexity, noticing in particular how strong emotions and raw, unreflected thoughts and fantasies lie hidden in our ideas. We can catch ourselves when we hear such simple, judgmental pronouncements coming out of our mouths. That is the time to reflect more deeply, take the matter a notch or two further, and speak in a reflective mode rather than in edict or axiom.

A general principle in soul-work is to bring the endless fertility of imagination to whatever is under consideration. Pronouncements such as those I've quoted stop imagination. Their purpose is to prevent the pain that a liberated imagination brings. For imagination is not only creative, it is also iconoclastic. It breaks down our simplistic ideologies, our self-protective principles, and our fearful rigidities. It opens us up to abundant life, and therefore, although it is liberating, it is also frightening and challenging.

Another source of one's personal mythology of love is past experience. At the cultural level, the past is often the basis for a myth: Columbus sails to a new world, and quickly his adventure takes on mythic proportions. At the personal level, too, experiences of the past quickly become a living mythology. Experience turns into belief. Because up until now I have always found it so, I may believe that a successful relationship is simply impossible. I may think that all women are untrustworthy or that all men are out to dominate women. My experience of family may have convinced me that family relationships are always painful, or always blissful.

Through this process, personal history becomes philosophy, and though built upon fact, memory becomes fantasy, important fantasy, and ultimately the mythology by which we make our choices and live our lives. We may dislike hearing a friend or relative offer a different reading of a shared experience, because then our mythology is put into question. We are shown that our own point of view is only one of many options, and that perception alone can be threatening.

For this reason, though, it is helpful to have a friend or counselor who can hear and point out to us the fear and rigidity that may characterize our grand conclusions about life and relationship, and offer a different set of perspectives, or even simply an opportunity for conversation in which our defensive beliefs can be examined and perhaps relaxed. A major part of soul-work involves just getting out of the way so that life can go on. We may hang on fiercely to our own interpretations and programs, as if we knew best what we should do, but care of the soul is more a process of listening and following, not without choice and responsibility, but with an intimate familiarity with the deep roots of our own thoughts and emotions. It recognizes that we all have old stories, guiding voices, raw emotions, and unfathomable natures that make our lives ultimately inexplicable and rich beyond imagining.

An Eye for the Soul's Manifestations

EVERY PERSON is infinitely more vast in scope than appears to the naked eye, and so to have a good sense of who we are and who our partner is, we have to employ an unnaked eye: a point of view that is penetrating, that catches, like radar, images that might otherwise pass unnoticed. We need an eye that can see the invisible world that affects the visible—the fantasies locked in the past, values hidden in the storehouses of family tradition, assumptions about the way things work, and the worldview that emanates from the culture all around us.

If we have no artful relationship to this world of invisibles, then we are subject to self-division and self-alienation—two maladies endemic to modern life. We can imagine this alienation not only as a fracturing of the ego, but also as a disaffection between those elements of our nature we live out and know well, and those that remain strangers.

Often, people who are in a close relationship, whether they are married, in a family, or just good friends, are one day shocked to discover something important about the other. A woman will say, "I never realized my husband was so angry until the day he punched his fist through the living-room wall." Several men and women have told me the story of their divorce coming as a complete shock. One man was getting ready to go out to dinner with his wife when she came downstairs from the bedroom with suitcases in her hands. He said he had no inkling that separation was in the works.

How is it that a couple who have lived together for twenty or thirty years could surprise each other so vividly? The stock answer is "lack of communication," but the problem must have deeper roots. One partner habitually may not let her thoughts and feelings come into the open. Another may be blind to all the signals that are being expressed by his partner. Some individuals live as if there were no interior life, as though anything but the most superficial exchanges were insignificant. The distraught man who told me that he had no idea his wife was planning to divorce him mentioned offhandedly that he and his wife had not had sex in five years because they were angry at each other.

The problem in such relationships is not simply a lack of communication, but a sense that experience is meaningless. There seems to be a widespread tendency in modern life to observe events as they happen passively, with gauze in front of one's eyes, like Camus's "stranger," whose detached passivity stems from a complete equalization of values. Nothing is shocking, there are no problems, things happen, there is nothing to be done, said, or thought. Yet certain situations cry out for reflection, such as five angry years without sex in a marriage that from both inside and out appeared placid.

Intimacy means living in the "very within" place of the relationship; it means looking into and beneath the surfaces. Without being coldly analytical, we can learn over time to glimpse another's interiority, to read between the lines of that person's words and actions. Intimacy requires some perspicacity in relation to ourselves and another. The person who can't read his partner of several years probably has little idea of the themes buried within his own life and emotions. Conversely, a person attuned to the mysteries of her own soul will know how to respond to her partner's as well.

Jung felt that none of us really wants to know who we are. In a letter of 1951 he writes to a man who apparently tried to understand his wife and met with considerable resistance: "In the end people don't want to know what secrets are slumbering in their souls. If you struggle too much to penetrate into another person, you find that you have thrust him into a defensive position."[2]

As we saw in the myth of Apollo and Daphne, this resistance to being penetrated by another person may be archetypal; that is to say, the resistance may have a necessary and valuable role to play, and may not be personal and defensive. Both the quest for knowledge and resistance to it have to be given a place. After years of doing therapy, I've come to the conclusion that when a person enters therapy there is something in him that honestly desires self-knowledge, but there is something else, sometimes much more powerful, that would like to foil the process. Something works against the therapy, and that spirit is so entangled with positive intentions that it is difficult to detect. It does its work of sabotage quietly.

When, in the privacy of our own efforts, we are trying to attain a degree of self-knowledge, it is worthwhile to take note of intentions in ourselves that resist our work. In Jungian language, we could say this is the shadow of soul-work—that aspect of the self that for its own good reasons doesn't want consciousness and knowledge. If we do not know this contrary will in us, then we may go through the motions of soul-work for years without much effect, while its shadow works efficiently and quietly in the background, undoing everything that we think we've accomplished. Even in our soul-work, we have to be alert to the fantasies we are living out, and to the deeper story that underlies our stated intentions.

It is all too easy to approach soul-work from a point of view that does not have soul. For instance, some people seem desperate for explanations for their lives, and there is always a book or a person that will give them one more key phrase or idea, or one more theory to explain why they suffer as much as they do. This search for reasons, however, may have within it a defense against a change in awareness. In the most obvious instance, a person will find a convincing explanation for his or her behavior, and then discover an equally convincing reason why that explanation doesn't apply. Equally popular is landing on a wonderful theory that elegantly explains why you are who you are, and then moving no further in reflection. Many people tout whole complex schemata, from primal screams to childhood abuse to Jungian archetypes, as explanations for themselves, but these ready-made, off-the-rack interpretations may well serve to inhibit, rather than to promote, ongoing, soulful self-analysis.

I know a woman who always has a new explanation for her behavior. She is brilliant at fabricating sophisticated explanations for the conflicts in her life, but she never stops to let any of these thoughts sink in and awaken true awareness or insight. Each of her reasons exists for its own sake, and not as a means toward further, more personally relevant knowledge, and in the end, all these explanations serve as barriers to self-knowledge. They may look like awareness, and the person certainly appears to be busy in her studies of herself, but in the end all her efforts form yet another kind of defense. Freud says that often the display of a thing is a sign of its lack. Our clear and loudly championed self-interpretations can signal an effective move against soulful self-examination.

Another interesting form of this defense is reading about psychology. Let the reader of this book beware! For some people, soul-work takes the form of reading a chain of psychology books, each one giving a different picture of how life works and what is wrong with the reader. Someone should write a book about the psychology of psychology books; excessive reading of these books is a modern psychological disorder. Frequently I suggest to people in therapy that they take a year off from reading. Reading can serve as a strong distraction from attending to the soul, because someone else's ideas take the place of personal reflection. It might be better if each person had his or her own psychological lexicon, which would be much more effective than borrowing key phrases from an endless supply of self-help manuals.

Establishing intimacy with yourself or another is not a matter of finding new information or borrowing new words for your condition or your personality. Nor is it the application of these words and ideas to your experiences. New ideas about psychology often lead to suggested programs of self-improvement, but such programs work against the soul. For one thing, self-improvement is full of ego and conscious intention, but the whole idea of soul embraces much that is unknown, and in order to be soulful, we need some way of allowing for the unknown. The best kind of soul-work I know is to take a great deal of time in the phase of getting to know yourself. Life will follow upon reflection, if the reflection is deep and patient enough to touch upon the central issues of the soul. We can trust that a genuine shift in imagination will result in a change in life.

Another problem with the idea of self-improvement is that it implies there is something wrong with who we are. Everyone wants to be someone else, but getting to know and love yourself means accepting who you are, complete with your inadequacies and irrationalities. Only by loving the soul in its entirety can we really love ourselves. This doesn't mean that we can't hope to live a fuller life or become a better person, but there is a difference between self-improvement and the unfolding of the soul. In the latter we don't take on an attitude of perfection; rather, we draw closer to those things that we feel as imperfect and let them be the openings through which the potentiality of the soul enters into life.

This posture of acceptance, quite different from that of being passively resigned, acknowledges the power of the soul to work in mysterious ways. I remember that once, during a particularly tumultuous and shattering year of my life, a friend gave me a book to read that came at exactly the right time. It contained Paul Tillich's sermon "You Are Accepted." At the time, I wasn't able to understand changes taking place in my feelings, values, and direction in life. Everything seemed to be up in the air. Tillich offered the solace of accepting myself unconditionally, which I now understand as accepting my own mystery, acknowledging that there are things going on in me that I may never understand. I may even act in certain ways that disturb others, not out of some character failure, but because my soul is trying to move itself into my life, against my resistance and my ignorance.

In his moving sermon, Tillich talks about self-division and separation within the individual, and the effect this division has on relationships. "The depth of our separation lies in just the fact that we are not capable of a great and merciful divine love towards ourselves," he writes. "We are separated from the mystery, the depth, and the greatness of our existence." His solution is not knowledge, but love: "When the old compulsions reign within us as they have for decades, when despair destroys all joy and courage, sometimes at that moment a wave of light breaks into our darkness, and it is as though a voice were saying: 'You are accepted. You are accepted.' "[3]

It is typical of the soul's ways that a solution to a serious problem takes the form of paradox. We look at ourselves and don't like what we see. We imagine a better life, a more sensitive or stronger personality, deeper relationships. We try to change and to become someone better, but years pass and the old imperfections remain steadfast. One day we may learn Tillich's important lesson, to accept ourselves fundamentally, with a "merciful, divine love towards ourselves." Suddenly, things look different. I am the same person I have always been, and yet I am not. The world hasn't changed, and yet it feels different. The difficult truth to learn is that true change takes place in the imagination, and knowing this has everything to do with developing a good, intimate relationship to our own soul and the souls of others.

INTERMINGLED

SOULS

The bird a nest, the spider a web, man friendship.

WILLIAM BLAKE

Chapter Three

THE MAGIC AND
ALCHEMY OF MARRIAGE

MARRIAGE IS NOT only the expression of love between two people, it is also a profound evocation of one of life's greatest mysteries, the weaving together of many different strands of soul. Because marriage touches upon issues charged with emotion and connected to absolute meaning, it is filled with paradoxical feelings, far-flung fantasies, profound despair, blissful epiphanies, and bitter struggle—all signs of the active presence of soul.

Many people turn to marriage hoping to find ultimate happiness and grace for their lives. Some find a pot of gold, others face disillusionment and regret. Even "successful" marriages that offer many levels of fulfillment can sometimes be trying, and teeter on the edge of dissolution. Most disturbing of all, some people fall in love, create a family, and then turn violent toward each other.

In the midst of all these contradictions, it's easy to be cynical about marriage, or to come up with yet another plan for making marriages "work." It's more difficult to look at marriage as we actually experience it, taking note of its deep fantasies, its hidden emotions, and its place in the life of the soul; not looking for perfection, but asking what the soul is doing when it entices us toward such a demanding form of relationship.

The distance between our intentions and expectations of marriage on the one hand, and the reality it presents on the other, indicates how far removed from consciousness and reason marriage can be. Marriage has less to do with conscious intention and will than with deeper levels of soul. In order to gain insight into marriage and its problems, we have to dig deeper than the familiar therapeutic investigation into parental influences, childhood traumas, and the illusions of romantic love. The soul *always* reaches deeper than we expect, especially in marriage, which lies far beneath matters of communication and even interpersonal relationship, touching areas of absolute importance to a meaningful and soulful life. We approach its soul when we understand that marriage is a mystery, a sacrament, as some religions say—a sacred symbolic act.

In order to grasp this sacred symbolic level, we need to set aside the modern penchant for scientific social analysis and instead look to sacred stories for instruction. Scientific analysis and therapeutic theories leave out the sacred dimension, and therefore they always come up wanting in their portrayals of marriage. But stories that evoke a mythic imagination, however simple they may be, offer us an opportunity to look at the soul's role in what is sometimes treated merely as an interpersonal structure.

The Native American Cochiti people of New Mexico tell a strange story about marriage, a story that can lead our thoughts in a fresh direction. According to the story, a young girl living with her poor parents taught herself to make many fine items of clothing on a simple loom. Her weavings caught the attention of the young men of her village, many of whom wanted to marry her, but she kept her eyes focused on her work and showed no interest in the men, even though they offered her beautiful things. Then Coyote, that mischievous figure of the mythology of the American West, decided he wanted to marry her. "I shall offer her none of these things, but she will belong to me," he said proudly. Then he went off to the mountains to fetch some black currants.

He came to her village and ritually donned a human costume. Stamping four times with his foot, he drew on a pair of white buckskin moccasins. Looking down at his feet, he said, "Do I look pretty? Yes, I look pretty." Using the same magic, he dressed himself in all his finery. Then, after taking the black currants in his left hand, he went to the village center and danced.

The girl watched him dance and was charmed. She saw the currants in his left hand and asked him for them. Then she took him home, made love with him, and in no time had little coyote children. One day he took her away from her parents to a hole in the ground. "How can you go in?" she asked. "It's so small." But he crawled in effortlessly, followed by all the little coyotes. She looked into the hole and beheld a house not unlike that of her parents, filled with the kind of clothes she had been making. So she, too, went in and lived there forever after.[1]

This story "marries" two entirely different modes of experience—the mundane and the magical. Notice that the woman is not interested in an ordinary human marriage. When such opportunities arise, she keeps her mind on her weaving. In many traditions weaving is one of the preferred images for the imagination. It's an important image of a people making a culture—weaving together families, communities, and nations, as well as all kinds of work and creative endeavors. Among the Greeks, Athena was the great weaver, the goddess who brought all the artisans and families together as a city and a nation. A person, too, is woven from many influences, many fateful events, and many raw thematic materials.

As I have mentioned, the soul is *com-plicated*, a word whose literal meaning is "woven together." Our young woman is an excellent example of a person giving all of her effort to the work of soul-making. In some ways, she is like the Virgin Mary as she appears in paintings of the Annunciation: when the angel appears with his announcement, Mary is reading a book, preparing herself for her supernatural fate by becoming acquainted with the sacred stories and prayers of her people. The young Cochiti girl is also preparing herself for a remarkable marriage by waiting for the magical enticement of the black currants and by devoting herself wholly to making culture and to bringing her creative talents into the world.

We may learn from her that we can't enter marriage soulfully without first preparing ourselves, by being in the world creatively and by weaving the tapestry of our own talents and destiny. Marriage is not separate from other aspects of life; on the contrary, our capacity to knit all the many parts of life into a persona, our own way of being in the world, represented here by the clothes the young woman makes, culminates in marriage. Marriage itself is a kind of weaving, not only of two individuals, but of every aspect of personal, social, and even cosmic life.

This, then, is one lesson we can take from the story. An essential part of becoming marriageable is to be a maker, a person who cultivates a life of beauty, rich texture, and creative work. If we understand marriage only as the commitment of two individuals to each other, then we overlook its soul, but if we see that it also has to do with family, neighborhood, and the greater community, and with our own work and personal cultivation, then we begin to glimpse the *mystery* that is marriage. A person prepares for marriage by becoming a cultured person, not in the superficial sense of refinement in the higher forms of art and the sophisticated life, but as someone who has achieved an identity through cultural initiations and has found a unique way of being creative in the world. This creativity doesn't have to be grand. It may be no more than the discovery of how to make a simple yet individual contribution to the community, like the Cochiti bride making clothes on her loom.

The mate to this work of cultivation is a Panlike, devilish dancer who is fertile, interior, and magical—Coyote. Marriage is accomplished not only by human design and will, but also by grace and magic. Coyote is a magician who knows esoterically how to dress himself, how to clothe his magical, mythical being in human form. All intimate relationships require some degree of magic, because magic, not reason and will, accomplishes what the soul needs.

Every marriage has both an external life and an interior dimension. The externals may be dealt with by reasonable means, but the interior requires myth and magic. The Cochiti girl married an enchanting figure from the world of animal dream who was able to make by magic what she was used to making by her own industry and talent. His home was an interior version of her earthly home, a microcosm within the earth. In this kind of home she could live out the rest of her days, because he was a worthy mate, his home an appropriate fulfillment, a deep interior vision, of the mundane home she knew so well.

Our expectations of marriage, those profound and far-reaching fantasies we have of life in the perfect married state, hint at the depths of marriage itself. When we marry, we are not only linking our lives to another individual, we are also entering a myth that reaches far into the most meaning-giving areas of the heart. The "happiness" we hope for in marriage is a catchall word that embraces many spoken and unspoken wishes for fulfillment. In a sense, the person we marry offers us an opportunity to enter, explore, and fulfill essential notions of who we are and who we can be. In this sense marriage is not fundamentally the relationship between two persons, but rather an entry into destiny, an opening to the potential life that lies hidden from view until evoked by the particular thoughts and feelings of marriage.

The all-important mystery the Cochiti story teaches is not the kind of lesson one reads in modern books on marriage. Textbooks teach us how to get along in life, while myth shows us what the soul experiences in those same life events. Marriage seems to be about relationship with another person, but this mythical story reveals that marriage is also more mysterious, that it is a strange but fulfilling union with the world of dream and fantasy. Genuine marriage takes place in a realm that is not identical with outward life; our soul partner is always of another species—an angel, animal, or phantom. The familiar Beauty and the Beast theme hints at the way love and marriage bring us into communion with a realm far removed from human life. Perhaps the ultimate object of all desire is bestial, demanding from us a broadening of understanding and feeling beyond mere human sympathies.

In the ancient tale of Eros and Psyche, a story much prized by psychologists in recent years, Psyche, the young girl, falls in love with Eros, who is Love himself. She visits him nightly in his beautiful home at the bottom of a cliff. One of her sisters, jealous of Psyche's lover and the opulent life he gives her, tells her that he is really a beast. She convinces Psyche that she should light a lamp one night—breaking a promise she had made never to shed light on her lover—and see for herself. Psyche gives in to her sister's scheme, lights a lamp, and beholds a beautiful winged Eros in her bed. A drop of hot oil from the lamp spills onto Eros, waking him. When he sees that he has been betrayed, he gets up and rushes away. The rest of the story tells of Psyche's desperate attempts, through a series of trials, to recover her life with Eros.

It's tempting to see the sister's ploy as simply that, a ruse to spoil Psyche's good fortune, but the sister's observation is at least partly true. Eros *is* a beast, a dragon, and sometimes a coyote. Every marriage brings the soul in its innocence into union with an erotic sprite who may have some mischief in mind. Perhaps if we were to recognize that deep in the scheme of things the lure toward marriage is always mischievous, we wouldn't be so shocked and disillusioned when the animal appears. We think it's a human institution, when at least in part it has a mysterious dimension that not only transcends but may contradict our human intentions, a dimension that is as devilish as it is angelic.

The Cochiti girl is clever. Before Coyote makes an appearance, she will not be satisfied with an ordinary human marriage, even when it is dressed up with fine gifts and extraordinary human talent. She is attracted more powerfully, though less directly, by these seemingly insignificant indications of an underworld fruitfulness—the black currants in Coyote's left hand. These currants are reminiscent of the pomegranate seeds that, in the popular Greek tale of mystical marriage, keep Persephone married to the underworld lord. In that story, too, the ultimate seduction is not accomplished by something obvious; it's achieved by what is dark, sweet, and in seed form rather than fully matured. We are drawn into intimacy by possibilities rather than by realities, by the promise of things to come rather than by proven accomplishments, and perhaps by seductions that are darker than the bright reasons to which we admit.

From the point of view of our story, it is the primary task of the marriage partners not to create a life together, but to evoke the *soul's* lover, to stir up this magical fantasy of marriage and to sustain it, thus serving the particular all-important myth that lies deep in the lover's heart and that supplies a profound need for meaning, fulfillment, and relatedness. It isn't unusual to hear of marriages in which all the reasonable life elements are in order— a good home, fine children, happy days—and yet one or both of the partners is deeply dissatisfied and often charmed by an erotic attraction to someone else, usually someone quite different from the mate. Apparently it isn't enough to make a *human* marriage. In order to fulfill its need for divine coupling, the soul needs something less tangible than a happy home. The moral I take from the Cochiti story is that every soulful marriage requires Coyote's presence. It requires in the people involved a vivid sense of its own mystery and an awareness that purely human efforts to keep it alive and thriving always prove insufficient.

The young men in the story tried to entice the girl to them by giving her their best weavings, things she herself could make better. Coyote, on the other hand, offered her nothing except the deceptively simple currants. In marriage we may not all need a fully functioning home, several children, a hefty bank account—a fantasy that seems strong in our day. These human goals may even stand in the way of the more mysterious needs of the soul for an interior home. Oddly, the attempts of many married people to create an affluent environment might even be the cause of marital failure, because the point in marriage is not to create a material, human world, but rather to evoke a spirit of love that is not of this world.

Once again I'd like to amend, or at least interpret, Rilke's famous advice to couples that one should protect the solitude of the other. One should rather protect and feed the deep fantasies that surround the other's imagination of love and marriage. This is one way to understand the "solitude" of the other. Getting to know our partner's soul, we may discover what charms his or her imagination. We may glimpse deeper hopes our partner has for marriage, even those goals beneath conscious awareness.

As a marriage partner, I could ask myself, "How can I evoke Coyote and make him part of this marriage? What are the black currants my lover enjoys and appreciates? What simple but not necessarily obvious things stir her heart and feed her notions of love? What can I hold in my subtle left hand to charm her, as my right hand goes about the mundane business of making a living and building a home?"

The Cochiti girl wonders if she and her family can live in the small space of Coyote's home. The realm of soul sometimes appears small and even insignificant in comparison to "the big

world out there" in which our lives are lived out. Tradition sometimes calls the realm of soul a microcosm. It's tempting to focus
on the cosmic element rather than the micro, yet we might recognize that to the soul the most minute things can be crucial. In
several places in his writing, Jung discusses the "little people"—
gnomes, dactyls, elves, Tom Thumbs—the ones who do the
work of soul. The soul of marriage is no exception: it is created by
small acts, small words, and small, everyday interactions.

How do we keep Coyote dancing in our marriage? Marriage
works best not by keeping the contract up to date and doing all
the right things, but by stamping our feet four times on the
ground, by doing and saying things that touch the feelings and
the imagination, not just the mind. If we lose that power, then we
know Coyote has vanished. "The magic has gone out of my marriage," a person says, knowing intuitively and precisely that marriage, like all matters of soul, works by means of magic rather
than by effort.

This is not an easy idea for a twentieth-century, enlightened,
technologically and scientifically sophisticated person to accept,
yet it is crucial. In matters of soul, a well-conceived ritual act,
well-chosen words, an inspired gesture, a symbolic gift, even a
well-modulated tone of voice can achieve the desired effect. Often
a very small gesture or action will have great consequences—this
is one of the traditional rules of magic.

I find in therapy that couples often bring a mechanical and
structural image of their marriage. They believe that they can examine their behavior the way their mechanic studies the working
of their automobile, find what is wrong, and be assured that their
expert therapist will know how to fix it. Couples often try also to
find some new pattern of behavior that will inject the needed element into their marriage. They reassign household tasks, set
times for discussion, and look for balance in spending time with
the children or devoting attention to their careers. These struc-
tual approaches are sincere, but they depend on mechanical reso-

lutions that usually sustain a new vision for a surprisingly short time.

Over and over again as a therapist I have seen remarkable changes in a marriage take place when, after all the reasons and suggestions have been presented, some more intimate, more raw expression of the heart finds its words. As serious magicians over the centuries have taught, words, and sometimes the mere sounds of words, have a powerful effect. This is certainly true of the magic needed to keep soul in our marriages.

Genuine though they may be, the problems of mundane life are not always identical with the concerns of the soul. The soul of a marriage asks for intuitive insight into its ways and needs. It demands wisdom, the kind of knowledge that lies far deeper than information and understanding. Sometimes the demands of the soul are paradoxical, so that it may ask for something that on the surface may look contrary to a "good" marriage, but soulful marriages are often odd on the surface. People make unusual arrangements, as in the case of one friend of mine who lives in one town while her husband lives in another, or another friend who commutes two thousand miles to his wife's home. As we saw in the first chapter of this book, the soul may need periods of distance, poor communication, doubt, and regret. These need not threaten the marriage as such, but they do show that the soul of marriage is a more mottled weave than the plain, sentimental, structural image of marriage we often try to maintain.

The soul generally does not conform to the familiar patterns of life. Whenever the soul appears strongly—in love, passion, symptom—its mood and behaviors seem odd and are difficult to fit into life. It follows that a particularly soulful marriage may look oddly individual, its forms and structures contrary to accepted patterns. When soulfulness appears in any human institution, it asks of us unusual tolerance and broad imagination.

Mortification in Marriage

WE ALL KNOW some marriages that are living hells and many that are full of difficulties, and yet we enter marriage with the hope that our marriage will be different. We bring a degree of innocence to marriage, hoping that in spite of statistics about divorce we will find in marriage a meaningful and fulfilled life. While innocent hope and expectation are a natural part of getting married, they invite experiences that are wounding, that bring us unwillingly and usually unexpectedly into the crucible of marriage. We need some innocence in order to enter marriage in the first place, and then we discover that marriage is not unadulterated happiness, but is rather another of life's initiations.

Excessive innocence about marriage can breed trouble. We might see the sentimental view of marriage that is often presented in movies and in advertising as a defense against the dark challenges that marriage offers, or at least a compensation: the more we are aware that marriage can be hell, the more frivolous will be our conscious presentations of it.

On the other hand, humor is one of our best ways of acknowledging the shadow aspects of our lives, and so jokes, comic movies, funny greeting cards, and many family stories poke fun at marriage. Through humor we can admit that marriages are not made entirely in heaven, that the devil has a role as well.

When I was in college I paid my way in part by playing music for weddings in churches. I'm sure I played for over one hundred weddings, and one of the interesting things I saw on these occasions was the way the trickster and underworld spirits interfered with the sentimental perfection of the planned wedding. I wondered even then if these unholy visitations were an indication that the marriages themselves would be similarly thwarted in their perfectionistic fantasies.

One time, for instance, at a large and costly wedding, the bride was walking down the aisle behind her dozen or so attendants, her father at her side and slightly behind. At the middle of the church the father got nervous, lost his stately gait, and stepped on his daughter's train. The long train ripped off at the waist, taking with it a good part of the dress. There, in the middle of the church, the ceremonious music playing, the attendants swarmed around the bride, protecting her modesty like the nymphs of Artemis at her bath, while one of them stitched her up before the wedding continued.

At another wedding the bride fainted, not an unusual occurrence. I saw the attendants rush to her aid, while I also glimpsed a flash of the groom running out the side door of the church. This is not the idealistic image of the hero always standing by the side of his beloved, but it may be a good indication that marriage is as much about division as it is union. I also recall a wedding in which the soprano reached an extremely high sustained fortissimo note, and her voice cracked, creating a screech that gave shivers to all present. In sympathy, I suppose, babies began to cry, and the ceremony had to be interrupted until peace was restored.

What is particularly liberating about these incidents is that the wholesome, beautiful, and perfect image of marriage is spoiled at the very outset. A realistically rounded view of marriage might allow us to restore some human dimension to our very idea of what marriage is. Ambrose Bierce's *The Devil's Dictionary* defines marriage as "the state or condition of a community consisting of a master, a mistress and two slaves, making in all, two." Marriage *is* a bondage, and a degree of knowing masochism in approaching it may be in order. Our very idea of what marriage is needs to be broad enough to include much shadow and many difficulties.

According to the Swiss Jungian analyst Adolf Guggenbühl-Craig, marriage is not a route to happiness but rather a form of individuation process. *Individuation* is Jung's term for the lifelong process of becoming an individual, of working at the stuff of one's soul so as to be less identified with collective images and more a unique person. In this view marriage would also be a form of alchemy and the relationship a true crucible.

The value of Guggenbühl-Craig's analysis lies in taking us away from the sentimental image of marriage as instant happiness, reminding us that it is an arena in which the soul matures and ripens. At one level marriage is about relationship, but at another it is the creation of a vessel in which soul-making can be accomplished. At the same time, of course, marriage is much more than an opportunity for each individual to suffer his or her way toward individuality.

Marriage is an Athenic weaving together of families, of two souls with their individual fates and destinies, of time and eternity—everyday life married to the timeless mysteries of the soul. Life and culture get more complicated with every marriage. Not just personalities, but cultures, ideas, politics, emotions, myths are all being woven together by means of marriage, and each marriage in a community affects all of its members.

It's interesting to notice that society loves stories of trouble in marriage. The worm in marriage is the very core of gossip, sensational magazines and newspapers, soap operas, and movies. We hunger for an acknowledgment of the dark powers of marriage: its capacity to disillusion, to inflict severe emotional pain, and to make life miserable. Along with humorous depictions of marriage, these stories save us as well from the burden of sentimentality that surrounds marriage. Sentimentality may at first feel as if it defends us against the weight of life, and yet it eventually becomes an onus, an unbearable lightness.

Marriage in its fullness is a soul institution and as such necessarily carries the weight of life. There can be satisfaction in the grittiness of marriage and dissatisfaction in its being sentimentalized. The Cochiti story reminds us that merely working hard at having a "good" marriage may not be enough to make it work.

What the industrious young woman desires is the one who carries black currants—the darker animal world. The story is reminiscent of one of Wallace Stevens's thirteen ways of looking at a blackbird: "A man and a woman are one. A man and a woman and a blackbird are one." The dark animal figure always has an important role to play, for no profoundly affecting human institution is without its challenging mysteries that visit us as from another species.

Jung learned from alchemy an important yet easily avoided truth about the life of the soul: its presence and thriving depend upon mortifying experiences. Our sunny understandings and expectations, our reasonable efforts and methods, and our high values and convictions all are subject to mortification, which means "making dead" and which is pictured in Jung's alchemical sources as the slaying of the king or the sun. Those places from which we exercise control and our bright and healthy visions must submit in the work of soul to processes of dissolution, and the keystone of Jung's insight is realizing that these mortifications are necessary in the making of a soulful life.

Insofar as it serves as an initiatory structure in the service of soul, marriage can be expected to provide all kinds of mortifications, and it does. Through intimacy's very difficulties, our personhood deepens, the relationship becomes more solid, and life itself takes on added intensity as our too sunny thoughts and emotions fall victim to the corrupting and eroding processes of marriage. The source of our pain isn't just that our partner is "impossible"—such an attitude would be taking marriage too personally. Marriage itself places us in impossible situations, impossible because they can't be resolved by human ingenuity. If we had Coyote around, of course, he would merely stomp his feet and the dance would recommence. We need his crafty, hole-in-the-ground, mischievous art if we are to meet the mortifications of marriage with the necessary insight and craft.

Marriage requires of us the slaying of our initial ideals and values—about marriage, about our partners, about ourselves. How do we do this without developing a cynical view of marriage or without becoming literal victims of the abusive potential in marriage? What we need first is some way out of oppositional thinking. Perhaps if we widened our image of relationships to include their being occasionally blissful and occasionally mortifying, with a mixture of all possibilities between, we might not be so surprised when challenging difficulties appeared.

Still, it isn't enough to be prepared for trouble. What is required is an appreciation for the profundity of the ghostly beast we conjure up with such apparent innocence in a wedding ceremony. The intimacy we pledge at the wedding is an invitation to open the Pandora's box of soul's graces and perversities. Marriage digs deep into the stuff of the soul. Lifelong, intense, socially potent relationships don't exist without touching the deepest, rawest reservoirs of soul. Few experiences in life reach such remote and uncultivated regions of the heart, unearthing material that is both incredibly fertile and frighteningly primordial.

Marriage may look like an arrangement of persons, but at a deeper level it is a profound stirring of souls. Like all initiations, it marks a fundamental shift in perceptions of oneself and one's world. Just as initiations are often ritualized with blood and pain, so marriage rearranges the emotions and one's view of life itself, often with painful stretching of the heart and the imagination. Often people who expect to find bliss in the arrangement discover bitter confusion in the re-sorting of feelings and thoughts occasioned by the marriage. They may blame each other for being outrageously inappropriate, not realizing that they have evoked a maelstrom in the soul through the "simple" decision to live as a couple rather than as a single person.

In the soulful marriage cynicism and disillusionment are replaced by an appreciation for the impersonal powers at work in what we imprecisely call human relationship. The Native American story reminds us that the "other" in marriage is not only a human being. It is also an animal, and a special animal at that—a tricky, resourceful, earthy, dark, untamable coyote, who brings to a marriage the potential for joy and fun as well as fear and power. In a marriage cognizant of soul, the partners find a brand of intimacy that is deeper than personal trust and mutual understanding. Oddly, it is rooted in mistrust and lack of understanding, in a distance that allows the soul of the other and of the marriage to be unpredictable and inexplicable. Oscar Wilde once said, "Only the shallow know themselves." The same could be said about marriage partners.

Caring for the Soul in Marriage

IF WE ARE going to care for the soul of a marriage, we may want to keep in mind a saying of Heraclitus that I have been using as a guide: "The soul is its own source of unfolding." One false temptation is to take the initial intentions of the people getting married as a guide for how the marriage should be lived. For example, people blame each other for not living up to promises made at the time of their wedding or engagement, but this kind of blaming is only a defense against the soul's incessant movement. At the beginning of any form of life the soul is in a raw, undeveloped stage; it makes sense that the marriage will be significantly different a few years into it than it was at the start.

HONORING FATE

We can honor the fateful spirit that brought us together at the beginning. From the viewpoint of soul, nothing happens by accident. The fatefulness that surrounds the beginning of a profound relationship suggests an intentionality far beyond the ken of the people involved. In acknowledging this turn of fate, we may find some peace and grounding, and also some humility as the relationship continues to offer unexpected challenges. Throughout the relationship we could remember its fateful beginnings, and notice further signals that the marriage has an impetus beyond the couple's intentions. It may take unexpected turns, or reveal surprising elements that may be both satisfying and threatening. Naturally, some relationships and marriages turn out to be disasters; but even then we can respect whatever arrangement of stars brought us into this story.

The fatefulness of a relationship may appear not only as extraordinary circumstances or synchronicities, but also as an element in the most ordinary events where it isn't appropriate to take full credit for what has happened. If a person's career goes off in a certain direction, that development may be due in part to decisions and conscious choices, but also in part to a gradual unfolding of soul; unknown forces and the deeper motivations are involved. Couples sometimes spend a great deal of energy and time arguing over choices that have been made, whereas they might be better off examining together, with a degree of humility and receptivity, the mysterious elements that have entered their lives.

Responding to the fateful dimensions of their own experience and of the relationship itself, a couple can lay the foundation for genuine spirituality as an ingredient in their love. By reacting not only to the partner's choices and reasons but also to deep impersonal factors, they reach down into their soul and establish a kind of intimacy that is more profound than the kind mutual analysis can generate. Then the relationship can be founded on ground not fully human, on a bedrock that is much firmer than anything human ingenuity could create.

Our conscious intentions are often colored by neurotic material and may have underlying mechanisms and purposes that serve more to resist than to respect the soul. But when we express ourselves so as to reveal less conscious material, we approach the realm of fate and providence where a spiritual attitude respecting destiny and other transpersonal factors creates a much deeper intimacy. If we are going to tend the soul in a relationship, we have to use means that match the soul's sacred dimensions.

HONORING THE GENIUS OF THE MARRIAGE

Something deeply mysterious and profound, like an animal lying at the very heart of relationship, far within its marrow, keeps a marriage moving, changing, and shifting. This is what the Romans called the genius, others called the daimon, and still others the angel—an influential yet hidden presence that is impervious to our explanations and rationalizations.[2]

Traditionally the genius served procreation. We can understand *procreation* not only in the physical sense, but in the fuller sense of all kinds of creativity issuing from relationship. Marital creativity involves not only the making of children, but also the making of a new family culture, a home, and an intimate relationship that is vital, changing from season to season, and affecting the married people and their friends and communities.

When we respect the genius of our marriage, we focus as much on its own creativity as on our intentions for the relationship. In getting married, we lay ourselves open to the influence of the genius, not just to hold the marriage together but to make something out of it. Just as the Romans poured libations to this spirit, so we might honor and respect it in our attitude and in listening to its voice as a source of guidance. In this way, we tend the character of the marriage instead of our abstract ideas about what a marriage should be.

I once worked with a very sincere couple widely read in the field of psychology and practiced in the art of studying their relationship. The man told me that the reason their marriage was stagnant was that he had been raised in a home that was cold and unloving. The woman's idea was that she needed freedom in her life, more than her husband did, and so she was feeling tied down. My sense was that both explanations, though subtle and convincing to an extent, were rationalizations, protecting both people from looking more directly at their marriage itself and noticing what it was now asking of them. I didn't know exactly what this demand was, but I had the feeling that the marriage, like any living thing, was animate and now moving in a new direction. What better way to avoid the challenge of that development than to become preoccupied with reasons and explanations that in a very quiet way argued against the validity and value of the felt changes? Instead, I suggested that they read the changes they were sensing as expressions of the marriage's genius, and turn their focus away from pathologizing each other.

A return to an appreciation of genius, while drawing from archaic beliefs and practices, could enrich modern life. Some people might even be comfortable thinking of it as a "post-modern" way of living everyday life—a recovery of old soulful ways that can coexist with modern sophistication. Recognizing that every marriage has its own autonomous spirit could help us with the problems that inevitably appear, and also give marriage its own personality and deeper value.

TECHNIQUES FOR TENDING THE MARRIAGE SOUL

In marriage we need ways to keep the soul in mind. The details of daily life can so take over that we neglect the mysterious genius that holds it all together. Marriage requires many different kinds of reflection and mindfulness, ways of communicating not only to our partner but also to the daimon that gives marriage its character and dynamics. A famous saying of the sixth century B.C.E. Greek philosopher Heraclitus, "One's daimon is one's character," applies to marriage as well as to individuals. The daimonic charge or genius in a marriage reveals something of its unique character.

One simple way to glimpse the genius is to tell each other one's dreams. For this purpose it isn't necessary to interpret the dream as a whole, but merely to notice the various situations one's spouse finds herself in night after night. Without any overt analysis at a symbolic or mythic level, we might still come to appreciate the less predictable aspects of our partner's soul life. One way to understand the complexity and puzzle of a dream is to see it as a revelation of the soul that is far wider in scope than ordinary life. Simple talk about dreams might introduce partners to the idiosyncratic imagery and themes of each other's souls. Talk about dreams also moves conversation away from rational interpretations and solutions toward a more poetic style of reflection, an important move since the soul is motivated more by poetics than by reason.

Societies in which people build shrines to families or to marriages acknowledge the daimonic aspect of marriage and honor the residing spirit who cannot be controlled willfully or trusted naively. We might either actually build a shrine to our marriage—a sculpture, painting, tree, pile of stones, a ring—and thereby maintain an idol of sorts as a way of remembering this important truth, or, less physically, keep in mind the mystery that lies at the core of our partner and at the very base of the marriage.

Not only while discussing dreams, but also in ordinary conversations we could give attention and validity to the indwelling spirit of our partner and of the marriage. Plato describes Socrates as a person who was guided in his relationships by his daimon, always alert to signs as to whether the daimon would allow real conversation and community. In Plato's dialogue "Theatetus," Socrates is talking about students who come to him to learn. "When they return and with strong arguments ask for further conversation, sometimes the daimonic sign that comes to me doesn't allow it. With other persons it may be permitted, and these make progress." This is an example of living in tune with the genius, paying attention to signs that soul, through the daimonic presence, is involved. If it is, then the relationship has deep grounding. Otherwise, in spite of much talk, nothing significant will happen.

We can be alert to the genius in ourselves and in our partner. It may show itself in such simple things as preoccupation, a sense of being driven, strong desire often unsupported by good and convincing reasons, or a tinge of irrationality. Ficino, a follower of Plato's ideas, said that if we don't pay attention to the daimon, our efforts in the most ordinary areas of life will be wasted. We might take seriously our partner's intuitive, unreasoned, but strongly felt desires or inhibitions, giving them even more weight than she does. A life sensitive to the daimonic is overall based more on intuition than reason, allowing ephemeral inspirations a place of prominence, and inviting excursions into the unknown and unpracticed.

This soul-centered image of marriage I am advocating respects the less subjective, less intentional elements in a relationship. The result may be a life in which the individual has room to play out his or her eccentric potentialities. We may honor a marriage's soul by discovering what it wants. Some marriages characteristically ask for distance, others for closeness; some for children, some for the life of a couple. Some apparently want to be brief, some lifelong. Some want frequent changes, some get into a mold and want to stay there. Some accent emotions of bliss, some pain. Some are flat, others are peaked or gulched. Some marriages prefer sentimentality, others like pragmatism. We can find out these preferences only by bringing to our own marriage a spirit of openness and inquiry that will cut through preconceptions and society's models. Only through many small acts of trial and error will we learn the flavors of our own, unique marriage.

Precisely because fate is unpredictable and by definition doesn't reveal a chain of causes or offer explanations, it can throw a couple into confusion. At this time, the first thing the people can do is to talk from the heart so as to meet life exactly as it presents itself. We all have a tendency to defend ourselves first and look for justifications for our actions. Fate asks for some loyalty from us, so that we might find a way of talking about it that is suited to its mystery. Without evading responsibility, we can express our wonder at the progress of events, speak for what feels unexplainable, and acknowledge that the life fate is creating in us is something we are willing to take on and for which we have responsibility.

Sometimes the only way to open a path to soul is the negative way—by noting ways in which we are unconsciously protecting ourselves from the sting of life's intentions. We could explore what is painful and challenging in certain developments, where we feel most resistant, and ways we have of evading or fleeing the challenge. Without berating ourselves or looking for sympathy, we could reveal the impact of the soul on us, and in that way show our partner with unusual candor what is shaping us and influencing our lives. This kind of objective honesty about oneself may be more revealing than subjective, personal confession.

Another way to care for the soul in marriage, a way that seems to have been understood better in ancient times than today, is through praise and celebration. This can be done in obvious ways—anniversary dinners and gifts—or through less common ways. We could, as chapter 6 will discuss, find occasions to write letters to our mates, even though we live with them every day. The letter could be a simple, heartfelt expression of feeling; or it could take the form of a poem. Poetry doesn't have to be professional or even "good" in order to do the job of celebrating the marriage. It also offers an element of formality and thoughtfulness that is not at all removed from feeling.

Yet another way is to take opportunities when they present themselves to praise and celebrate our partners, either expressing our feelings directly to them or to others. It's easy to overlook such opportunities and end up speaking only about the problems. There is something in modern culture that distrusts praise; one often hears judgments about being selfish, self-centered, and narcissistic. This concern about narcissism is a modern problem in itself, wrapped up certainly in our equally difficult task of being genuinely humble. It has harmful results, because the heart craves recognition and appreciation; only a neurotically puritanical mind would deny the soul these graces.

Sometimes the soul wants something not quite as strong as praise, but more like interest. What an interesting thing marriage is! We could all take more interest in our marriages, becoming sensitive to what they ask for every day, noticing how each is unique, and day by day discovering what marriage in general is all about. Our standard ideas about marriage may be dull, but the lived relationship subjected to wonder may present an altogether unstandardized view of marriage. The interest itself can also unveil its soul by turning attention away from the persons to the process.

Marriage and the Sacred

TRADITION TEACHES that the soul has an important spiritual dimension, so that living soulfully, even in marriage, entails a spiritual life that emerges directly from the relationship. In many of his writings, Jung talked about the *hieros gamos*, or "sacred marriage," which is a union at a far deeper or higher level than personalities and lives. In a sense, every marriage evokes and participates in the "marriage" of all dualities. Work and play, night and day, feeling and thought—all contraries we can imagine come together in a holy wedding of qualities. At the beginning of his massive work on alchemy, *Mysterium Coniunctionis*, Jung lists some of the pairs that come together in the "soul wedding":

> moist / dry
> cold / warm
> upper / lower
> spirit / body
> heaven / earth
> fire / water

bright / dark
active / passive
gaseous / solid
precious / cheap
good / evil
open / hidden
East / West
living / dead
masculine / feminine
Sol / Luna

The marriage two individuals enter upon may be seen as a ritual and a common life in which over time these other "mystical" elements are successfully wedded. It might be worthwhile to meditate on these tandems in order to see beneath the surface of marriage to the elements that are in play in it. Working through the relationship is a way of performing an alchemy on these soul qualities, and ultimately this alchemy could prove to be more important for the marriage than working out personality problems.

It is not surprising that in the New Testament the first miracle of Jesus is set at a wedding, in Cana. There Jesus transmutes water into wine, the flat necessity of life into the spirited, Dionysian, active substance of spirit. All marriages take place at Cana, for in all marriages the necessary raw material of life (water) is changed into a sparkling, tingling, inspiriting element of the soul (wine).

It is entirely appropriate that at weddings and at renewals of vows couples celebrate the union of their lives and the qualities of their souls with traditional prayers, poetry, wine, and ritual actions. Marriage is holy not only because it is a precious and revered way of forming human lives, but also because it is a form of religion in itself, a special way in which spirituality pours into life.

There's no need, of course, to think about myth, theology, and alchemy in order to live the miracle of marriage. One need only enter into it fully and tend its soul, of whatever kind and in whatever direction it leads, even into darkness. Marriage is by nature miraculous and magical. We do not understand it and cannot know where it is headed. To care for its soul, it is more important to honor its mystery than to try to outwit its intentions for what we, with our small minds, may think is a better outcome. If you want to ensure the soulfulness of your marriage, it would be infinitely better to build a shrine to it, find its god or goddess, and tend its image than to follow the "manual" and do it all properly and intelligently. For all of us, of whatever religion or nonreligion, a marriage is a sacrament. To care for its soul we need to be priests rather than technicians, and to draw from the wellspring of ordinary piety rather than from theory or formula.

Chapter Four

THE FAMILY OF THE SOUL

THE KEY to giving the soul the family life it wants, and to giving family life the soul it needs, is to appreciate the poetry of what a family is. A family is not an abstract cultural ideal: a man, a woman, and children living blissfully in a mortgaged house on a quiet neighborhood street. The family the soul wants is a felt network of relationship, an evocation of a certain kind of interconnection that grounds, roots, and nestles. This connectedness doesn't have to be perfect or whole in order to do its business and give its gifts, but it has to be able to stir the imagination and move the emotions in a way that is particular to the family.

The soul family is an echo, a poetic reverberation of the literal family; it exists in the time of myth even before an actual family gives it life. Since, to the soul, family is not a literal entity, it may be evoked by many different things—a single parent, a satisfying house, even a school or some other institution. There is a constant dialectic between the soul family and the actual family, so that memories of our own childhood play a significant role in the forming of the imaginal family, and our imagination affects the way we relate to our actual families.

The soul needs a felt experience of family, whether we are children getting most of our family experience at home, or adults looking for a family in the workplace or neighborhood. In the extended sense, "family" is no mere metaphor, but a particular way of relating that can take many different forms. It always provides a fundamental relatedness that doesn't depend upon attraction or compatibility. People working on a project together, for example, may feel the presence of family as they talk, work, and get to know each other. When we hope that our nation can hold together as a family, or that the family of nations can live in peace, these are not metaphors, but rather the expressions of a profound need of the soul for a special grounded way of relating that offers deep, unconditional, and lasting security.

In psychology, sociology, and politics we talk so much about the importance of the family "unit"—a soulless, abstract term—that we may overlook the simple need the soul has for a vivid experience of family. In expressions of hope for a family of humankind, the soul is calling out for one of its most longed-for pleasures. Jung referred to the archetypes of mother, father, child, husband, and wife as the "supreme regulating principles of religious and even of political life," which have "tremendous psychic power."[1] A deep image of family, residing effectively in our hearts and imaginations, can help us work and live together in ways that no rational principle can. But in order to nurture family to this degree of depth, we have to regard family with a poetic mind that is tuned to the deepest emotional needs and yet be able to imagine the nature of the family broadly.

Since it is so easy to literalize the family and neglect its soulfulness, it might be better for us to deal first with our image of family, arriving at a profound sense of what this is in the life of the soul, and only then think about our actual families and homes. It is possible to live in a family structure that doesn't evoke the image of family that the soul craves; soul doesn't automatically follow structure. We may also discover that a particular family doesn't need to reproduce the ideal family in order to give the soul what it needs.

Seen as a basic structure in life, a family offers children shelter, guidance, education, physical and emotional security, and love. Parents may find in family life the meaningful work of raising children and providing for them. Other members—grandparents, cousins, uncles, aunts, nephews, and nieces—are connected through the family to others, no matter where they live and how they behave. The soul is nourished in other ways as well. A child receives a history and culture from his family, and his identity, values, worldview, and life habits are profoundly influenced by his experience of growing up in a particular family. Elders see in their families the way that their individual lives will extend forward in time. In the life of the family, past and future meet.

The culture of a family is not only a shaping influence, it is also a resource into which a person may dip throughout her life for direction, meaning, and style. People living the modern life often complain about a loss of traditional values and about feeling aimless, rootless, and adrift. If we were to see the family as a wealthy source of traditions, stories, characters, and values, we might not feel so alone and abandoned to a life that has to be manufactured every day. We can't make a life out of nothing; we need raw material, some of which may come from our own inner resources, but the rest is provided by life. Our families, even though they rarely seem to be perfect models for us, offer plenty of raw material that we can shape into a life in our own creative fashion.

When we become parents and create our own families, we may want to be conscious of the importance of family traditions and other aspects of our family heritage to the souls of our children. In many societies, rituals, manners, and customs preserve traditional ways of raising children and keeping the family together. Our culture has become so devoted to productivity, mobility, communications, and information that we seem to have lost any sense of the importance of family traditions. In many cases, young people feel antagonistic toward them, breaking away from them and going off on their own as a way of avoiding what they feel as the burden and restriction of traditions. They may gain some freedom, and certainly traditions can be exploited in families as a means of maintaining power, but the loss of family traditions can leave wide emotional gaps and holes that may contribute to feelings of emptiness and aimlessness.

In part, the problem in current family life is one of "the chicken and the egg." In order to live a satisfying life of soul, we need a rich experience of family, at home and in every aspect of life; but in order to appreciate the family in depth, we need a general intensification of soulful living. The only solution is to give increased attention to both of these needs, realizing that we could bring more soulfulness to our dealings with our own families, and that we could also turn to the family more frequently for our soul needs of security, guidance, relatedness, and tradition.

In family therapy one often sees ruptures in all the many relationships that make up a family. Husband and wife can't agree on how to deal with issues of work and home, and so they engage in arguments and fights that are disruptive and disturbing. Parents don't understand how their children could be living lives so different from their own and feel cut off from them. Adolescent children in turn feel utterly misunderstood by their parents; feeling no trust and security in their family, they are left without guidance and support. Siblings also often feel alienated from each other through jealousy, envy, or endless rivalry.

One way to deal with all these ruptures would be to begin accepting the difficult truth that all expressions of soul ultimately speak for its needs. These many bitter feelings are part of family life; still, they may be raw and undeveloped. Family members may need to create for one another the time and space to give these feelings a hearing, without judgment and expectation, so that they can be sorted through, refined, and translated into a communal life. Such a process could bring imagination and reflection to all these difficult tensions, acknowledging both their necessity and their rawness.

The fundamental problem with the family is one of imagination. We need an appreciation of the family shadow—the tensions, differences, antagonisms, and clashes—that plays a constitutive role in the family soul. It's often a struggle for family members to forge a new imagination of what they are, especially as various members go through their individual rites of passage and life transitions. But if they have the courage to reimagine themselves continually as a family, while remaining loyal to their traditions, they will be caring for the family soul. They may not discover happiness—happiness pure and simple isn't the goal of soul-work anyway—but they may find the deep, rich rewards of meaning, belonging, direction, and history simply by honoring the soul of their family.

Failures of the Family

WHEN WE lose the soul in any aspect of life, the result is always a deeply divided way of living. In the case of the family, not sensing its depths, we consider it either sentimentally or judgmentally. We talk about the family as though it were the most honored institution in society, and we blame it for many of our adult ills. In fact, the family is neither as exalted as we make it out to be, nor is it the main source of our failure in life. One way to restore the family soul might be to find a way out of this split attitude and deal with the family more realistically.

The question "Why doesn't life match our ideals and expectations?" is a fundamental one, as basic and as mysterious as "Why is there evil in the world?" If our thinking runs along the lines of cause and effect, and if we think human life is mainly the result of external influences, then of course we'll look to the personal past—to family life and childhood trauma—in order to deal with these most difficult questions. It may seem logical that if we're having emotional or relational problems now as an adult, we must have picked up some neurosis from our parents, or had a debilitating experience as a child.

Questions about evil and suffering are the most profound mysteries we can tackle, but blaming our struggling human parents for these utterly deep mysteries distracts us from our own responsibilities. The result is that we lay a huge burden on our parents and other relatives, one they cannot bear successfully, and we also avoid facing the mysteries of evil and suffering in our own lives, and as our own individual, life-shaping challenges. James Hillman has made the interesting observation that by divinizing our parents, we dehumanize them. Or, to put it another way, when we idealize the family, we also demonize it. When we resolve our own questions of absolute meaning by reducing them to family dynamics, ultimately blaming our parents for life's difficulties, we dehumanize our parents and oversimplify the challenge of our own existence.

Philosophers and founders of religion have considered these absolute questions about evil and suffering and have offered far more substantive answers. Buddhism, for instance, looks for the sources of suffering and points a finger at our own cravings. Native American traditions wonder about suffering and understand it as the work of an evil community in the dim past of prehistory, like the Bow clan of the Hopi, whose corruption brought about the destruction of the world. Christianity asks the question and answers it with the mythological story of Adam and Eve.

What if, instead of thinking obsessively about our own family histories, we looked instead to the old stories for explanations of our suffering? For example, to imagine that Adam and Eve, our mythological parents, are responsible for evil and suffering is, first of all, to acknowledge that these matters are not really problems, but rather mysteries. Second, we might recognize that the roots of these mysteries do not lie in any temporal dimension but are eternally located in the human heart, mysteriously part of the human condition.

When we're children, our parents may seem so large to us as to be of mythical proportions, but as we grow older they assume human dimensions. Still, even as adults we may confuse the two people who are our parents with the mythological couple who go by various names in different cultures. Mom and Dad may evoke the myth of family, but they are not identical with Adam and Eve.

Adam and Eve are the true, and perhaps only, dysfunctional family. The story says that they had paradise in their grasp, but they lost it because they broke the rule God had given them against eating from the tree of the knowledge of good and evil. The thought that life could be paradise visits us often, but something always happens to make paradise vanish. Mythical and archetypal, this pattern is in the very nature of things. Because it is lived out in the details of personal life, it is tempting to understand it in personal terms; and so we blame our parents for the fact that we are not children of paradise—guiltless and perfect. But a deeper and truer response would be to understand that both paradise and the Fall are pieces of the same mystery, and both are essential to the human condition.

Our task as adults, then, might be to search for whatever it takes to forgive our parents for being imperfect. In some families those imperfections might be slight, in others severe, but in any case, we each have to deal with evil and suffering in our own lives, without benefit of a scapegoat. In fact, our lives would be all the richer if we could let go of the excuse of parental failure; we could make interesting adult lives out of the challenge of a world in which evil and suffering play a role. And if on a larger level we allow social science to blame parents for the mythic challenges of human life, we will remain an immature society, suffering many of the symptoms of a culture not ripe enough to deal with life's shadow elements.

Another benefit of releasing our parents and other family members from responsibility for our fate is the possibility of establishing a satisfying relationship with them—no small achievement for the soul. Thinking negatively and pathologically about the family distances us from family members, and so we lose the opportunity to be enriched by them. Forgiveness clears the way for some kind of connection—tenuous and slight in some situations, profoundly satisfying in others. Certainly the family would fare better if we all grew up and faced the eternal challenges of human existence squarely on our own terms, taking full responsibility for living our own lives.

Another difficulty in blaming our parents for our archetypal suffering is that our very blaming locks us into a stagnant pattern with them. We are tied to them not because of dependency, but because of blame; yet even slight movements toward living our own lives could liberate us from this static condition. Often, when people have been stuck for years in a sterile deadlock with their parents and then find some movement in their emotions toward an individual life, they suddenly feel free to move to a new geographical region, away from their parents, or they enact their liberation less literally by doing things they have put off for years. Often, too, these people notice how breaking the pattern allows them to have positive feelings toward their parents that they have never allowed themselves before.

Parents, for their part, might realize the importance of encouraging their children to live their own lives responsibly. Maybe the best way to teach this lesson is to offer a good example. Parents at times avoid responsibility for their own lives by hiding behind their children, taking responsibility for them rather than for themselves. Living our own lives is not only a good example, it creates genuine community within a family, for community can exist only where people are free to be individuals.

In dealing with the discouraging mistakes and bad judgments that we encounter in raising children, parents might also note that the story of Adam and Eve applies to parenthood: as much as we wish to be perfect parents and as much as we hope that our family will be paradise for our children, the Fall is inevitable. For centuries, theologians have warned us that paradise is also a form of prison—we need to be expelled from it. According to one tradition, Adam and Eve's fall was *felix culpa*, a "fortunate error." The ordinary mistakes parents make, the "negative" feelings they may have about being parents, such as selfishness and disgust, all play a role in raising children. The soul doesn't distinguish between good and bad as much as between what is nutritious and what isn't.

Family in the Sacred Imagination

WHILE WE need to appreciate the family's shadow as part of its creativity, and we need to distinguish between what is personal and what is fateful in family life, we also need inspiring images that show us the sacredness of the family. Our books, magazines, and films are permeated with images of the family as a sociological construct or as a hygienic hothouse for human development. But this humanistic family does not necessarily have soul, because soul requires a spiritual vision and a solid appreciation for the sacred.

One of the more interesting methods Jung employed in his writings was to interpret teachings, rituals, and images from various religions as expressions of the soul that apply to everyone. For example, for him the promulgation of the Catholic doctrine of the Assumption of the Virgin Mary was a moment of importance to the whole world, signifying a turning point in history when the feminine aspect of life was given a place of highest importance. In the same spirit, we could look at the Christian notion of the Holy Family as pointing out and celebrating the holiness of the human family.

Some Catholic churches are named after the Holy Family, and a day of the year is dedicated to its celebration. A prayer in the Mass for that day quite beautifully petitions an awareness of the truly sacred nature of the family:

> Lord Jesus Christ, who was subject to Joseph and Mary, you have consecrated domestic life with unspeakable power. Teach us by the example of your Holy Family and with the help of each member, and help us live in eternal community.

This prayer not only acknowledges the sacredness of family life, it also takes note of its extraordinary power. This power is not political or personal, rather it is a power of soul. The capacity of a family to strengthen, educate, and enrich a child or another of its members goes far beyond any measurable authority or influence. By its very nature, family has an inherent power to foster human life. This power, according to the prayer, is "ineffable"—it cannot be spoken, it is so profound and mysterious. No psychological or sociological analysis can explain its source, but religion can attest to it. Like all powers that rise from such a deep source, it has the potential for good or evil: one family prepares a person to deal effectively with challenges throughout life, while another inflicts such deep wounds that one wonders if they can ever be healed.

When we are taken aback by personal problems or overwhelmed by social ills that seem impervious to all our efforts, we might remember the sentiment in the prayer from the Holy Family Mass: the family contains power that reaches beyond human effort. There is something magical in the power of the family, a magic that we can employ effectively with respect and humility.

Living in tune with the soul means trusting such powers as those of the family that are beyond understanding and that transcend human efforts. This could be a strange idea for those who follow the modern way of relying on one's own personal understanding and skills; yet cultures around the world know the effectiveness of ritual, magic, pilgrimage, song, prayer, and sacred arts in dealing with life's difficulties. Like these, the power of the family is a method of dealing with the most mysterious and demanding challenges to human life. Throughout history families have gathered together not only for physical protection, but because of the special power of soul that can be found within a family. We, too, in our modern world could turn to our families, not only for reasonable advice or financial assistance, but for the mysterious creative power that is to be found there.

An extraordinary prayer from the Native American tradition celebrates the sacred power of the family to hold our world together. Every age has seen divisions and antagonisms among nations, and has sought political and military solutions to those divisions. The prayer of Black Elk, given in his account of the seven rites of the Sioux nation, offers a religious answer to the problem:

> He who is our Grandfather and Father, has established a relationship with my people the Sioux; it is our duty to make a rite which should extend this relationship to the different people of different nations. . . . O Grandfather, *Wakan-Tanka*, behold us! Here we shall make relatives and peace; it is your will that this be done. With this sweet grass which is Yours, I am now making smoke, which will rise to you. In everything that we do, You are first, and this our sacred Mother Earth is second.[2]

By acknowledging the divinity of motherhood and fatherhood, this prayer extends the feeling of family to all nations and creatures. The family of humankind here unfolds from a sacred relationship between a community and its spiritual parents and grandparents. Black Elk is not asking for a world government or international agreements. These are important, but first we need to recognize and acknowledge family in the deepest sense. In his view, we can create an international family only by developing in ourselves a profoundly spiritual notion of family.

Our secular idea of family, so taken for granted in our time, easily turns inward, becoming excessively personal and ultimately xenophobic. It pathologizes the people who raised us, rather than honoring them as having performed a sacred duty, and by extension it pathologizes humankind in general. If our idea of the family is narrow, limited, and secular, we may be defensive about our own attachments, and on the global scene it will be difficult if not impossible to live in peace. But if we could appreciate the family as truly sacred, as a way in which life could be lived effectively and powerfully, then we would have a profound basis for relating on an international level.

If our smoke does not rise, as does Black Elk's, to the divine, mythic Father and Mother, then we will not have the sensibility required for a broad appreciation of family that extends to include nations. Yet we need this global sensibility, not only for our survival, but also for the soulful life that such a richly diverse global family could give us. With the scientific discoveries of the past hundred years, and with continuing technological inventions, it is evident to all that we live in a "global village." Apparently it is not yet evident that we could live in a "global family," with all the feelings of connectedness, support, security, love, and community that a genuine family can provide.

The international family envisioned by Black Elk is not a utopian pipe dream. It can be an evolving community, filled with struggles and antagonisms, and set back occasionally with great failures. What is required is a soulful feeling of connectedness, inspired by broad familial piety. I use this old word *piety* positively, to stress the importance of *honoring* the family. We need devotion, rites of remembrance and respect, images of holiness, and even prayers like those of the Catholic liturgy and of Black Elk to nurture this creative, familial piety.

When as a child I learned the commandment "Honor thy father and thy mother," I thought of it as a rule of conduct toward my own mother and father. Now I see it as the expression of a tremendous mystery as well. If we could truly honor our parents, and discover in that experience the "holy family," we would find an infinite resource for meaning, direction, security, and community in our lives, a power rooted more in honor than obedience, and more in a poetic mind like Black Elk's than in the literalizing mind of social science.

Because this theme is so important, I would like to add a final example. In the Jewish *Zohar*, a medieval Kabbalistic text, the following teaching is abundantly clear about the divine nature of the family.

> When is a man called complete in his resemblance to the Supernal? When he couples with his spouse in oneness, joy, and pleasure, and a son and a daughter issue from him and his female. This is the complete man resembling the Above.[3]

Here is another strong religious affirmation of the family, pointing to a parallel between the human experience of family and the very nature of divinity: we are most divine when we are sexual couples and when we have a family. As is often the case, religious statements are remarkably different in tone and emphasis from our secular, scientific points of view.

The *Zohar* prayer could correct our common secularization of sex and family by reminding us that in both of these areas we have the privilege of participating in the greatest mystery of human life—procreation. How much closer to divinity can we come than to bring new life into existence and to play a fundamental role in making that life meaningful, creative, individual, and communal? If there is anything in life that is inherently sacred, it is having sex and giving birth.

How do we lose sight of this sacredness? Both men and women often say that the most transformative and powerful moments in their lives were giving birth to their children. In the privacy of our thoughts we might also have similar feelings about our sexual experiences. But we forget the inherent numinosity—the awesome sensation of sacredness—of these experiences as we get caught up in the everyday struggles with children and family.

Worse, we live in a society that prides itself on secularizing the most awe-inspiring aspects of life. We have made birth primarily a medical experience, and we see sex as the expression of personal feelings. The family has become a social organization and parenthood a skill for which one can be effectively trained. These pragmatic approaches to the family do not do much for its soul, because while the soul is always fully involved in the day-to-day concerns of life, it also always has an eternal dimension that demands equal attention and care. We do need to enjoy a secular life, but that life is incomplete without its spiritual counterpart.

Religious traditions have long recognized the tendency in human life to get caught up in the mundane and to forget the eternal. Rites, rules, sacred arts, and holy literature form an "art of memory," aimed at keeping the spiritual dimension alive in our minds and hearts. Maybe we need ways of remembering the "holy family," as well as symbolic and poetic means of honoring it.

We can always begin with the "negative way": resisting the antisoul tendencies of our time and culture. We could also find ways to sacramentalize our sexual lives and the birth of our children. It doesn't take much to evoke the eternal: carefully chosen music, candles, paintings, poetry, stories, fabrics, clothing—religion has always used these as tools for evoking the sacred. We could easily find ways to honor and celebrate the family: parties, conversations, cards and letters, visits to gravesites, journeys to see family members, honoring family homesteads and possessions, handing furniture and clothing down from generation to generation. These acts are not only practical, they help sustain the family's particular spirituality, and they can be motivated at least in part by a sensitivity to the family's holiness.

Caring for the Soul of the Family

A MAJOR PART of caring for the soul of the family involves doing whatever is necessary to honor its sacredness, but there are other ways, too. First, a family is a form of community and so we could discover ways to honor both self and other in it. Gatherings of a family help nuture the group aspect, but it is equally important to respect and promote the individuality of the members. It often happens in families that one member lives a life quite different from the rest, or sometimes one member will be visited by an extraordinary difficulty that may seem unusual to everyone else. These occasions are fertile opportunities to care for the family soul by responding to the individual, knowing that the soul manifests itself more in unique expressions than in what is normal and expected.

I have always felt that one of the strengths of my own family is that, even though it traditionally supports values typical of the Irish Catholic way of life, when unusual events occur—divorce, children born out of wedlock, emotional disturbance—it rallies around the individual and offers warm acceptance and support. As someone who drifts quite far from familiar patterns of life and thought, I have appreciated this grace of my own family, and know that it comes from deep religious faith at the family's very core.

Another part of caring for the soul of the family is tending its particular cultural hearth. Just as regions and nations have certain ways of doing things, certain beliefs and values, and their own heroes and villains, so a family has its own cultural materials. Soul benefits from the richness and particularity of family stories and mores. To the soul, the places, events, characters, and themes of the family stories are what mythologies and literature are to a society. They are history, myth, and an ever-present resource for imagination. Psychology may self-consciously look to a person's family experience in order to find the causes of current disorder and disruption, but at a less conscious level it may simply be seeking out the stories as such; for our family stories account a great deal for who we are, and our soul is to be found in the details of those stories. In this sense, too, those biographies and autobiographies that explore childhood in great detail are a search for the soul that lies so abundantly within family life.

To care for the soul, then, we might make every effort to keep stories alive and to provide opportunities for the family to get together to renew its culture. We might pass on to our spouse, our children, and our friends the stories of our own experience with family and its early history. This narrative not only promotes intimacy with those close to us, it also keeps us in touch with that large piece of our own soul that is located in the family.

Since our families are so much a part of our identity, it may be especially soulful to avoid separating our work and professional lives from family. When I was a boy, my father would sometimes take me on a field trip with one of his classes—he taught plumbing in a trade school. I remember visiting a factory where toilet seats were manufactured—not every young person has the opportunity to get a behind-the-scenes peek at this process—and many other plumbing businesses. I'm sure my father saw these excursions as educational opportunities for me, but they were more than that. I came to know his persona as a professional man, and this made a profound impression on me. On one occasion, he gave me a tour of the county morgue, where he happened to be doing some special plumbing designs. This was a true adventure that showed the depth of his interest in my soul, since he obviously wanted me to have experiences that would serve as powerful initiations into life.

Except for the occasional company-sponsored family picnic and in family-owned businesses, our culture tends to keep family separate from work. Maybe we sense some potential contamination: work is often done in a soulless manner on behalf of efficiency and productivity, and the presence of family could interfere with these goals. Some businesses seem almost monastic in expecting employees on the work site to be individuals cut off from their families; but corporations and businesses could find more soul by sincerely taking the family life of their employees into account when making corporate decisions, and by re-imagining the very nature of work in ways that include the family.

Modern life seems to value the uncluttered and simple, and yet families complicate life. In some countries, trains, and even an occasional plane, will be filled with families seeing that their relatives are comfortably seated and given full farewells—not a common American practice. Sometimes a family will "invade" a restaurant, gathered boisterously around a large table for a celebration. I take special pleasure in meeting the parents and other relatives, not only the spouse and children, of people I know professionally. The inclusion of family in ordinary life, especially in areas where the family is customarily invisible, is an easy and effective way of introducing soul, and I believe it is good for the family, too, who feel their place of importance and have a more public representation. Government leaders may also eventually be able to leave behind the image of the solitary individual, whose family is oddly denied by the very notoriety it may have in the press, and include a spouse and other family members at the focus of their work. "Bring the family along" is a way of breaking out of our neat, solitary puritanism and allowing the soul to shine.

When we emphasize one aspect of a person's life, such as position or profession, the rest may fall into the gutter, to become the stuff of gossip, speculation, and rumor. The family is sometimes to be found in this gutter, where a great deal of other soul stuff lies, like a compost heap full of fertile humus. If we ever feel as though soul is missing in some significant part of life, we might look into our own emotional compost and see what lies there, waiting to make our lives more fertile.

Bringing the family more into the life of the individual not only enriches the individual, but it may help us regard with due complexity as well the varying roles family members take on. We could always move deeper into the mystery of the person who is mother, father, brother, sister, son, or daughter, and find paradoxes and contradictions that are signs of soul. The person who is known as a kind father may have a powerful rage in the deeper levels of his heart. The giving mother may hide a self-preserving streak of selfishness. The strict, cold parent may hold deep, unexpressed reservoirs of love.

My wife tells the story of how helpful it was at her father's funeral to hear stories from his old friends of times long ago. A more complicated picture of her father was drawn by those stories told by people who knew him in ways she did not. In many families, individuals are blurred by the roles they play or by the strong feelings we have for them on the basis of a certain structure of relationship. The revelation of a parent's or child's larger personality might foster intimacy by making the soul more fully available. There may, of course, be a price to pay—the surrender of a simpler image of who this person is—but the reward can be much deeper contact with the soul of the other.

In more general terms, we care for the soul of the family by allowing it to reveal itself gradually over many years, in the individuals who make up the family and in the family as a whole. Soul is not a static object, but an endless source of changing life. One reason it is difficult to live a soulful life is that it isn't always assuring to be confronted with change. Because soul is usually in movement, forward or backward, it's necessary to observe it carefully. We might watch with interest as our parents and grandparents go through life changes, deal with illness and crisis, and find some of the goals they are seeking. We might notice the flowering of our brothers, sisters, and cousins as they ride the bumpy road of soul-making. We might be fully present to our children and grandchildren, nieces and nephews, and our godchildren, not interfering as they find their way, but always offering involvement:

our care, our attention, and our stories of experience. Finally, we might see the family spirit and myth alive within ourselves, being fulfilled once again in a unique way, and, loyal to that spirit, we might be proud of it and weave it consciously and artfully further into our lives.

These are all simple ways to care for the family soul, and they are all marked by a spirit of restrained ambition and by a style that is not full of striving and effort. The point in soul care is to let soul emerge on its own, to tend it in times of blockage and wounding, and to honor and celebrate its slightest manifestations and modest initiations. In such a milieu, this ordinary entity, the family, may show itself to be one of the most powerful creative forces in our lives.

Chapter Five

FRIENDSHIP AND COMMUNITY

MUCH OF MY work is based on the insights, imagery, and worldview of the Florentine Academy headed by Marsilio Ficino in the later decades of the fifteenth century. Scholars debate about the nature of the structure of this academy, but for Ficino himself it was clearly not a simple institute of teaching, but a living community of friends.[1] It's easy to pass over a distinction like this lightly, or to treat it as an insignificant, sentimental thought, but imagine how radically our social structures would change if we made friendship our highest priority and considered our functional purposes secondary.

When we make the effort to place soul at the center of our concerns, as Ficino did in his reconstruction of culture, values shift significantly. In every gathering of people, from business to politics, community would be considered more important than organization, and friendship more valuable than productivity. If

this idea seems anachronistic or impossible to live in our culture,
then it is apparent how far we have to go to make our lives more
soulful.

Friendship

SOME OF our oldest literature attests to the importance of
friendship to human life. In the ancient Sumerian epic of Gilgamesh, the eponymous proud hero is brought to tearful self-
reflection when his friend Enkidu dies at the hand of a giant they
had battled. He has a statue made for his friend—"of lapis is thy
breast, of gold thy body"—the precious materials of the sculpture displaying the high value of friendship. Then Gilgamesh re-
alizes, in the death of his friend, his own mortality. "When I die,
shall I not be like Enkidu? Woe has entered my belly. Fearing
death, I roam over the steppe." So begins Gilgamesh's epic quest
for immortality: an indication of just how deeply friendship is located in the soul.

In the Old Testament, the great King David enjoyed a celebrated love with Jonathan, the son of King Saul. On several occasions Jonathan protected David from harm. But Jonathan and
his father were killed in battle, and at Jonathan's death, David,
composer of sacred songs, sang a dirge: "O Jonathan! by your
death am I mortally wounded" (2 Samuel 1:25). Again we find
the theme: the death of a friend equated with one's own mortality
and woundedness.

It is not surprising that the loss of a friend affects us so deeply:
such deep relationships become part of our very makeup. In a letter about the death of her dear friend Judge Lord, Emily Dickinson wrote: "Forgive the Tears that fell for few, but that few too
many, for was not each a World?"[2] Each friend is indeed a world,
a special sphere of certain emotions, experiences, memories, and
qualities of personality. Each friend takes us into a world that is

ourselves as well. We are all made up of many worlds and each friendship brings one or more of those worlds to life. Friendship "constellates" (the word means "an arranging of stars") one's universe of meaning and value. One shares with a friend a unique way of looking at life and experiencing it, and so our friendships perform a kind of astrology of the soul, opening planetary worlds for us, to give our lives culture and articulation. To lose a friend is to suffer the loss of worlds, and to be lacking in friendship altogether is to be cut off, in a deeply felt way, from a richly self-defining way of being in the world.

If the body is in pain, one of the first things to look for is infection; if the soul is in pain, we might look for lack of friendship. Friendship creates the cosmologies in which we live, and if we do not have a cultivated world made through the conversations and exchanges of friendship, we will necessarily feel detached, unmoored, and unplaced. We may believe that friendship, like so many things of the soul, is tangential to life, an added boon, or an accessory. But if we were to take Epicurus, Ficino, Thomas More, Emily Dickinson, and many other writers at their word, we would realize that friendship is a necessity. If we neglect it, we will feel its lack as a morbidity of soul. Friendship makes a major contribution to the process of soul-making, and without it we feel a painful lack and a debilitating weakness of heart.

Friendship: A Vessel of Soul-making

IN ADDITION to whole worlds of imagination, friendship offers the soul intimacy and relatedness. Many parts of life go along fine without intimate connections. Work doesn't necessarily ask for intimate relationships, and it is possible for political and social life to be carried out without intimacy, too. But without intimacy, soul goes starving, for the closeness provided by intimate relationships fulfills the soul's very nature. Family, home, marriage, hometown, memories, personal and family stories—each gives the soul the containment it requires. Jung described the ideal setting of soul-work as an alchemical *vas*, a glass vessel in which all the stuff of the soul could be contained. Friendship is one such vessel, keeping the soul stuff together where it can go through its operations and processes. In times of emotional struggle, our first recourse might be to talk with friends, for we know that our most difficult material is safe with a friend, and that the friendship can hold our thoughts and feelings, no matter how painful or unusual, as we sift through them and watch them unfold.

In the practice of friendship, we might keep this important aspect of soul in mind: its need for containment. Our capacity to keep a secret could be important to a friend who may feel free to talk to us in a spirit of confidentiality. It often happens, too, that what goes on among certain friends has to be protected from other friendships. Emily Dickinson's biographer Richard Sewall notes that Emily made a separate world of her various correspondents and friends: "The letters to Higginson say nothing about Bowles; the letters to Bowles say nothing about Higginson; the letters to Helen Hunt Jackson say nothing about either of them."[3]

A friend could also offer containment by receiving another's feelings and thoughts without a strong need for interpretation or commentary. Sometimes, of course, we ask friends to offer their opinions and judgments, but even then we expect a high degree of acceptance and recognition of who we are. In friendship, we want to receive and to be received.

In the years of my work as a therapist, many people asked me to be their friend rather than their therapist. "Couldn't we just meet at a coffee shop," they would say, or, "If you talked to me about yourself, this conversation wouldn't be so one-sided." Clearly there is a difference between being a friend and being a therapist, the latter role lacking the mutuality of friendship. I have come to understand this common distaste for the therapeutic role and the desire for friendship as the soul asking for what it knows is best. To the soul, there is hardly anything more healing than friendship. I suspect that a patient's wish for friendship with a therapist is more a correct intuition than a defense.

In friendship there may be more not-doing than doing. Friendship doesn't ask for a great deal of activity, but it does require loyalty and presence. After all, what the soul wants is attachment—a detached friendship is a contradiction in terms. Therefore, like all forms of soulful living, friendship demands attention. We may be present to our friend through visits, phone calls, letters, or postcards. Using any methods at hand, we can nurture a friendship through simple heartfelt expressions. Some of my most treasured tokens of friendship are postcards with only a half-sentence on them, best if the half-sentence is thoughtful, or if it conjures up some intimacy between me and the sender. I have a treasured postcard from James Hillman that reads simply, "My health? Root canal and spreading bad poison ivy, and yours?"

A friendship doesn't require compatibility. The soul can reach out and make its connections through and in spite of differences of politics, opinions, convictions, and beliefs. Friendship is the container of soul, not the process of weaving compatible companionships. The *Tao Te Ching*, employing an image that applies to all aspects of life, says, "It is precisely where there's no substance, that we find the usefulness of clay pots." It is precisely where there's no effort toward homogeneity, but simply a space shaped with a sensitivity to intimacy, that we find the usefulness of a friendship. The soul requires many varieties of vessels and many kinds of spaces in order to work day by day with the raw material life serves up. Friendship is one of the most effective and precious of those containers.

Cultivating Friendships

FRIENDSHIP IS not essentially a union of personalities, it is an attraction and magnetism of souls. Friendships often begin in a soulful way through the workings of fate. We might "just happen" to meet a person and find even the slimmest basis for a relationship. Over the years, each of us encounters many, many people, and yet only a few become friends, and over a lifetime maybe only a very few become truly intimate friends—soul mates.

The fact that it's impossible to explain just what makes someone a great friend, or that we can't go out and apply a formula for finding true friends, indicates how deep and unintentional friendship can be. It is as though souls recognize the hidden treasure in each other and forge the alliance, while the conscious mind goes on with its intentions, hopes, and expectations.

It may be wise, then, to cultivate friendship in an indirect manner. Friendship may not respond well to pressure. It may be more fruitful to notice signs of potential friendship, and allow them to incubate. Sometimes it seems as though "others" in us make friends, and we then enjoy the glow of their acquaintance. As is often the case, it is better to stand out of the way and see whether or not a friendship will seed. And yet, eventually even this kind of friendship, established far from consciousness, will need devoted tending from us as part of our work of caring for the soul.

Sometimes it seems as though friendship is actually established counter to our will and expectations. I once did a radio interview with a man who seemed exactly in tune with my sensitivities, and I wished that we could be friends. I even made a mild overture, but so far nothing has come of it. On the other hand, several years ago I received a telephone call from a man inquiring about Renaissance philosophy. He turned out to be a former professional football player, a member of a world I knew little about. But we have been fast friends ever since, by the magic and grace that pays no heed to our respective backgrounds.

Sometimes friendships come into blossom in what seems like an instant. An extraordinary moment in my life was a few hours spent with my football-playing friend, and another friend who is a playwright. The three of us spent a summer afternoon floating in a swimming pool, talking about our early experiences and some of the father figures in our lives. It was a surreal moment of exquisite friendship, one I will never forget, but that moment was also ephemeral.

Eternity makes itself felt in both lasting relationships and those that last for only a time. In neither case is the soul concerned with literal time, but rather with the tone of the event. If it evokes eternity, then the friendship itself remains in imagination for endless time, even if the personal relationship does not. In a variant of the eternal/ephemeral nature of friendship, Lou Andreas-Salomé enjoyed a profound relationship with the poet Rainer Maria Rilke for nine or ten years. After their second major breakup, she wrote to him, "I am faithful to memories forever; to people I shall never be faithful."[4] We could take this statement as a testimony to sexual freedom, or more deeply as a reflection on the soul in relationship: its emotions remain forever, long after the visible relationship has ended.

Friendship Within Structured Relationships

FRIENDSHIP MAY sometimes describe the structure of a relationship, while at other times it refers to the quality of intimacy. Friends may have nothing to hold their relationship together except strong feelings of intimacy. They may not be neighbors or coworkers, and they may live thousands of miles from each other. Then, of course, loyalty to feeling sustains the friendship, and if the loyalty or the feeling should weaken, the friendship may fade. Often, though, people feel that their closest

friends are those with whom they have a solidly structured relationship. A person might well say, "My father is my best friend."
Or it may be a wife or husband, a brother or sister, the boss, or a
neighbor. In those moments when we remark on how a significant
structured relationship is also a friendship, we might sense the
unique gift friendship offers, over and above relationship.

A woman says proudly and with feeling, "My husband is also
my best friend." She means that she is close to him only in ways
one is to a spouse, but also in a way that has special qualities—a
high degree of mutual understanding, a common concern for
each other as individuals, and perhaps a sensitivity to the soul-
work of the other. Ultimately, this kind of friendship may be the
most soulful relationship, because the outer structures that bind
people together are less important to the soul than its own deeply
experienced life.

There may be a hint in this idea of how we might respond to
what many perceive as the breakup of the modern family. Families in which there is no friendship among the members will lack
the glue of soul to hold them together. Instead of friendship, one
sometimes sees mostly power struggles in families, where parents
expect their children to have certain values and children want
their parents to behave in a certain way.

Friendship entails a paradoxical blending of intimacy and individuality. Friends, unlike families, have no claim on each other
to live in certain ways. They enjoy an element of distance in that
regard that sustains their necessary individuality, and given that
distance, friends can choose to be close. In families, and in other
structured relationships, we could foster deep friendship by eas-
ing up on power issues inherent in those structures and by giving
more attention to the ways of freely chosen friendship. We can
also, of course, bring friends into the structures of the family.

In religious communal life I experienced a sense of brother-
hood in the community as a whole that was tangible and strongly
felt, but I also had close friends, individuals who stood out as spe-

cial soul mates. In my family, my mother's sisters are her friends; they can go out together or gather in each other's homes not only as family but in an obvious and powerful bond of friendship. On the job, subtle signs of potential friendships appear quickly, and people discover possible friends among their coworkers. Corporations might be well advised to consider the importance of these friendships in nurturing and sustaining the soul of the business.

Marriage counseling, too, might benefit from reflection on the importance of friendship within the structure of marriage. As soon as we think of two people as friends, rather than as a married couple, different values and expectations come to the foreground. Again, the paradox of individual separateness and intimacy comes into play. It may be as important to give a place to the individual soul life of one's spouse as to foster closeness and togetherness. An interest in developments in the other's soul provides distance and objectivity, and also familiarity at a deep level. Seen within the context of friendship, a marriage can be freed to discover its own unique nature outside of society's fixed preconceptions.

The intimacy created by attention to soul is different from interpersonal closeness. For one thing, attending to the soul, two friends look together at a third thing, the soul. The soul is autonomous, to use Jung's word, or, to use Heraclitean language, develops according to its own laws. Friends interested in each other at the soul level do not simply look at each other's lives and listen to each other's intentions and explanations. They look together at this third thing that is the soul, and in that mutual gaze they find and sustain their friendship.

If this sounds like a romantic goal and an easy thing to accomplish, then the challenge offered by the soul's autonomy has not been taken into account. In pursuit of friendship, I am asked to regard my wife's soul without any sense of ownership or possessiveness as it constantly shifts and moves and stops. My ideas of what a marriage should be, how a partner should act, what the future will bring all have to move into the background so the soul can take center stage. The spirit of possessiveness has a place in marriage, sometimes as a strong shadow element, but friendship asks for a more objective intimacy. While the soul is the absolute source of our individuality and our personal, subjective life, it also has a degree of objectivity. It is a "what" as much as a "who." It is what makes our partner who she is, and yet it has its own purposes, most of which lie far beneath the surface of awareness.

Friendliness and Paranoia

IT ISN'T easy in modern culture to cultivate friendships, not only because life is so fast and busy, but also because many of the values that at one time sustained friendships have waned. In many cases neighborhoods, a great breeding ground for friendships, have given way to housing developments in which each house is either a palace or a safe haven protecting its occupants from violent streets—not a particularly good arrangement for fostering friendships. A soulful activity like friendship requires a soulful ambience: a neighborhood of stores, porches, and safe walkways where people can see and get to know one another.

Friendship lies on a long continuum of intensity, from the true soul mate to the friendly neighbor or deliveryman. On the lower levels of that continuum it's sometimes difficult to distinguish between real friends and mere acquaintances. Sometimes we use the word *friend* for someone and then take it back, realizing that we've only talked to the person once. Still, even low-intensity friendships are valuable, especially in the way that they lend a soulful quality to everyday life. A sense of general friendliness in a community is related to the capacity to make and keep true friends in that community, so that a brief exchange with a letter carrier can become a thread that, in mysterious ways, binds a neighborhood together.

Friendship is threatened in many places by a paranoid spirit that worries about danger or threat in the world at large. The world is indeed a dangerous place, but broad and indiscriminating paranoia is not a realistic response to actual danger. Instead of perceiving real danger and real opportunities for friendship, paranoia simply creates a bland atmosphere of general mistrust. Instead of maintaining faith in the world and human life in the face of evil, it looks first for reasons to be defensive. In short, paranoia is a way of avoiding being present to life with its full range of safety and danger, its potential for good and evil.

Like all symptoms, paranoia contains a profound truth and yet has a great amount of soul locked up in the literalism of its symptomatology. The word *paranoia* means "knowledge on the side"; we might loosely translate it as "parallel mind." In paranoia there is a knowing that is not direct, not purely intellectual and conscious. In its symptomatic form, paranoia is an unreflected, uncultivated, dark suspicion that there is more going on in the world than we are aware of. Of course, it's also true that we don't know everything that is happening around us, so there may be ways of working our paranoia and fears until they become useful and effective, even soulful, parallel knowledge.

The idea that important knowledge may be unconscious is the conclusion and solution in James Hillman's remarkable essay on paranoia.[5] Less rational cultures, he says, have acknowledged the limits of conscious ways of knowing and have relied upon oracles, seers, augurs, and prophets for vision and insight. As a society they were not without paranoia, he says, but that is because they read the oracles too literally. "Nonetheless," he writes, "the idea of an unconscious shifts attention to the Others beyond human control and away from fixation upon the enemy's hidden intentions." He is referring to the kind of knowledge we can obtain from less rational sources such as dreams, intuitions, and fantasy, as well as by indirect means such as modern equivalents of seers and prophets.

As a way to regain our sense of friendship and friendliness in this world, we could deal with our pervasive paranoia by placing more value on intuition, serendipity, and imaginal ways of reading experience. If we were to do what many people in the past have done—build shrines to the spirits that affect everyday life, and tell stories of the angels, devils, sprites, and gnomes who enchant the natural world—then we might find a way out of paranoia and prepare the ground for a friendly life. Acknowledging the "familiars," the spirits of a place, makes nature itself familiar and friendly.

In our day the word *friendly* may sound too light and insignificant to be taken seriously. We seem to prefer the *Sturm und Drang* of heart-wrenching relationship; yet a friendly world is necessary for the cultivation of soul. Friendliness is a sign that life with all its highs and lows is taken with a dose of Mercury, with imagination and wit, and is not literally and generically adverse to human intercourse. Some say that friendliness in a community is shallow and only covers over bad feelings, but maybe we could even learn to value a certain kind of shallowness. The spirit of simple community friendliness certainly can be shallow and still do its work of preparing the ground for relatedness. And in a deeper way, friendliness doesn't have to preclude honesty and negativity in our relationships; it can coexist with them and perhaps allow us to be more open with our negative feelings without destroying the fabric of our families and communities.

Manners as a Way to Community

A FRIENDLY world is maintained by manners, a sphere of human interaction that seems anachronistic in our time. In a democratic, pragmatic, bottom-line society, manners that show some appreciation for humanity in general disappear, and we find instead oppressive rules and procedures on one side, and uncaring rudeness on the other. Going into the world these days often means standing at a store counter trying to make a purchase while the clerk chats on the telephone, or driving on an expressway as cars speed up behind you to force you over so that they can drive faster. It's difficult to be friendly in such situations.

Courtesy, literally the style of life at court, is not much in evidence in our time when efficiency has replaced style, and our democratic society is proud not to have any royalty or a court; instead, our model is a "chief executive," or "head bureaucrat." But as with Hillman's recommendation to find some remedy for our paranoia in oracles without resorting to literal auguries, we might imagine courtliness, too, with poetic license and, without building castles, restore some graciousness of soul to everyday life.

Our home is our court, and might run somewhat less efficiently but with more grace if only we knew the value of manners. Modern American homes have lost two soulful, courtly rooms, for example: the dining room and the parlor. The dining room allows for a different experience of eating than does a nook or kitchen table. The parlor, too, once created an imaginal space entirely different from the living room and family room. But even without these rooms, we can bring an imagination of friendliness to our homes and artful, stylistic thinking to our most ordinary activities, steering shy of excessive formalism or artificiality, while inviting some measure of friendliness and soul.

Anything done without imagination is impervious to soul, and yet it takes little effort to move from practicality to style. A flower on a table, color on a wall, or an imposing rock in front of the house go a long way toward evoking the spirits who animate both nature and manufactured things. Stores could end their single-minded worship of cost-efficiency and play inviting music on good P.A. systems, use a little less plastic, and show some signs of individuality. I know of a restaurant in which the staff has been ordered not to replace a napkin even when it is requested by a customer, because of the cost of laundering. But such simple things as a clean cloth napkin, some good lace, or a well-oiled piece of grained hardwood add grace to ordinary life and invite manners on the part of all who come into contact with it.

Ficino not only celebrated manners as a major aspect of the soulful life, he presented an elaborate philosophy and instructions for making life more artful. One means he used was the *convivium*, a celebration commemorating Plato's *Symposium*. *Convivium* means "living together," or, as Ficino put it, "the sweet communion of life," so what he says about the celebration applies as well to life in friendship and community in general. Here is how he describes convivium: "The convivium is rest from labours, release from cares and nourishment of genius; it is the demonstration of love and splendour, the food of good will, the seasoning of friendship, the leavening of grace and the solace of life. . . . Everything should be seasoned with the salt of genius and illumined by the rays of mind and manners."[6]

Of course, manners can be merely superficial and formalistic, but they can also be an effective way of making the ordinary details of life correspond to human sensitivity. Genuine style in a dinner or in gathering people together elicits an environment in which souls can mingle, creating genuine convivium. If we only emphasize personal interactions in our reflections on relationship, we burden ourselves with excessive responsibility; the settings and rituals of our interactions are equally important. They are the context and the culture in which relationship takes hold. They feed the souls whose purpose is to mingle, and they nurture the friendliness that can lead to genuine community.

If it seems odd to recommend friendliness and manners in a world of starving people, ubiquitous wars, and crime on the streets, recall that Ficino was writing at a time when conspiracy was all around him, and the losers in a plot with which he had a distant connection were hanged at city hall for all to see. There may be a direct relationship between loss of soul in daily life and the atrocities of international struggles and the barbarism on our streets. Only in a thoroughly unrelated world can we poison nature without conscience, neglect our children and the poor, and righteously slay thousands of enemy soldiers because we don't have the patience or imagination for negotiation.

As a tonic for our troubled world, friendship and behaving with consideration and care may seem light and even frivolous, but that could be because we have lost a sensitivity to the values of soul. Our soullessness appears in our tough pragmatism and in our bottom-line thinking. Even our social sciences seem more secure studying hard issues such as chemicals, traumas, and direct family influences as sources of our problems, instead of the philosophical issues that lie deep in society. In compensation, some turn to otherworldly spirituality, seeking to transcend the limits of human knowledge and effort through preternatural means. In neither case is soul nurtured. We need a return to the simple virtues of friendship and manners if we are to restore life to humane dimensions and values.

Conviviality: A Renaissance Idea of Community

*F*ICINO'S IDEA of convivium leads us to a soul-centered image of community. From the point of view of soul, identity is not a solitary achievement but a communal experience, always implying a relationship to others. Soulful identity is not so singular when we define it in egotistic terms, nor does it suggest a polarizing of individual and community. When I see that my very identity is always shaped in part by those I am with, then I can glimpse my soul as fluid and multiple. Some people worry about not having good boundaries for themselves, but I suspect that that kind of concern hides a failure to be truly communal as well as truly individual.

At the practical level this theory of soulful identity means that I can be most myself when I am engaged with other people. I sense myself as an individual in context, in relationship to another. I don't have to insist on my separateness, thinking that only by protecting my individuality will I be an independent person. Nervous defensiveness in relation to community is not an effective way to feel secure and grounded.

When we are leading the soulful life, our very nature, if we follow Ficino's thinking, is convivial. With convivial values, we live in a world of both clear and blurred boundaries between ourselves and others. We go about our work and play on behalf of conviviality, rather than for individual success alone. If they are soulful and not egotistic, our efforts to have our own unique talents brought into the world and embodied in our own personal culture will have a convivial dimension. In Ficinian style, this would involve celebrating our common humanity, ancestors, family, and friends, and it would mean arranging our physical world to foster conviviality. Conviviality is not the heavy onus of taking responsibility for the rest of the world, but rather the pleasure of living within a web of relationships.[7]

This soulful approach to community is not concerned primarily with literally gathering people together. Current notions of community literalize the idea by grouping people according to their political preferences or other causes, according to problems that are shared, or in a utopian way of experimenting with human social relationships based on a set of beliefs and principles. A group is not necessarily a community.

We can apply two tests to discover if a group is really a community: (1) Is there a working together, affection and discord, and commonality? (2) Are the members truly individuals, or are they expected to think alike, have shared goals and values, speak the same language, or hold to a party line? Community is born when individual and group are no longer felt to be two independent realities. Like all soul entities, community is a paradox. The convivium, a richer word perhaps than community, remains "the sweet communion of life" even in the presence of differences and disagreements. It doesn't operate on the level of personalities and ideas, but from a deeper location in the soul.

One of my most powerful experiences of conviviality in the Ficinian sense was my life in a religious order. Like many young Catholic men in the 1950s, I entered the order in a preparatory seminary when I was thirteen. I left at twenty-five, after living the vows of religious life for seven years. I was fortunate to be in a community that appreciated the intellectual life, had a definite epicurean love of simple pleasures, and recognized the importance of beauty in spiritual practice. A sign of the soulfulness of this life was, as usual, the paradoxes: withdrawal from the world fostering an intensification of life, affirmation of pleasure accompanied by an unusual amount of asceticism, and a common life that allowed me to find my individuality.

While I left that life behind many years ago, it now seems to me that its principles still apply in our world at large. I can see how the vows of poverty, chastity, and obedience which shaped our quasi-monastic way of life could guide us all, in a nonliteral way, in whatever style of life we are living. We could take those vows and live them according to our positions in life, and I believe our lives would find soul through their wisdom.

In monasticism as I understood it, poverty did not mean having little or going without necessities. A toning down of materialism and consumerism was certainly part of the spirit of the vow, but its essence was common ownership. Living under this vow, I didn't own anything, not even my shirt or my pencil, yet I was never without a shirt and I usually had several pencils. Owning things in common generates a vivid sense of conviviality, taking away much of the ego that is invested in property, without denigrating property or material goods as such.

The idea of common ownership and doing without material things could become so spiritually ambitious that soul would suffer, but I believe there is a way to imagine common ownership as a way of fostering soul. If our city leaders, for instance, lived under this vow, they would do their best to preserve public places such as parks, riverways, and lakefronts. They would know that it isn't enough to ensure people's survival, but that such simple pleasures of communal living are also essential. They would see that the championing of conviviality would be much more important than the support of private enterprises. To a great extent, the quality of life in this highly technological society is succumbing to constant entropy because the public is served less and less with the bounty of corporate wealth. When the division of money and resources is split widely between the rich and the poor, the signs are clear that the soulful potential in money has been lost. We all lose, even the wealthy, when the spirit of the commons breaks down in our public and civic life.

In a condition of conviviality, individual possession and common ownership are fulfilled together. The person who makes money is in a position to be responsive to the community, and the person who has little money can still "own" the lakes, the air, and the earth. Problems of money, in any case, do not depend entirely upon quantity. A poor person can be controlling and a wealthy person can be convivial.

Chastity, another of the vows, also has interesting implications for conviviality in the modern world. People are often curious about how a monk or nun could live a life of chastity without feeling hopelessly repressed. Certainly there are problems in the celibate life, as there are in married life or in the singles world, but the withdrawal of a certain kind of sexuality can elicit another kind of eroticism, the kind that emanates from and sustains conviviality.

I can't speak for the experience of others, but I found not just community life but also convivial life within the chastity of the religious order. I suspect that our world could use some of this chastity, not as a literal way of life, but as a quality of relationship. We place so many demands upon sexuality that it is not surprising to find much of our emotional distress focused around it. Yet chastity can be seen not as a repression of eros, but as a form of soulful sublimation, a spreading of eros throughout life, not restricting it to sex as it is usually understood. Chastity is a form of loving, a way of letting others into your life that is not limited by a relationship to a single individual. Monks and priests do this literally, but we can all do it in our relationships.

Just as the vow of poverty does not mean strictly living without things, and yet its spirit requires a measure of asceticism, so with chastity there may be a reserve, ways of limiting sexual activity and concern. This spirit of asceticism, applied to sex, can serve the soulful life, provided that it is not literalized into an antisoul, antibody withdrawal from the erotic life. If we could imagine chastity as an essential ingredient in the sexual life, we would not get so caught up in various excesses and repressions. Boticelli's famous painting *Primavera* displays the world of Venus and includes both Eros and Chastity, Chastity dancing with Pleasure and Beauty as one of the three graces of human life. Chastity increases pleasure and actually reveals beauty, which might otherwise be drowned in lust, playing a necessary role in the full range of the convivial sexual life.

In recent decades we've heard and read much about the importance of not repressing sexuality, and that is certainly a necessary emphasis. But at the same time we could insist upon the importance and necessity of chastity, especially in the name of community. Our hearts can be opened by a kind of chastity that is deeply believed in and enjoyed, even as we live out our sexuality as fully as possible. In this way we find a way to community that is erotic and pleasurable. Our participation in community is not based then on cold principle, heavy responsibility, or ambitious idealism. It is rooted in pleasure, in the sheer, erotic pleasure of another's company.

The third vow is one of obedience. Many in religious life confess that this is the most difficult vow to observe: surrendering one's will to the divine will heard sometimes as an interior call, sometimes as the scripture and structure of religion, or sometimes as the voice of the current authority. One reason why this vow can be so difficult is that it raises the issue of power and sub-mission. It's important, of course, not to have your own voice and identity wiped out though submission to another, and yet the in-sistence on one's own will also seems one-sided. We need to find our way to a condition in which submitting and individual power are contained in the very same act.

The understanding in religious life is that we may eventually find our own destiny and discover deep-seated personal power not in the practice of willfulness, but through a holy kind of obedi-ence. This is seen not as literal surrender to another person, but rather the discovery of the divine will through obedience to an-other. Clearly, this could be taken in the wrong spirit, leading to disempowerment of the worst kind and to masochistic symp-toms. But there is a way to imagine obedience with sufficient depth and subtlety that we avoid the dangers of literalism in this area and find the necessary paradoxes surrounding willfulness and submission.

Where the monk looks for the divine will in the orders of his or her superior, we may detect our destiny, the seeds of our life, and our calling in the needs of the world around us. With this kind of "obedience," we move toward community in a deep way. We see our own fulfillment as entangled in that of the people around us. As we find our true calling and live it out, others prosper; and as others fulfill themselves as a community, they provide us with an irreplaceable context for our own unfolding and self-discovery.

In more immediate ways as well we can find ourselves in the others of our community. We pay attention to the will of others because that attitude of respect is the essence of community. We discover by living the "sweet communion of life" that it isn't nec-essary to honor only one's own will in all things. Community arises when we discover the interesting, if radical, alternative: finding guidance for our own lives by giving attention to the de-sires and intentions of others. This is not an obligation, it's a way of being that invites soul in place of ego. I find no difficulty seeing marriage as one person obeying the other, when obedience is defined in this soulful way. Our partner is essential to the discovery of our own calling, and in a curious way shows us what we want, or more exactly, shows us what is wanted of us from within ourselves and our world. As this kind of obedience develops and matures, we make the move from community to conviviality, for we find joy and pleasure in the points of view, desires, and demands of others, even though sometimes they may be frustrating. The appreciation of these paradoxes can be the foundation of conviviality.

Once again, caring for the soul proves to be a rather radical position, going against the popular currents of private ownership, sexual abandon/repression, and a strong-willed ego. We confuse openness of imagination with neurotic passivity, and yet our emphasis on individual will fails to provide the active, initiating sense of self we value so highly. The paradox is that the source of independent existence we all crave is set infinitely deep in the soul, so that no amount of muscle-flexing egotism can waken it. Only the surrender of the very idea of self can evoke the soul's rare gift of self-reliance.

In his essay by that name, "Self Reliance," Emerson goes to the heart of individuality and finds there the universe of things: "For the sense of being which in calm hours rises, we know not how, in the soul, is not diverse from things, from space, from light, from time, from man, but one with them and proceeds obviously from the same source whence their life and being also proceed."[8] Individuality is thus fulfilled in the discovery of "self" as the community of all things. I am the microcosm. The deepest, most mysterious well of soul holds the secret I seek and cherish: a strong, solid, rooted, creative sense of self.

This paradox of community and individuality is yet another *koan*, an insoluble puzzle to stew over for a lifetime. Stretching imagination so as to contain this mystery is a good opening move toward living with a strong sense of identity in convivial union with others. It also helps to soak our notion of friendship in the same mystery: when I have opened my heart to a friend, I am more myself than ever. When I can find a place for chastity in the ways of my daily life, then I may discover the soul pleasures of sex, and when I can relax my desperate hunger for possessions, I will find a profoundly satisfying horde of life at my disposal. These mysteries monasticism discovered centuries ago, and it would do us no harm to revive them in our day.

THE INTIMATE

IMAGINATION

But as all severall soules containe
   Mixtures of things, they know not what,
Love, these mixt soules, doth mixe againe,
   And makes both one, each this and that.

The Extasie, JOHN DONNE

Chapter Six

CONVERSATIONS AND

LETTERS

"TECHNOLOGIES OF INTIMACY" are the ways we go about creating and sustaining closeness in our relationships, expressing and evoking the "withinness" in community and friendship. It isn't enough to be concerned with intimacy in an abstract way, or to see it only as a feeling that comes and goes without our participating in its design. Intimacy, like everything else, requires art.

I am not talking here about communication in any superficial or rational sense. "Communication" has become a catchword in discussions about relationship, and it is a truism to observe that the trouble within a relationship is a failure of communication. But what passes for communication can be to relationship what information is to education—a soulless exchange of facts. We sometimes think we are educated when we have compiled a certain quantum of data, and we may think we're being intimate when we "communicate well." Good communication allows us to express our thoughts and our feelings to another clearly and adequately, but it's worth remembering that intimacy may also develop in the gaps in communication, in silences and in awkwardness, in muddy attempts at expression, and even in the lies and subterfuges that sometimes appear in a relationship.

In order to cultivate intimacy we need to find forms of expression that emerge from and touch the soul. For the most part these things are obvious: a gift that is particularly meaningful, a late-night conversation in which feelings rise to the surface, a letter at a time of deep emotion, or a quiet walk with another through a woods with few words exchanged. We *know* that these forms of intimacy are valuable, and yet in our modern world we seem to forget their importance. We accept the current concern for communication—we may have an extremely sophisticated telephone system in our home or we may use the latest lingo from pop psychology—but neglect the kind of interchange that is primarily for the soul. We may also confuse bare self-expression with honesty, and think that by being outspoken we are being intimate.

Our task in this technological era is not to invent a new theory of communication or a new method of therapy, but to develop the art and craft of intimate expression. In most cases it is a matter of giving value to simple forms of exchange: taking the time needed to write a letter, to buy or make a special gift; spending money on textured paper and a high-quality pen; allowing meaningful nuances in our gifts and in our choice of words to reach the soul of the other. Once we shift our attention from communicating to expressing intimacy, we are on the way toward soulfulness in our relationships.

Conversation

TRUE CONVERSATION is an interpenetration of worlds, a genuine intercourse of souls, which doesn't have to be self-consciously profound but does have to touch matters of concern to the soul. The following brief passage, from a letter by Ralph Waldo Emerson dated September 30, 1842, alludes to several elements in soulful conversation:

> Hawthorne and I set forth on a walk. . . . Our walk had no incidents. It needed none, for we were both in excellent spirits, had much conversation, for we were both old collectors who had never had opportunity before to show each other our cabinets.

First is the idea of taking a walk while talking. Walking can be a soul activity, so long as it is not done for some heroic purpose such as getting somewhere, losing weight, or winning a race. It was easier, perhaps, in days past to exercise the soul this way because there were good places in which to do it—no danger from fast automobiles and more access to nature—and not as many alternative forms of travel. Walking inspires and promotes conversation that is grounded in the body, and so it gives the soul a place where it can thrive. I think I could write an interesting memoir of significant walks I have taken with others, in which intimacy was not only experienced but set fondly into the landscape of memory. When I was a child, I used to walk with my Uncle Tom on his farm, across fields and up and down hills. We talked of many things, some informative and some completely outrageous, and quite a few very tall stories emerged on those bucolic walks. Whatever the content of the talking, those conversations remain important memories for me of my attachment to my family, to a remarkable personality, and to nature.

While I was a student in a Catholic seminary, regular walks were built into our schedule, and I believe that much of the learning I did in those days took place on pleasurable walks around the grounds of the monastery. I also recall a recent walk with a friend across Hampstead Heath in London, followed by a visit to the home of John Keats. This walk stays in my heart both because of the pleasure of the company and the connection it forged with a soul mate of sorts, Keats, whose work, though he died over a hundred years before I was born, inspires and guides my own. I also have painful memories of walks undertaken during the heartache of separation and divorce. In certain kinds of walking and talking, the soul comes out of hiding and shows itself with unusual intensity of emotion.

Emerson also notes that his walk with Hawthorne had no incidents and that it needed no incidents. The soul is not nearly as concerned with events and action as the conscious mind is. It has no need for events, and in fact incidents can get in the way of the soul's emergence in conversation. For Emerson, the important thing was that both men were "collectors," that they had thoughts in their "cabinets"—memories to exchange, ideas to discuss. The soul is more a container than an instrument, and these two soulful men must have had much to bring out for each other's enjoyment as they walked the forty miles Emerson tabulates for their two days' journey.

Conversation does not have to be confessional in order to be soulful. I notice that sometimes people who are just beginning to become more psychologically aware feel compelled to speak whatever is on their mind or in their heart too directly and too innocently. Some people play a game of "I've bared my heart, now you bare yours." But soulfulness is not created by naive exposure. What matters is not how much you expose about yourself in conversation, but that your soul is engaged. Two people working on the plans for a house or immersed in a recipe can be caught up in a soulful conversation—the topic doesn't have to be personal.

In another letter, written to Thomas Carlyle on March 13, 1839, Emerson makes this point:

The office of conversation is to give me self-possession. I lie torpid as a clod. Then comes by a safe and gentle spirit who spreads out in order before me his own life and aims, *not as experience*, but as the good and desirable. Straightway I feel the presence of a new and yet old, a genial, a native element. . . . I regain, one by one, my faculties, my organs; life returns to a finger, a hand, a foot. A new nimbleness—almost wings—unfold at my side.

Talk from and about the soul may be about "the good and desirable," about the direction in which we are all going as human beings, about the life and world we commonly know. The soul seems to prefer talk that is close to life and yet not only pragmatic and technical. Its favorite modes are reverie, reminiscence, reflection—those *re-* words that point to the soul's task of working imagination into past experience. Conversation restores blood to the limbs and gives wings to the body precisely because it is one of the chief conduits of soul, and it is soul that quickens the body and lightens the weight of literal life.

Conversation may also relieve us from the pressures of everyday activity and decision-making, opening us up to undisclosed levels of our experience. Soul resides in the overtones and undertones, not in the flat body of literal events. Conversation performs a pleasurable and gentle alchemy on experience, sublimating it into forms that can be examined. Experience itself takes wing from conversation.

I would reverse the notion that conversation is important because it is therapeutic, and say instead that therapy is helpful because it is conversational. To the soul the important thing is talk, not healing. It is much more significant to the soul to talk than it is to find some technique for repairing life. Conversation might be an Emersonian mode of psychoanalysis, lifting experience into the somewhat higher regions of imagination and making us feel more alive.

From Emerson's point of view, conversation is a way of coming to oneself, a mode of relating to oneself as much as to another. Maybe this is one of the reasons why conversation can be so pleasurable: we become reacquainted with ourselves. How often we've heard people say, "I didn't know I had this thought until I spoke it."

When he describes his conversations with Hawthorne, Emerson uses the intriguing image of the cabinet. In Jungian terms, the cabinet is a womb, a woman's way of containment and incubation. Beyond that, a cabinet suggests a way of keeping things that are personally important, perhaps old and filled with memories. A great deal of *anima*—the mood and presence of soul— surrounds a cabinet, and in that sense Emerson is suggesting that in our conversations we can bring along our treasures of memory and thought: all those things that are inextricably ours, that we take with us as we go from place to place. This treasury of inner, personal materials is the stuff of conversation and is the basis for developing a soul mate.

James Hillman makes the important point that not all of our ideas are soul ideas. Some are purely intellectual, cut off from soul. These may be interesting and may provide their own pleasures, but they do not engage the soul. The soul is always rooted, not necessarily in relevancy and application, but in the particulars of life and personality. In conversation with a soul mate, we can explore ideas in a way that is not limited by the special demands of the solitary intellect. We can include our opinions, our life stories, our prejudices, and our own style of expression. Soulful ideas connect to the everyday events of life without necessarily being about them. They have capillaries in touch with the deep emotions and fantasies that run through a personal life or a culture.

Conversation is different from discussion and argument. It is less pointed and focused. In its early history, the word *converse* meant not only to talk, but also to live and to dwell, and was sometimes also used to mean sexual intercourse. We can retain these old echoes of the word even as we use it to denote talk. Conversation is the kind of talk in which one feels one is really living. A good conversation may give us a sense of dwelling in a place even more strongly than its architecture or natural setting. Some rooms only come alive as rooms when people are enjoying conversations in them, and no matter how grand a room may be, if it does not nurture conversation, it may seem empty and cold. If the soul is not served, architecture has failed.

A few aspects of talking that I have observed during my years of doing psychotherapy apply to ordinary conversation, not least because a certain kind of intimacy is created in the private setting of therapy. First of all is the therapist's office itself, where we have a place to sit and talk that is not open to interruption and is designated only for talk. It isn't easy in this world to find such places. Restaurants and cafés sometimes fulfill this role, but they can also be filled with too much activity, and the people sitting and talking in them may feel rushed.

It's difficult to find places, whether public or private, without televisions, telephones, and radios, all of which seem to be designed to stop conversation. Not long ago I found myself in the large waiting room of a hospital where I tried to gather my thoughts about an illness, but the television was blaring so loudly, as twenty people watched it intently, that I couldn't focus, let alone make any contact with anyone else there.

Another aspect of talk in therapy can also be a model for ordinary conversation: what is particularly striking about therapy is that at least one person present is doing an exceptional job of listening. The person who cannot listen cannot converse. One has to take in what the other presents. Conversation involves holding the material the other has taken from his "cabinet," treating it with attention and respect. I have attended many formal events in my professional life called "conversations," often structured discussions in an educational setting, in which no one really listens to the other. Someone may be taking notes, or more likely there is a tape recorder endlessly magnetizing all the talk, but no one is truly hearing what is said. There is little sense of the erotic in these discussions because there is no receiving, no pleasure in holding the thoughts and stories being offered—the body is not involved.

I find that among couples having marital difficulties, conversation is often difficult, if not impossible. One party wants to hear certain things from the other, but he will not really listen. Or one person wants to hear certain confessions or admissions, but she will not confess her own state of being. In place of conversation, we have a talking game in which a power struggle is the most obvious focus. "I will not take the burden of speaking," an irate husband declares. "She has to admit what she has done first, then I will talk." Power issues dominate this kind of exchange, precluding any possibility for conversation. It's no surprise that couples having sexual difficulties can't converse.

Another aspect of therapeutic talk that has relevance to ordinary conversation is the allowance of painful and shadowy matters into the dialogue. "Polite conversation," a superficial exchange of pleasantries, may not be enough to evoke soul. Just as in a highly intellectual discussion the heart of the matter may be at the very peak of an idea, when the discussion has reached a point of abstraction when insight dawns, so in intimate conversation soul is evoked often at the very darkest core, the place both or all parties may wish to avoid. Going for the sore point is sometimes the shortest route to soul.

An interesting metaphor from modern life, "the bottom line," betrays our exaggerated attention to conclusions and applications. Conversation has no bottom line, it doesn't have to arrive anywhere, and more often than not it will lead to even further talk instead of a solution or an answer. It may take some fundamental shifts in our very idea of talk in order to appreciate the value of true conversation that turns ideas and experiences over and over, satisfying the soul with its nuances rather than with extraordinary insights or explanations.

Since the material discussed is of paramount importance in conversation, there is little ego involved. People trying to win an argument, make a point, preach a sermon, hold forth on a theory, or give testimony to a belief are not engaged in conversation. These agendas are burdened with narcissism and offer little room for soul. Conversation is an inherently soulful activity, and therefore requires that the ego be given a limited place.

Conversation hovers between people, takes its time to get in motion, finds its rhythm, and slows to an ending. A quick conversation is possible, I suppose, but it will always be truncated, a substitute for the genuine thing. A conversation tends to grow at its own tempo and in its own directions. Notice that when a conversation is under way, the links between topics are not always logical or predictable.

Perhaps the most important thing of all is simply to value conversation, to realize how valuable it is for the soul, and to recognize that some of the complaints we feel in our bodies and in our moods could be alleviated by giving the soul what it needs, including something as simple as conversation. Many of the things that nourish the soul are quite ordinary, and therefore easily overlooked or set aside when seemingly more important matters demand attention. It may seem more important to go to a lecture than to sit around talking, when in fact the soul may need the latter much more than the mind needs more information or stimulation.

Some soul complaints clearly indicate the kind of lack that conversation could fill. Loneliness, busy-ness, a craving for love, hyperactivity—all these suggest the need for something that would feed intimacy and ground the soul. A Renaissance historian once made the observation that Marsilio Ficino, master of the arts of the soul, was the "least active person in recorded history." Oscar Wilde once wrote about his story *The Picture of Dorian Gray*, "I am afraid it is rather like my own life—all conversation and no action."[1] This doesn't mean we have to become ultrasedate in order to tend the soul, but it does suggest that we give more attention to ordinary, purposeless, soul-pleasing activities such as conversation. Conversation is the sex act of the soul, and as such it is supremely conducive to the cultivation of intimacy.

Hermes the Postman: A Return to Letters

ONE OF the most potentially soulful aspects of modern life is mail and all that attends it: letters, envelopes, mailboxes, postage stamps, and of course the man or woman who delivers the mail. Junk mail and bills are only the shadow of an otherwise blissful institution. A great deal of pleasurable fantasy surrounds the important soul task of writing letters. An envelope is one of the few things in the modern world we seal, thus creating a private space for expression. Stamps are usually not mere tokens of monetary exchange, but small paintings, the closest thing we have to medieval miniature art, and they are also of interest to collectors, partly because of the variety of fantasy they contain, from national figures to local flora and fauna.

The mailbox is a mysterious item, too. For the most part, we place our treasured letters in this box, and mysteriously our letters find their way around the world. I sometimes have the fanciful idea that the box is a black hole into which my thoughts and feelings fall, to be retrieved somewhat magically by another person participating in this ritual of self-expression. I can understand why people in other ages sealed their letters with wax—not only to keep them private, but also to acknowledge the sacredness of a letter through the ritual of stamping one's seal with fire and a material, wax, that is not just functional, like glue, but has aesthetic and religious properties.

I don't mean to mystify letter writing, but rather to highlight some of the fantasy and ritual that go into this important technology of intimacy. Something happens to our thoughts and emotions when we put them into a letter; they are then not the same as spoken words. They are placed in a different, special context, and they speak at a different level, serving the soul's organ of rumination rather than the mind's capacity for understanding.

A woman who was in a touch-and-go struggle in her marriage, not sure if it was going to survive, told me that even after hours of conversation with her husband, she would sometimes write him a letter, feeling an added dimension of intimacy in that form. Another woman described how in moments of extreme frustration she would stop talking to her husband and instead sit down and write him a letter, delivering it from the kitchen to the living room. Each of these women felt that a letter might somehow touch her mate's heart more deeply than the spoken word. A young man who was in therapy with me was telling me about the difficulty he was having trying to convince a woman he worked with that he wanted more intimacy with her. "Maybe I'll write her a letter," he said, "so she'll know how I feel." I don't think it's enough to say that a letter is just one more style of communication. These people were driven by their desire to mingle their souls with another, and to each of them a letter seemed the most appropriate way to do that.

I have had many clients in therapy who would write letters to me between their weekly sessions. I'm aware of the suspicion therapists sometimes place on this practice, believing that it is a way for the client to have power over the therapist, but I see this interest in letters more as an awareness that speech alone is not in itself adequate to the enormous work with soul that is the aim of therapy.

Letters take time to write, usually much more time than talk. They require a certain level of artfulness and thoughtfulness in expression. Then they remain, to be reread, perhaps to be stored away for another day of reading, or even to be encountered at some distant time by a future, unknown eavesdropper. All these aspects of the letter invite soulfulness: rereading is a form of reflective meditation; keeping letters honors memory and not only daily living; and speaking to a reader not yet present in this life respects the soul's eternal nature.

How interesting it is to read the letters of artists and writers who reveal themselves in a special way in letters to friends, lovers, family, and strangers. For myself, I love to read the letters of great men and women, hoping to find a piece of soul revealed in a way different from that in their formal art, and even to find fresh insight into their work through the special forms of expression that a letter invites.

The limitations of the letter, much discussed over the ages in essays on letter writing, also contribute to the soul-weight of a letter. Ordinarily in letters we do not ramble on and on, as we can in speech. We choose our words more carefully, even in informal letters, and give thought to what we will or will not include. These everyday aesthetic judgments give art to letters, and it is art above all that opens a channel to soul.

It has often been noted, too, that although letters are addressed to a specific person, they are also at times the occasion for the writer to engage in some serious thought, with the addressed person in mind shaping and coloring the writer's reflections. Emily Dickinson observed that "a letter always feels to me like immortality because it is the mind alone without a corporeal friend."[2] To some extent, and probably more than we imagine, the person to whom we write our letters is more imaginal than actual. We have this person in mind as we write the thoughts that are ours, and to a large extent intended for our own eyes. Many people tell me they write letters that they never mail.

In letters we tend to follow the same illusion we do in speech: we don't realize that the other about whom and to whom we speak is in large measure the same soul we experience inwardly. Every day a client tells me with some passion about a partner, a mate, a friend, or a business associate who is doing something outrageous, and I sense from the way the words are spoken that fully externalizing the matter in another is a way of avoiding looking at the same issues in oneself. So in letters, perhaps in a milder way, we can deal with some issue of the soul *as if* it concerned another. I read the graceful letters of Marsilio Ficino not to find out about his relationships with his friends, but to gain more insight into *his* life and thought.

There is a wonderful scene in Paul Cox's extraordinary film *The Man of Flowers* in which the very strange antihero anxiously goes to the postman who is delivering a letter from the man's "mother," a letter the man had written and mailed himself the day before. In a sense, all our letters are of this kind: we hear another's words in the colors and tones of our own soul figures, and we write to our friends by expressing our thoughts to other soul figures we know internally. I am reminded of those mysterious words at the beginning of Jung's *Memories, Dreams, Reflections*: "Other people are established inalienably in my memories only if their names were entered in the scrolls of my destiny from the beginning, so that encountering them was at the same time a kind of recollection." Central to Ficino's highly developed theory of friendship was the idea that friends live in each other's hearts. In our letters we are recollecting and conversing with the soul, through both our friends and ourselves.[3]

Reading the letters of another, whether published letters intended for someone else or letters written to us, we are listening in on the recollections of our friend. This is the nature of intimacy: in specific ways the boundaries between self and other soften. The woman who stops arguing with her husband and turns instead to the letter form is trying to get him to see and hear her more profoundly. She knows intuitively that a letter straddles the boundary between them, while her spoken words might aim at penetrating the other in an exchange that is more polarized by issues of power.

I have said that in doing therapy with a couple I often ask one to talk while the other listens. I don't try to help them communicate to each other, but to listen to what is going on in the other, to glimpse the other's soul. A letter by its very nature sets up this kind of arrangement: we don't read part of a letter and then send back a reply midstream, as we do in talk. We take the letter in, think about it, reread it, and then respond after having observed the recollections of the other.

In the history of painting all over the world the letter has been a favorite subject. Often these paintings, such as Vermeer's *The Letter*, capture the moment when we see the emotional effect the letter has on the one reading it. These paintings sometimes let us know the content of the letter by means of symbolic elements in the painting, or in paintings on the walls that clearly depict a certain theme or emotion.[4] The painter uses an intriguingly indirect way of conveying the letter's content, hinting at the gist of the message but also respecting that the letter itself is private, reflective, and internal.

In movies, when a letter is important to the story we, the audience, are sometimes allowed to read the letter ourselves, over the shoulder of the reader or writer within the film; at other times, we hear the writer's voice as he or she writes the letter or as the recipient reads it. The "voice-over" in film is a curious figure, a disembodied voice, a voice that the audience is allowed to hear but which in life would not be heard except in imagination. That is, as we read a letter, we may imagine the voice of the writer speaking to us, but that voice is out of our own fantasy.

In a letter we "presence" our thoughts, giving them an existence outside ourselves. Our spoken words often have a function to perform, while our soulful letters are meant more for reflection. The move from function to reflection invites soul into the process, allowing more time to ponder the words and offering an opportunity for repeated consideration of the text. In a letter, speech becomes everyday literature, and so imagination can play a significant role.

The postman is Hermes not simply because he carries a physical letter from one place to another, but because he is a go-between of the soul; and Mercury, the spirit of letter writing, is truly a *psychopomp*—a guide of souls. With good reason flower and message agencies use an image of Mercury with his winged sandals as a logo. One of the great needs of the soul is for Mercury/ Hermes, for a means of connecting one soul to another, and for making necessary bridges between the surfaces of life and its underworld depths. These are the classical functions of Mercury, and they suggest that letters, insofar as they are the work of Mercury, speak to a depth of soul and at a level of imagination far beyond the literal—thus, their importance in the fostering of soulfulness.

Another soul aspect of letters is the rite of saving them, placing them in a box or some other container, stuffing them into a closet or placing them neatly on a bookshelf, filing them. In these ways letters are prized, taken out of the realms of time and function—they no longer serve as communication. By saving letters we keep our reflections with us, acknowledging, if only in a slight intuitive way, their objective nature and their eternal relevance. The soul wants to be accorded a reality beyond our own internal ruminations and ideas. It needs to find a home in objects, and for the soul of intimacy there is no better home than letters of intimate value saved over a lifetime.

The boxes in which our letters are safeguarded and stored are true holy containers, of the kind Lynda Sexson describes in her book *Ordinarily Sacred* as echoes of the ark of the covenant or the tabernacle. Whenever we return to these letters, our attention is taken away from our modern (for the day) concerns, and placed in an eternal framework. Such movements out of time serve the soul by feeding it its necessary diet of memory and melancholy. From the point of view of the soul, it's not good to let go of the past; better to revisit its painful and pleasurable moments, thus keeping ourselves intact, full, and nourished within.

A long history of essays on letter writing stresses the importance of the form we give to our thoughts and feelings. Erasmus of Rotterdam, a prolific letter writer himself, entered into this traditional discussion, saying, "A letter is a mutual conversation between absent friends, which should be neither unpolished, rough, nor artificial, nor confined to a single topic, nor tediously long. Thus the epistolary form favours simplicity, frankness, humour, and wit."

These four virtues are also hallmarks of soul. I often emphasize the fact that the soul is complicated and is most present during those moments when life becomes complicated, and I usually recommend not escaping complexity in the name of some simplistic interpretation or solution. However, there is another kind of simplicity that *is* soulful: using plain, frank language, speaking directly about emotions and situations, allowing oneself to be transparent and visible. These simple forms of expression allow the soul to be seen, and are therefore valuable in letter writing.

Humor and wit, the other two qualities Erasmus prizes, are also signs of soul. The person being stern and sober obviously lacks the ironic perspective of soul. Soul is always polycentric, always capable of seeing any situation from more than one point of view. Humor can be defined in part as enjoying a multiple viewpoint, so that even tragic and unhappy events can be seen from another angle, liberating us from the tyranny of narrow vision.

Humor allows two people to enjoy each other's company even as they consider some of the serious and painful aspects of everyday living without falling into despair. People who have to be perfect, or who can't admit to each other the difficult or impossible situations life presents, can hardly be intimate. What they share is the common artifice of perfection, but they overlook the fuller soul, which prospers in the failure of perfection. Humor allows us to entertain failure and inadequacy in life without being literally undone by them. Because letters provide some distance and perspective on experience, and since they are a quotidian art form, they invite the imagination and breadth of vision necessary for humor.

The final signal of soul mentioned by Erasmus is a commodity I take as a litmus test of soulfulness: wit. A certain kind of wit can of course be shallow, merely mental, and obviously lacking in soul; but there is another kind of wit, closely aligned with humor and mercurial in tone, that is full of soul. It is to be found in all the great writers on soul, as in Ficino's endless wordplays upon the names of his friends and in Emerson's ever resourceful turns of phrase. It isn't easy to get wit right—not too bitter or clever, not too light or dumb—but when it is right it allows soul to enter through the cracks in our seriousness.

In a letter to his cousin Sebastiano Salvini, Ficino lists qualities he wishes to find in letters: "In letters I desire clarity and brevity, penetration and grace, wit and gravity."[5] These qualities are to be found in Ficino's letters, and in the letters of many others who have brought artfulness and feeling to their letters, but Ficino omits another quality that we find in him and other masters of letter writing: a breathtaking openness of heart and expression of affection. In a letter to his close friend Giovanni Cavalcanti, Ficino writes, "Tonight I had decided to write to you in the morning like this: 'Come back, my hero! Hurry! Fly to me, I beg you!' Then, on more mature reflection, I deemed it wiser to dissemble my longing so that you would return all the more speedily, thinking me angry. Well, I am! But what's the point: Will anger stir him whom love has not moved? I don't think so. So I don't know which way to turn—to entreaty or to scolding."[6]

With similar openness of heart Proust writes to Antoine Bibesco, "I don't know anything about you—and yet I know too much, because when I think of you, which is all the time, I have the same feeling as in jealousy, though there's no connection. I mean that, without knowing anything precisely, I keep imagining everything best calculated to torture me, at every moment I see you either so shaken by sobs that it drives me to despair or so terrifyingly calm that it depresses me not to see you weeping."[7]

These expiations of feeling may seem unusually revealing, yet they clearly provide an opportunity for the writer to reflect on his emotions and experiences at the same time he's expressing them. The deeper we move into experiences of soul, the more vivid the feeling, and in general our emotional life is nourished when the imagination is vivid. We need words, pictures, and gestures that are in unison with the soul, not dissonant because of their weakness and shallowness.

The celebrated friend of Erasmus, Thomas More, an artful writer of letters and a complicated and sophisticated man, in the most dire circumstances could write and speak with humor, wit, utter compassion, and heartfelt simplicity. In his last letter to his beloved daughter, written on the day before his death, he wrote, "I cumber {burden} you good Margaret much, but I would be sorry, if it should be any longer than tomorrow, for it is St. Thomas eve and the octave of St. Peter and therefore tomorrow long I to go to God, it were a day very meet and convenient for me. I never liked your manner toward me better than when you kissed me last for I love when daughterly love and dear charity has no need to look to worldly courtesy."

These passages, written with simplicity of emotion and elegance of language, demonstrate how affection, fear, and conviction can be shaped by the written language so that they are not merely expressed, but are contained in a way that deepens their import and allows them to sing for centuries, stirring all who read these words hundreds of years later in the direction of those same emotions. The soulfulness in these words consists in part in their capacity to touch other souls, to create a community across the centuries of strong sentiment and faith.

Letters offer the opportunity to express our feelings, especially when the soul is undergoing a particularly disturbing attack, as when Virginia Woolf writes to her sister, Vanessa Bell, about her jealousy, "Do you like Helen Anrep better than me? The green goddess, Jealousy, alit on my pillow this very dawn and shot this bitter shaft through my heart. I believe you do. It's not so much the private wound I mind—it's the deficiency of taste on your part. All the same I admit she has her moss rose charm; and in her breast instead of dew is a heart, I admit."[8]

Emily Dickinson's last letter, to Louise and Frances Norcross, written in the month of her death, brings together the classical qualities of the soulful letter—brevity, clarity, affection, and penetration—in a terse farewell: "Little Cousins, Called back, Emily."[9]

People often ask, in matters of psychotherapy or care of the soul, "What can I do for my soul? Can you give me some practical suggestions?" It's difficult to translate ideas about re-imagining the entirety of life into daily practices that would make sense for everyone. Usually the questions concern problem-solving— "How can I get out of this mess?" But in this chapter we've considered some matters of practice that anyone can try. They may not seem therapeutic, but that is only because we've come to think of therapy as quasi-medical treatment or the removal of symptoms. These more artful ways of caring for the soul not only offer a tonic against some of the emotional suffering we endure, they also more positively show a way toward a more pleasurable and more soulful life.

They all involve thoughtful and artful self-expression. Finding words that truly express our feelings and experiences is an achievement of a high order. Bringing a dimension of style to our conversations and letters, diaries and gatherings, homes and workplaces, goes a long way toward making life more soulful. In these areas, too, of course, we are always dealing with individual taste, but that is the beauty of it. Individuality is an important aspect of the soul, and one of the products of living with genuine style is self-expressiveness and personality.

The examples of speaking and writing I've given are all from the realm of the personal, but there is no reason why we can't bring some of the same attention to style, careful use of words, and poignant expression of feeling to our business letters and to all our forms of communication. The point is to make all of life soulful, not just the private areas.

Simply realizing that style and artfulness invite soul, making life immeasurably richer, is an excellent first step toward caring for the soul in our dealings with one another. When style is wedded to heartfelt expression, nothing could be more potent, nothing more creative. In the age that is dawning, in which problem-solving may not be granted so much importance, it may be possible finally to set aside our drivenness about understanding and change, and instead aim for beauty and heartfelt expression as we present ourselves to the world and to those who are intimate with us.

Chapter Seven

CREATIVE ILLUSIONS IN

ROMANTIC LOVE

it was the west wind caught her up, as
she rose
from the genital
wave, and bore her from the delicate
foam, home
to her isle

and those lovers
of the difficult, the hours
of the golden day welcomed her, clad her, were
as though they had made her, were wild
to bring this new thing born
of the ring of the sea pink . . .

Intimacy is sometimes born of elements so inward, so part of nature and deeply embodied, that the accompanying emotions feel impossibly strong and overwhelming. The American poet Charles Olson describes this elemental nature beautifully in his poem "The Ring Of," his hymn to Aphrodite Anadyomene, Venus rising from the foam of the sea, an image known best perhaps through Botticelli's *The Birth of Venus*.

Aphrodite, the goddess who generates the lusty, sensual emotions of romantic love, blows into a life as though on a wind, and she rises from the waves of genital feelings that are so central to sexual attraction. Olson's poem, like an ancient Greek hymn, praises this goddess whom the modern world finds difficult to appreciate in her full complexity and power. Olson implies that there is divinity in our waves of lust and in elemental, perhaps impersonal, feelings of attraction. Something eternally valid comes to us in the sensations of sex and romance.

The hard part, as the poem suggests, is to clothe this divinity with the particulars of everyday life—the Hours. Botticelli shows a nymph of the Hours holding a flowery robe in her hands, ready to place it on the goddess's body. Our task is to find a way to weave deep-seated emotions into our daily lives, to clothe eternity in the garments of time. But how is it done? Do we marry the person who stirs our passion? Do we live out our sexual fantasies? Do we move from partner to partner in search of the goddess? Do we break up a marriage because the west wind has done its work once again, blowing in another visitation of this being "of the sea pink"?

We are often divided in our approach to the rising of Aphrodite's passions. On the one hand, we may look for them frantically, joining social groups for that reason alone, or placing ads in the personal columns. Advertisers are confident that we will buy almost any item they can invent and package, as long as they also promise that Aphrodite comes with it. The tried and true method of placing scantily clad models—men or women—near the object of consumer desire is effective because they evoke naked, elemental Beauty rising from the sea, which most of us want at all costs.

On the other hand, religious purists complain of Aphrodite's nakedness, and even psychologists sometimes moralize against her when they warn that romantic love is an illusion, a projection, an obsession, a parental fixation, or an *anima* possession. The ancient historian Eusebius recounts that when the crusaders were attacking and razing the pagan temples of the Mediterranean, they would not only tear down the temples to Aphrodite, they would even dig up the earth under them, as if to completely uproot any remnant of this scandalous deity. In our psychological moralism, we, too, may try to eradicate ("take up by the roots") the challenging call to pleasure and beauty.

To heal this split attitude toward romance and sexual attraction, we might try granting each side its own validity and value. Obviously sexual attraction can lead to intimacy between people, a lifelong partnership in marriage, and family. On the other hand, the appeal of Venus in adultery can also disturb and destroy a marriage, and a person may confuse a passing sexual or romantic attraction with the possibility of marriage or deep friendship.

Sex and romance are both enticing and dangerous. This quality of ambiguity and even duplicity is inherent in their nature. Aphrodite was sometimes called "the goddess of the sidelong glance," suggesting that she and the sphere of life she governs are not always straightforward. We are right to be wary; but there is so much potential beauty, attractiveness, and vitality in these things that, in spite of their dangers, we are forcefully drawn to them.

We might distinguish between wise circumspection and a moralistic, defensive resistance to the power of sex and romance. Moralism of any kind usually serves as self-protection in the face of life's enormous force. Just as we might retreat in the face of overwhelming depression, or look for a quick way out of deeply disturbing jealousy, so we might naturally seek relief in moralism from the power of sexual and romantic feelings. But, unlike wise caution, moralism offers no entry into the sphere of life that is presenting itself. Opting against the moralistic defense, we could try instead to be aware of what we're getting into, without taking a defensive posture of condemnation.

We may need to take time, for example, in order to find out precisely how a particular love wants to be in life. Our early images of the relationship may prove too optimistic or too literal. "Love at first sight" doesn't always signal a lifelong relationship. The soul's "purpose" in our attractions may only be revealed in due time, and the final picture may be entirely different from our initial impressions and expectations. In the "Homeric Hymn to Aphrodite," written in the early centuries of our era, Aphrodite, driven by desire for the mortal Anchises, tells him a tall tale about her supposed adventures and her innocence. It's difficult for those of us who were raised on sacred stories fully devoted to truth and virtue to appreciate the point of such a tale of deception. Still, this is an important observation: sexual attraction, for all its beauty and grace, may have within it seductions and deceptions that help give sex its rich texture and dimension but also make it difficult sometimes to bring into life. As Ficino said, we taste love, but we find it difficult to distinguish its flavors.

This doesn't mean we should avoid sex and romance because of their duplicity, but we might understand that deception is an inherent and necessary ingredient. Knowing the wiles of Aphrodite, we might enter her sphere not with naïveté, but with keen discrimination and awareness. We might even imagine that part of the initiation in sexual relationship is a sharpening of perception, a loss of innocence, the discovery that life demands penetrating perceptions and unsentimental judgments. Or, in another way altogether, romance may lead us into a more abandoned life, where we find experiences more intense and more complicated than we had ever known before. In the maelstrom of this new, exciting life, we may feel confused and may make some foolish decisions, but we may have also crossed a threshold into a richer level of experience, having abandoned childlike simplicity and discovered adult complexity.

The shadow of Aphrodite is not always easy to see. A sexual attraction may at first seem innocent and light, and a new romance may be filled with positive images of the other person and of the future. Yet we all know that both sex and romance can lead into difficult relationships that are suffered and endured for years, and that sex can lead to parenthood or abortion, to sexually transmitted disease, or, utterly dark, to abusive and even murderous relationships.

The enticements of Aphrodite are indeed deceptive, and yet they obviously serve a profound purpose in the raw designs of nature. Understandably, Venus is goddess of gardens, and as in Botticelli's renowned painting of spring, *Primavera*, she stands deep in the green shadows of forest and garden, a nature goddess as well as patroness of the civilized dance of the humane graces. Through the seductions of romance we are brought to the most physical, elemental, and life-defining events of life—from dating to giving birth, from courtship to family, from the frivolous joys of flirtation to the heart-wrenching pain of separation and death.

It does no good to shun Aphrodite's temptations as illusory. The exquisite truth of her myth is the paradox that life thrives on the illusions it spins, and that the most serious challenges are entered through our willingness to fall and to be foolish. This is another way of picturing the old wisdom that to say yes to exuberant life is to invite the most painful initiations into its darkest mysteries. The surface deceptions, it turns out, are in the service of the most rooted ways of our nature.

Another way to approach the problem of romantic love in mythological imagery is to note that in a polytheistic arrangement each of the gods and goddesses has his or her own code of morality. Each has a tablet of ten commandments that sometimes contradict the others. The commandment of the virgin goddess Artemis says, "Thou shalt not surrender to the compulsions of sex." The commandment of Aphrodite says, "Thou shalt not *resist* the compulsions of sex."

How are we to live these contradictions? There are several possibilities that are basically quite simple in theory. At one time in our lives, for example, we may be ruled by one code rather than another. A young man once told me that he tried several times to have a long-term relationship with a woman, which was obviously, he said, the best thing to do, but he just couldn't do it because his real desire was to have sex with as many different women as possible.

In response, something in me no doubt connected to my Catholic past felt a moral twinge, and my sensitivities to feminist criticism of male sexual anarchy also issued a complaint. Still, committed to honoring the expressions of the soul, I could see the Aphroditic direction in this man's strong feeling. I tried to help him sort out his feelings and fantasies so that he might live the code of Venus with some depth and subtlety, instead of acting it out at the expense of either the women in his life or his own deep desire for variety.

Variety is a polytheistic delight. A problem can arise, however, if at the immediate, existential level we forget that Aphrodite is a cosmic goddess as well as a personal one. Pleasure, beauty, sex, sensuality, attraction, and lust are attributes of life, of being itself. Sometimes what we imagine to be a personal affair of the heart has cosmic dimensions: in looking on the surface for variety in sexual partners, we may in fact be desiring variety at a deeper level, at the very foundation of our experience.

In 1484, Marsilio Ficino published a book on love in which he explores this question of personal and cosmic sexuality in the imagery of two Venuses, the heavenly and the earthly. The two, he says, ordinarily go together, so that when we behold a person who is beautiful to us, we are led to reflect on beauty itself. He warns that it is sometimes tempting to divide these two and focus only on physical beauty, neglecting the cosmic Venus. Whenever we do this we are guilty of the abuse of love.[1]

It is useful to remember this platonic conception of love in our concrete, personal experience. My young man was interpreting his Venusian fantasies of sexual variety as a purely physical, literal matter. As his therapist, I was trying to evoke the sister Venus, the heavenly one, she who makes a soul beautiful and pleasurable. I was doing this by fostering a sublimation of his concrete thoughts about sex, not into rational and defensive forms, but into more subtle versions of themselves. Together we allowed his particular sexual wishes to lead us into discussions on beauty, variety, and pleasure in the depths of his soul and in many areas of his life. This was not to deny the issue of actual sex, but rather to deepen it, to give it greater dimension. In the end, this man could bring greater imagination to his efforts to come up with a sexual life that would meet both his pressing desires and the deeper needs of his soul.

Another way to respect the contradictions in a polytheistic approach to life is simply to stay with the feelings evoked by them. Sometimes values collide. We may feel a strong desire to live a life of satisfying sex and sensuality while at the same time something in us longs for solitude and even chastity. In this collision of values our only option may be to remain within the tension. The modern tendency to resolve tension as soon as possible is so unconscious and feels so natural to us that at first it may seem strange to consider remaining willingly in our discomfort. We want solutions and resolutions, and we want them quickly, but there are several benefits to being patient with contradictions and paradoxes.

The first is an expansion of soul. Over time tension gives rise to thoughts, memories, and images that bring greater breadth to imagination. The soul grows bigger as it holds more thoughts, instead of shrinking them all down to the size of a single solution. And as we become more abundant in our souls, we can bring increased wisdom and acceptance to many areas of life.

Another benefit is the possibility of finding more profound and lasting solutions to our life problems. If we rush to solve a problem, the solution will need to be something ready-made or quickly put together, and will most likely be a project of the ego; but if we sustain the tension created by two worlds colliding, an unexpected solution will emerge eventually from the opening to soul that tension creates. If we tolerate moments of chaos and confusion, something truly new can come to light.

Taking this approach to our contradictions, we don't have to choose sides, either dismissing moralistic attacks on sex and romantic love or championing free love without inhibition. We may need to listen openmindedly to all the fantasies that come to us in moments of confusion. One voice says, "Your life will be ruined if you pursue the route of promiscuity." Another voice says, "Don't be as tight and repressed as your family was. Enjoy life and give yourself what you need in order to feel sexually fulfilled." Listening to both of these voices over time, a person might be guided toward a point free of oppositions and contradictions, and yet not a place of balance in which all ambiguity is resolved. Feeling the tension created by various claims of the soul, gradually we move toward a new perspective in which the struggle of competing values turns into an appreciation for unresolved complexity. There, the old arguments are irrelevant because they simply have no place in the newly achieved point of view. There may be new tensions and unfamiliar ambiguities to deal with, but having won a fresh vantage point through the courageous endurance of tension, we may be better equipped to understand the process, realizing that illusions and follies have their own roles to play in the mysterious alchemy of the soulful life.

The Future of Our Illusions

ROMANTIC LOVE is an illusion. Most of us discover this truth painfully at the end of a love affair or else when the sweet emotions of love lead us into marriage and then turn down their flames. Some couples are graced with a lifelong "illusion" of love, living out their marriage with eyes at least partially blinded to the "realistic" nature of their partner. We may well wonder whether these illusions are a necessary part of life, or whether we should try to avoid them in the future.

Illusion comes from the Latin *in ludere*, "in play." For hundreds of years the English word has meant mockery, deception, and even hallucination. Let us keep the Latin in mind, to help us remember that illusion can have a playful, even sporting aspect. Johan Huizinga's celebrated book *Homo Ludens* defines the human essentially as a being who plays. In his analysis, all our serious activities, from war to business to setting up house, are a form of play. They are play because, setting aside the serious elements of literal life, we find pleasure in the drama of our actions, in the stories we are living out *through* the events of serious life, in the game aspects of business and politics. The soul enjoys the playful side of life because play elevates the otherwise heavy literalness of day-to-day existence to the realm of imagination. Something in us—psychologists call it ego—loves the literal aspect of our activities, while the soul loves the imaginal level, which may take the form of poetics, dream, or play. What nourishes the soul is not exactly the same as the preoccupations and concerns of everyday life.

Play is an ingredient in the most important aspects of life. In war, the theaters of engagement, the strategies, the odds of winning or losing, the uniforms, the theatrical names (general, lieutenant, corporal) are all signs of play, dangerous and horrible though it may be. In religion, the holy objects, language, stories, actions, colors, foods, and garments of ritual are signals that what is taking place is sacred play. In his ground-breaking book *Gods and Games*, David Miller describes religious faith itself as play: "Faith is being gripped by a story, by a vision, by a ritual (game). It is being seized, being gripped by a pattern of meaning, a pattern of meaning that affects one's life-pattern, that becomes a paradigm for the way one sees the world."[2]

Romantic love is one of the most powerful means for pulling us out of literal life and into play. In the trance of love, we may neglect our life duties and obligations, we may make heroic efforts to be with our beloved, we may look at the beloved and see someone without the blemishes that always appear to the realistic eye. To be in love is to be in play, to be taken by illusions. We *are* deceived so that soul can create something out of the stuff of our emotions and fantasies.

Freud's reading of depression could apply to love. When a person is depressed, he says, even though outward appearances suggest that nothing is going on, a great deal of inner work is being accomplished. In romantic love, even though consciousness appears deluded and the serious business of life is being hampered, nevertheless a great deal of inner work, soul-work, may be taking place. From the point of view of the soul, romantic love is trustworthy precisely because the literal concerns of life are set aside. The soul has room to go into action, and its action is always in the nature of play, whether comic or tragic.

Our elders and counselors often warn us of the dangers of love's illusions. Romantic love is no way to enter a genuine relationship, they say. We can be led astray. We will end up with the wrong partner. We will be disillusioned with marriage. It is a short step, we are warned, from romantic love to divorce.

All these things are true, of course. Illusion is a dangerous condition, and yet we continue to place naive trust in this kind of love, and we enjoy movies and novels that depict these illusions. Critics complain about the unrealistic way in which love is portrayed in romantic stories, but audiences and readers continue to watch these movies and read these books avidly. In our childish attachment to romance, we are championing the way of the soul—its thirst for pleasure, and its inescapable need for experiences that may or may not be conducive to productive lives.

Several people have told me stories of a love given up in order to protect family or a mate. These buried loves then smoldered in their hearts, creating the resentful acid that is concocted by repressed pleasure. Their lives remained orderly, all right, but their souls went into hiding. In more than one instance I recall, it proved impossible to sustain the repression.

"I had been married for five years," Stephen said, "when I met a woman who made my heart come to life. I still loved my wife and more than anything I wanted to keep my family together, but this new experience was so sweet, so enlivening, that I risked losing my wife and my children over it."

"What did you do?" I asked.

"At first, we had a brief affair. But I couldn't stand the lying and the cheating. I told her I had to go back to my wife and family."

"Then what happened?"

"I felt relieved, of course, not to be living a double life. But I also saw that there were real problems in my marriage. Nothing improved there, even though I never stopped loving my wife and still wanted to be with my family. I had fantasies about being with the other person, but if I had to choose, I wanted my home."

"And where do things stand now?"

"The other person has shown up again. I'm back to the lying and cheating. I feel terrible about it. I hate what I'm doing, and yet I can't seem to be able to stop it. I have no choice in the matter."

Over many years of doing therapy, I've worked with many men and women in similar circumstances. These are good people who feel torn apart by the conflict between their love for their partner and their need for another relationship. Sometimes it looks like a battle between solid, deeply personal love and affection at home, and light, fluffy yet indispensable romantic love away from home—a description that makes the situation all the more confusing and painful. People caught in the sweet net of romance sometimes denigrate it theoretically, while at the same time throwing themselves into it wholeheartedly.

If a conflict of this kind is imagined only on the level of literal relationship, the tension can become unbearable, or a solution is forced and the problem never truly resolved.

If we understand that the soul has strong needs that go against the commitments of our lives, and that these needs can be met without necessarily making drastic life changes, then we may find a way to satisfy the demand for romantic love. No matter how unrealistic in relation to the structures of life, no matter how illusory and dangerous, romantic love is as important to the soul as any other kind of love. When therapeutic thinking, professional or personal, sees its task primarily as making life work out according to some preconceived idea of what is proper and correct, then we miss the point of many developments that concern the soul. In the case of romantic love, we have no idea where the "illusion" is taking us, what it implies, or how it is best lived out.

"Either I leave my wife," Stephen told me, "or I give up my desire."

Now, when I hear an impossible situation like this presented out of confusion and pain, I get suspicious. To imagine life in such a divided manner serves to preserve the status quo. There is no way to turn, nothing to do but to remain in limbo. Apparently Stephen preferred static limbo to its alternative—affirming both sides intellectually and emotionally so that a solution might present itself.

I was reminded of another man, Arthur, whose wife was in Stephen's position. Arthur told me there were only two alternatives available to him: an illusory, romanticized idea of the perfectly monogamous marriage, or a sexually "open" marriage. The first had proved itself sterile and impossible to live, and the second had no appeal to him at all.

In both cases my response was "Maybe there is a third alternative." Two wants to finds its way into a third.

"How can there be a third alternative?" Stephen said incredulously. "I have to decide either to go back home for good, or get out and start all over again with someone else."

"I can't possibly imagine a third alternative," Arthur said. "It has to be either monogamy or its opposite, whatever that is."

In his book *Three Faces of God*, on the trinity as a structure in all of life, David Miller discusses the necessity of the triangle in all loves. "There is one man, one woman, and love. If this fails, then perhaps there will be one man, one woman, and a pet animal or a mutual hobby. Or there may come a time when she notes, not without appropriate jealousy, that he seems wed to his work, which is now a third in the marriage."[3] All love is a ménage à trois, Miller concludes.

The third, I would say, is always the soul. Traditionally the soul was always considered the third factor between mind and body, between spirit and matter. It is the medium, the mediating element, that holds everything together. Stephen can't find his way out of the dualism of his attractions because he hasn't considered the soul. Arthur can't see a way beyond the monogamy/ nonmonogamy dilemma because he is not allowing the soul to enter the equation. What does this mean to the person facing the problem, and exactly how do you introduce soul as a third way?

Problem-solving is not an effective way to introduce soul into life. Soul appears in the opening made when a person finally gives up the effort, or when logic has finally exploded away, or when frustration has reached a level where the attempt to gain control gives way. Soul appears when we shift to a different level of perception altogether. The heroics of problem-solving keep soul at a distance, while the very defeat of our heroism lets soul in.

Arthur consistently took an engineer's approach to his marriage. He wanted to know which *structure* would work. "I don't think it's a matter of monogamy or nonmonogamy," I said to him more than once. His first response was to try to vanquish me with logic: "It has to be one or the other. There can't be any other alternatives." A few weeks later he said, "I can just begin to imagine a third alternative, but even if I find one, the marriage still has to be monogamous or nonmonogamous." He still wouldn't let go of the structural, bifurcated view of his relationship.

After several conversations about intimacy, I said to him, "What if marriage were a matter of getting to know your wife's soul, and of her getting to know yours, if the two of you watched life emerge from that mutual knowledge and love?"

"Maybe," he said haltingly, "maybe there would be no room for thinking about monogamy."

"Maybe," I said. "And no room for worry."

Just as imagination is a sign of the soul at work, so worry is a sign of the ego doing everything it can, especially through rational understanding and control, to keep soul locked away.

The soul is not meant to be understood. The only way to understand with soul is to imagine, to watch structures take form as our love and attachment deepen. At the level of soul, the way to understand is to "stand under," to move closer and closer toward that which has our interest. One of the many axioms I have learned from archetypal psychology is the wisdom of entering more fully into whatever it is that has captivated the soul, and one way of doing that is to let the current passion or preoccupation get on top, to stand under it until it tells us who or what it is.

The point in responding therapeutically to the soul is not only to "stick to the image," but to stay with those specific images that lie at the heart of the matter and therefore tend to be the most painful. We might imagine the soul, as many traditions have, as an immense space, an innerscape as vast as the outerscape of the universe. What appears to be a small problem, like a tiff in a relationship, may touch on some grand theme in the soul's deep universe. The move to that level can be disorienting and sometimes full of fear and disturbance. We may wish to avoid the journey and the visitation to an unfamiliar or frightening place. Yet precisely this kind of movement gives the soul its desired spaciousness and acquaints us with its territory. Daring to consider the most painful images, what the British analyst Neil Micklem calls "the intolerable image," is an intense and unusually productive form of soul work.

Both Stephen's feeling of being stuck in an uncomfortable affair and Arthur's struggle to choose between monogamy and an open relationship are examples of avoidance of soul. I don't mean to blame these men, or criticize them; it isn't easy for any of us to respond to the call of soul. Defending against soul, however, can be extremely subtle. Defenses wouldn't work so well if they were not tailored so carefully and convincingly. To remain stuck between two unacceptable alternatives preserves us from movement into a new region of imagination and experience.

With this in mind, I am careful in my practice not to take sides in such splits. To side with one, however gently, is to serve the defense and work against soul. On the other hand, to speak against one of the alternatives is also to serve the division. The only effective response I know is to deepen each side, to imagine each alternative further, giving each more substance and seriousness. Eventually, the alternatives will change character, and will not be so far removed from each other. Eventually the dilemma may diminish as a third possibility comes into view.

Stephen had to enter more deeply into his desire for his affair and into the attraction for the other woman in his life. He also had to include and intensify his genuine feelings of revulsion about the affair. In matters of soul, all feelings and fantasies deserve an equal hearing. Being stuck in a dilemma is often a sign of superficial involvement in whatever has stirred in the soul. The temptation is to remain stuck, to spend hours of thought and conversation and weeks, months, and even years luxuriating in the dilemma. As long as we are thus occupied, we don't have to dare the soul's invitation to explore new territory.

I tried to help him enter more deeply into both aspects of his dilemma.

"There's no denying, is there," I said, "that something of your soul longs for some of the affection and romance you are finding in the affair?"

"I wish I could be faithful and honest, but the feelings are too strong."

"Well, you tried once before to shove these feelings down and force yourself to live the principled life you always wanted."

"Yes, but it didn't work out."

"Tell me about your negative feelings about having an affair," I said. "How genuine are they?"

"They're very genuine," he responded. "I truly don't believe in living this way."

"Is it a matter of belief, or feeling, or just an accepted norm from society?"

"It's definitely more than conventional morality. I don't like the person I am when I'm doing this, and yet I feel compelled to do it."

"Does this discomfort you feel have an effect on the affair?"

"Of course it does," he said. "I'm always thinking I should end it, and I can never give myself to it fully. My lover isn't very happy about my attitude, but still she stays in there with me."

We talked more like this, letting his fantasies and emotions come to the surface in greater detail. Soul work doesn't require grand revelations, superior interpretations, or ultimate conclusions. On the contrary, slow, steady exploration of the person's *imagination* of his situation more reliably allows the soul to show itself, and only then do "solutions" become possible. As presented in the poem of Charles Olson that began this chapter, our Venusian entanglements need to be clothed in the "hours." That is, we have to bring our hidden fantasies into the arena of life, where, visible and palpable, they show us the powerfully motivating forces at work in our compulsions and inhibitions.

Over time, Stephen decided that his feelings of revulsion about his affair did not stem from guilt or from superficial inhibition. As he considered being influenced more strongly by his revulsion and by his love of home and family, he discovered some issues about home life and about his wife that interfered with these intimacies. Ever since he was a young man, he realized, he had thought of conventional home life and marriage as a limitation on freedom. These new thoughts complicated the entire picture for him. He had to meditate for a long time on his attitudes toward family life. Eventually he concluded that at least at one level his affair was a way of avoiding the confinements of marriage and family, and that he himself was responsible for the absence of affection and romance in his marriage. Eventually he ended the affair and went back to his wife and family, but with a new attitude about life's limits and the possibilities for freedom. He slowly discovered a way to feel free and yet at the same time embrace his family life. He now understood, he said, that freedom included the possibility of living the life that had been given to him, complete with its limitations.

Arthur had a more difficult time. It wasn't easy for him to learn to trust the soul. He wanted to understand everything analytically. He could even reflect on his need to be analytical, but he couldn't give it up. As we discussed his way of being in a relationship, he began to see that behind his love of analysis was a power struggle. Whenever we leave the realm of soul, where opposites melt into each other, divisions tend to appear, often in the form of power and control. Arthur felt thoroughly destroyed by his wife's love for another man, and his way of restoring the balance of power was to come up with unassailable interpretations, followed by firm expectations and demands.

One problem with a rational approach to romantic love is that love is treated as a purely interpersonal matter of human dimensions. Mythology and poetry teach us to imagine this kind of love differently, sometimes as a meeting with a goddess. In romantic love we are all like Anchises, a mere mortal faced with overpowering divinity. Love *is* divine, and if we don't recognize this fact and treat it with some piety, then clearly we will be its victims.

We need nonrational approaches to this kind of love, because rationality fails to apprehend the divine. Arthur gradually began to loosen his reliance on reason and control, and as he did so, his anxiety diminished. His wife became more interested in him and less in her affair. Although he didn't have much of a perspective on the whole process, to me it seemed that this love conflict worked on his soul, making him a more secure man by forcing him to allow life to happen. Insecurity may develop out of a fear of what life can bring if it's allowed to be free. He had much to learn about love and marriage, and the means of this learning was his struggle with jealousy. The only way through his jealousy was not, as he imagined at first, capitulation on the part of his wife, but a change in his own attitude toward relationship. As his attitudes changed, his life problems eased.

The French symbolist poet Rimbaud makes the point about finding a way out of such unnecessary divisions and power plays in his poem "Vigils":

> It is the friend neither violent nor weak. The friend.
> It is the beloved neither tormenting nor tormented.
>   The beloved.
> Air and the world not sought. Life.[4]

To arrive at the life that stirs in romantic love requires finding a way through the power plays to the person we love, through the pains that almost always accompany such love to a pure experience of love, through the things we are intentionally looking for in love and in another, to the life and vitality that have been generated by means of love's illusions. Our thoughts about not getting into trouble, being foolish, or making a mistake get in the way of love. Our attempts to prevent illusion make us blind to the love that is present and to the life that is stirring, and so our self-protection only creates *de*-lusions.

I'm not saying that it isn't important to be circumspect about love, but that the way we exercise caution is crucial. If inhibition comes from fear of love's power, and if it is made up only of rational thoughts whose purpose is to protect us from moving into life, then both the desired love and safety will be out of reach. First we have to find our way into the presence of love; then we will be able to decide what to do. In all psychological matters it's necessary to discriminate, to know the difference between nervous avoidance and a firm intuition that we are heading in the wrong direction.

Stern, moralistic warnings about not falling into the illusions of romantic love come from a place foreign to love. They are not messages from erotic life, but from a place that devalues eros. When we are close to love, then we can discern the authentic partner from the stand-in, the empty rush of feeling from the invitation to create life. The best way to know if our caution is erotic or not is to sense the source of the inhibition: does it come from within love, or does it stand outside the sphere of love making fearful judgments?

If we have the habit of living the least bit soulfully, then to that extent we can trust our romantic illusions and our unjustifiable desires. William Blake says, "Sooner murder an infant in its cradle than nurse unacted desires." Just as logic leads the mind, desire guides the soul. We live in a world that trusts logic, and from that commitment we distrust desire; but if we lived in a world that validated desire, we would know how to trust it.

Desire often asks that we abandon logic and perhaps appear foolish to our logical friends. Euripides presents a marvelous scene of foolishness at the opening of *The Bacchai*, when two high-placed old men, Tiresias and Cadmos, walk onto the scene dressed in women's clothes, ready to celebrate the mystery of Dionysus. Standing there like two fools in a modern absurd drama, one of them says, "We're two sane men in a mad city." That is what we must say in our illusions: from the soul point of view, our madness is sanity, and so we embrace it. A Dionysian life is one that gives itself over to illogic, the transgression of borders, and the pursuit of frenzy.

When our caution is not defensive, our leap into illusion will not be literally crazy. Its madness will be the foolishness of the soul reaching for nurturance and joy. The soul needs true pleasure and genuine joy, just as the mind needs ideas and information and the body needs food and exercise. It asks for abandonment to its illusions, its serious playfulness and its purposeful games.

We don't have to justify our pleasure in the illusions of love. Dalliance and flirtation don't have to lead to a longstanding relationship or to marriage in order to prove themselves. If we had this thought in mind, perhaps we would be able to enjoy our passing fancies without worrying so much about their implications. The soul thrives on ephemeral fantasies of love as much as it does on lifelong partnerships.

One way to discern the movements of eros is to be in the habit of listening to our intuitions and to the various voices that speak in imagination. Eros moves and settles in the area of the heart. If we are confused by this strong rush of new spirit, it may be because we are not familiar with our own interior life. If we can't distinguish illusion from opportunity, then maybe we don't know our own hearts well enough. An intense romance could provide an opportunity to get to know ourselves, but how much better it would be if we were familiar with the ways of our soul in the first place.

One of the most remarkable ideas I have found in the writings of James Hillman about the soul is his work on *anima*; he calls *anima*, the feminine image of the soul, a guide to unconsciousness, as though we needed help in finding our way into the unknown.

In moving further into soul we are stepping in a positive way into unconsciousness. Eros fits snugly into this picture of soul-making, for eros, too, leads us into mysterious places—unfamiliar feelings and moods, unexpected relationships, and unfathomable complexities. The passions of attraction, attachment, and jealousy initiate us deeper into life and soul, where understanding is elusive and in the end unnecessary.

According to John of the Cross, if you want certainty in your path, walk in darkness. In a story told in many traditions and versions, a man is crouched over the ground at night under a lamppost obviously looking for something. A passerby asks him, "Have you lost something?" "Yes, my key," he says. "Did you lose it here?" "No," he says, "over there, but there's light here."

Our attempts to understand eros try to keep it in the light, while for the most part it lies in darkness. Eros invites us into darkness, because the darkness of unknowing is beneficial to the soul. Much of life takes place in that darkness, and so it's not a bad thing to be led into it. I recall hearing a dream many years ago—I've forgotten most of the details—in which the dreamer saw a beautiful blue light at the bottom of a well. He was attracted by the light, and in spite of his considerable fear he crawled down into the well.

This blue light is the kind of twilight consciousness that romantic love creates. Although our practical eye may be dimmed, at the same time we see things we've never seen before. Emotions are turned high, and fantasy goes into high gear. Practical awareness diminishes, so that overall there is an enlightenment of sorts, but its light is subdued, bluish.

Eros plays our lives in blue, taking us to an aesthetic plane where fantasy is more pronounced than so-called reality, where we find ourselves and yet more than ourselves, where the black and white of reality give way to the colors of imagination. When love stirs in life, we are like that dreamer who goes into a deep well chasing the beautiful in the form of a blue light. In his poem "The

Man with the Blue Guitar," which is all about living in the blue light of imagination, Wallace Stevens refers to blue as "The amorous Adjective aflame . . ." Love makes life light and fiery, but with a blue shade. It's no accident that the anthology of Hillman's writings, a book of soul and eros, is entitled *A Blue Fire*.

Romantic love is not only a necessary illusion, it is a desirable deception. Naturally, if we enter that illusion without an imagination for poetry and music, we may literally play the fool as love buffets us; but if we appreciate its theatrics, we could be profoundly deepened by it. People who have been stung by Cupid's arrow are invited to live on the edge between the lure of love's promises and the ordinary demands of life, allowing illusory love to keep life "in play," close to imagination, aflame with the heart's passions. It is one of the most powerful and most effective forms of soul-making. Its potential danger is only the other side of its spectacular capacity to transform a life and to resurrect the soul.

Chapter Eight

SEX AND IMAGINATION

SEVERAL YEARS ago I attended a dazzling exhibition of the sacred art of Pompeii at the Dallas Museum of Art. The rooms in the museum were crowded, and at one point I found myself shoved up close behind a man and woman who were admiring the beautiful objects closely and having animated discussions about them. We came, the three of us, to a small sculpture of the Greco-Roman god Priapus. In traditional fashion, he was depicted as a short, fat, balding figure having an enormous phallus that curved up over his head. It was taller than he was by half. The woman laughed, not anxiously, I thought, but appreciatively when she saw it, while her companion looked embarrassed and ushered her quickly to the next piece, and our threesome was broken up.[1]

I remembered reading that in ancient times a statue of Priapus was often placed in a garden, where sometimes it was used as a scarecrow to keep the birds away. I wondered if this man had something in common with birds and felt the scarecrow power, forcing him to move away. Maybe he was lofty in his thoughts and tastes, while his companion was more comfortable with earthy matters.

As we have seen, sex is a great mystery of life that resists our many attempts to explain and control it. Along with money and death, it represents one of the few elements left in life that virtually pulsate with divinity, easily overwhelm our feelings and thoughts, and sometimes lead to profound compulsions.

Emotional compulsion is often regarded negatively as a failure of control or a sign of irrationality. We might see it rather as the soul yearning for expression and trying to thrust itself into life. Sexual compulsion may show us where and to what extent we have neglected this particular need. Compulsion asks for a response from us, but we might be careful lest we simply react to the felt need. Some respond by advocating "free love," as though the best way to deal with the compulsion were to give in to it literally. This is the way of compensation, which doesn't solve the problem but only places us at the other end of it. The soulful way is to bring imagination to sex, so that by fulfilling the need at a deep level, the compulsion is brought to term.

We may try to keep the power of sex at bay through many clever maneuvers. Our moralism, for example, helps keep us clean of the mess sex can make of an otherwise ordered life. Sex education tries to teach us to avoid "venereal diseases"—the pathologies of Venus—by placing sex under the strong, white, Apollonic light of science. Yet in spite of all our efforts, sexual compulsion interferes with marriages, draws people into strange liaisons, and continues to offend propriety, morality, and religion. Its dynamic is too big to fit into the cages we make for it.

We are in a difficult position in relation to sex: we believe it's important to have a "healthy" sex life, at least within marriage, and yet we also believe that the tendency of sex to spread easily into unwanted areas—pornography, homosexuality, extramarital affairs—is a sign of cultural decadence or moral and religious breakdown. We want sex to be robust, but not too robust.

The man and woman standing in front of Priapus represent two common responses to sex: humor and anxiety. Sex is exceedingly human—bodily, passionate, often satisfyingly improper. Some theories of humor suggest that sex often provides material for humor precisely because it liberates us from the burden of propriety and the repression of passion. Sex also offers the rare gift of deeply felt, unreasoned joy, and laughter can sometimes be the expression of pure joy. On the other hand, perhaps because it is difficult to contain and mold into stable forms, sex can also bring with it considerable anxiety. Sometimes we laugh as a way of reassuring ourselves in the face of anxiety. It is the very potency of sex that suggests it is one of the most significant springs of soulfulness in modern life.

The Holiness of Sex

IN MY school days I was given two messages about sex: one, that it is holy, and two, that it is usually sinful. My father tried hard to give me a positive attitude about sex, and during a few of my adolescent years talked to me about it, with the best of motives and with utmost sensitivity, on every possible occasion. Yet, in spite of his caring and enlightened efforts to counter the teaching I got at school, I still felt guilty about sexual feelings and fantasies. This guilt didn't lessen the intensity of the erotic images that insisted themselves in my imagination, but it robbed them of some of their pleasure and made me uneasy in the presence of anything remotely sexual. The religious teaching I received painted sex as a holy part of creation—anything created by God, even sex, must be holy—but in all practical ways sex was presented as the absolute epitome of sin.

From my vantage point now, it appears to me that this splitting of sex into holiness and evil did neither element justice. I could never feel the holiness in any other than an abstract theological approval of God's creation, and I also never truly appreciated the dark, destructive capacities of sex except as a source of personal guilt. If we can restore both the holiness and the real darkness—for paradox is usually a sign of the presence of soul—then we might be able more fully to enter the mystery that is sex, and find in it a genuine route to intimacy, both with ourselves and with others.

What does it mean "to enter the mystery that is sex"? It doesn't mean compulsion, although carefully following the lead of our compulsions could lead us to soulful sex. It doesn't mean withdrawing from sex in fear. We might ask ourselves in what ways we could respond more affirmatively to our own sexuality, to desire and fantasy. We could also look closely both at the obvious and at the microscopic resistances we feel in relation to sex. The point is not to become sexually liberated in a literal sense, but to recognize that the soulful life may be barricaded behind the walls of our resistance.

Sex asks something of us. It can be the means through which we allow the archetype of life to show itself, so that we live more fully and manifest ourselves more transparently. This demand is so central and powerful that our resistances to it are also strong—our moralism, indirection, rationalization, and acting out. It would help if we would stop thinking of sex as in the slightest way medical or biological. The whole sphere of sex—emotion, body, fantasy, and relationship—falls within the domain of soul.

To broaden our imagination of the holiness of sex, I turn once again to mythology. In Greek and Roman polytheism, interestingly, each of the deities is sexual in a particular way, showing us how sex is divine in as many ways as there are gods and goddesses. I use this word *divine* of sex as a way of describing its unfathomable mystery and its absolutely profound place in the nature of things. A whole book could, and perhaps should, be written about the mythologies of sex; here I will give just three examples to suggest how such an approach can help us.

HERMES

The Greek god Hermes was known chiefly as the "guide of souls," but he was also a strong sexual deity. A *herm* was originally a pile of stones that rose up from the earth like nature's phallus, used by travelers as a guidepost. From a Hermes point of view, sex offers guidance toward soulfulness, especially toward the deep places of the soul where strong emotions arise. For instance, we might look closely at shifts in our sexual fantasies for signals of what is going on deep in the soul, as though these fantasies were herms showing us the way. Our usual tendency is to judge these fantasies, or to move quickly into either repressing them or acting them out; we don't think to take them as indications of movements in the soul. Yet it's quite evident that the soul has its own sexual poetics. Our sexual fantasies and curiosity, even our inhibitions and repressions, have far-reaching resonance and many levels of meaning. In sexual imagination the soul is alive and fertile, not only in relation to physical pleasure but as an expression of its own quickening of life.

Sexual dreams can also be seen as the work of Hermes. It's all too tempting to take these dreams literally, assuming that last night's dream of making love to my teacher means that I must be attracted to her in waking life. But dreams can also take the material of life and give it a context and dimension that place it at the very heart of our identity and at the core of our emotions. Each sexual dream offers a glimpse of our deep nature and fate. This particular dream could suggest that my personal fate is to be drawn to teaching, that there is an erotic magnetism at work between myself and education, or it could also allude to the learning that goes on in sex. Sex is certainly a form of education, which is not the same as "sex education." Taken Hermetically, sexual dreams implicate all areas of life, while at the same time they hint at the innumerable ways in which sex gives meaning to life.

Hermes was known as the god of communication and connections, so we could also explore these more commonly recognized aspects of sex as well. Through sex we may be able to express feelings more revealingly than in language. As desire and pleasure take over in the rush of sexual feelings, we are unveiled in ways not possible outside of sex. Our partner can see us with a transparency uncluttered by ego and manipulation. In this way sex communicates who we are, in a seizure of imagination that is uniquely expressive and therefore powerfully Hermetic.

When we look to sex for hints at the meaning of a relationship, or as the expression of love, we are imagining sex Hermetically. Modern studies that explore the sexuality of language are also sniffing out the presence of Hermes. Not only is sex a language of sorts, language is also sexual. Poets know well that language is both erotic and genital. Wallace Stevens says, "A poet looks at the world somewhat as a man looks at a woman."[2] In *Love's Body*, Norman O. Brown describes the sexual nature of language: "The little word 'is' is the hallmark of Eros, even as, Freud said, the little word 'no' is the hallmark of Death. Every sentence is dialectics, an act of love."[3]

Every aspect of life has its sexual dimension, and sex in the strict sense gives rise to life's poetics, whether in the form of art—music, paintings, dance—or the intimacies of everyday life. When people say that they can express certain feelings and thoughts only through physical sex, they are describing the Hermetic capacity of sex to serve as intercourse in all senses of the word. As such, sex can bring magic into a relationship, and anchor it in a way that no amount of talking or doing things together can. On the other hand, because sex touches such deep places in the soul, sexual failure can be devastating.

The image of Hermes suggests that connections can be made between people in ways that are not reasonable and fully intentional. Indeed, sex is one of the means Hermes uses to make these magical relationships. The worst thing would be to replace Hermes by "using" sex for communication or by intellectualizing it. The only thing required is to be open to Hermes in sex, and let him do his work. We could develop an awareness allowing us to distinguish when we are manipulating and forcing, and when we are letting ourselves be revealed and communicated. This passive form, "being communicated," is a pious way of letting the god have his way with us. The best way is not to reveal ourselves, but to be revealed.

We might want to keep in mind as well that Hermes, noble guide of souls, was also a thief, a liar, a cheat, and a lusty philanderer. The magical power of sex to link hearts has a shadow side which we overlook at our own peril. We may be drawn sexually to people who in every other respect do not make good partners. The Hermes element in sex also leads to very dark experiences. I knew a quite innocent man who found sexual fulfillment only by having sex in dangerous criminal communities and settings. I've worked with several women of little experience in the world who have described an allure they felt toward men who were violent or were involved with crime. If we see this magnetism as a draw toward Hermes, we might be able to evoke him in his trickster aspect without exposing ourselves to the danger of his literal underworld stand-ins.

On the other hand, there is no way to enter soulful sexuality without being soiled by its Hermetic shadow. As we answer the call of the sexual spirits, we will likely find ourselves in one mess or other, but this fall into sexual darkness may not be a literal fault. It may simply signal that we are getting close to the soul, which in its Hermetic sexual expression is never fully clean or bright.

APHRODITE

Aphrodite is an obvious goddess of sex, especially of its alluring and seductive elements. We have already noted her important role in love. One of the Homeric hymns in her honor says, "That seductive face of hers is always smiling, always carrying its seductive flower." The hymn honors this important dimension of sex and the sexual nature of life itself. Aphrodite was known not only as the goddess of human love and beauty, but of the seductiveness and attractiveness of the world. When we are seduced to smell a flower or to watch a sunset, we have given in to the charms of this beguiling figure, and at such times we might reflect on the relationship between our own personal sexuality and sex in a much greater sense.

When our sexual thoughts excite us toward new liaisons and new experiences, we may consider honoring these thoughts not by establishing new interpersonal relationships, but by being in life more sexually. A person can live erotically every minute of the day by valuing deep pleasures, beauty, body, adornment, decoration, texture, and color—all things we too often consider secondary or even frivolous. But to an Aphroditic sensibility, they are of primary importance and deserve our sincere attention.

If it seems impossible to imagine seduction as a holy thing, try to imagine a world without it: without the lure of travel and exploration, without the beguiling beauty that entices us to look at photographs of enchanting places, without a desire for a rich experience of this life. Teachers know the importance of presenting ideas in such a way that they are seductive. Advertising geniuses obviously know the particulars of an Aphroditic world well. All of this is Aphrodite's sexual domain.

By seeing the cosmic aspects of Aphrodite, whom the ancients also called Ourania, or sky goddess, we might break through some of the compartmentalization that attaches to our personal experiences of sex. She divinizes the mirror—vanity, and the pleasure to be found in cosmetics and fashion, ornament, and jewelry. Of course many people have no trouble indulging vanity and fashion, but as a society we lack a full appreciation, especially in a public way, of these Aphroditic virtues. It isn't easy to find traces of Aphrodite in our modern cities—in our civic buildings or in the language of politics. Yet if we are not sexual in all of life, how can we expect sexual fulfillment in our relationships? We might also go a long way toward an ecological consciousness through a greater appreciation of the Aphrodite myth: we might take better care of the natural world if we could see her spirit in our hills and countryside. In a phrase that could serve as an inspiring mantra, Ficino said that it's terribly important to feel the "breath of Venus" in the world, for she is one of the primary sources of graciousness in this life.

A dose of vanity is a blessing from this goddess. It can motivate people to take care of themselves, to present themselves to the world attractively, and to become people of visibility and effectiveness. Vanity can feed fashion in a soulful way and motivate us to bring beauty and care to our homes and our persons. Obviously, when vanity is a symptom rather than a character trait it can render life literally shallow and superficial, but in that case the problem is not with vanity itself. Besides, excessive modesty can be just as narcissistic and equally unattractive.

Another easily overlooked virtue of the Aphroditic life is attention to adornment and decoration. As a people we have lost this simple aesthetic sensibility that many societies take for granted. Old machines and furniture are alive with decoration, while it is the very hallmark of late-twentieth-century life to use machines, utensils, and appliances that are sleek, gray, and decoration-free.

On a recent trip to Rome I had an opportunity to attend a *presentazione*, a public celebration of a poet who had just published a small volume of poetry. After a reading of the poems, three substantive minilectures by two professors, and some good wine and cheese, we examined the lovely old printing press on which the poems had been printed. It was made of imposing cast iron, was a hand-operated machine, and was alive with decorations and animal motifs. The paper on which the poems were printed was also exceptional, thick and textured, so from the words of the poet to the physical object to the way it was publicly presented, the entire event demonstrated the possibilities of an Aphroditic approach to poetry.

Imagine computer terminals multicolored and supported on little animal feet. If that image is difficult to conjure up, then you know how far removed our boxlike machines are from the animated, sensual, image-filled mechanical paraphernalia of the past. When Aphrodite is evoked in such everyday objects and activities, life is given soul. Too often we think that the psyche is nourished only by means of mental analysis and personal behavioral changes, but as Jung said, soul is more outside than inside. We can care for the soul by eroticizing our lives and sexualizing our environment—invoking a blessing from the goddess who has always been both a scandal and a grace.

ARTEMIS

Another goddess, quite different from Aphrodite in that she is sometimes considered asexual, is Artemis, in Rome known as Diana. Although Artemis is a virgin goddess, she also represents a sometimes overlooked dimension of sexuality. We have already seen the story of one of her "daughters," Daphne, being chased by Apollo, who is filled with desire for her. There are other stories as well of Artemis figures who are obviously sexually attractive and have to run away from their pursuers: Britomartis flees from the advances of King Minos, Atalanta runs a race hoping to achieve freedom from sexual entanglements. There must be something terribly alluring in these virgin goddesses to inspire such lust.

We might think of these virgin figures of myth as evoking our own modest, inexperienced, and innocent spirit, as well as the integrity of nature. The goal of some pursuers may be to spoil that innocence, while others may wish to claim it as a life companion, to learn from it and be affected by it. Many people seek out partners whose innocence is their most beguiling charm. Others choose to live as near as possible to nature, assuming that nature's purity will maintain their own. Some people even like to make their sexual relationship virginal in some fashion. They may appreciate personal privacy and restraint in lovemaking, or they enjoy the eroticism that comes from sexual abstinence.

Chastity has a place in a sexual relationship. But we literalize the soul's virginity when we polarize chastity and sex as two opposing ways of life, and not as two dimensions in a relationship. I would think that even so small a thing as the statement "I don't feel like it right now" may be a visitation from Artemis and may serve a sexual relationship in its own way. Reserve, withdrawal, and withholding are part of the dance of sex. If they are seen only as a failure of sex or as an aberration, then the sexual relationship, perceiving Artemis as a threat, could suffer.

Artemis, the tall goddess, could often be found in the mountains. She has a high and exalted air, as do the Artemis elements in life, such as meditation, solitude, moral conviction, spiritual practice, and purity of life-style. We may glimpse this spiritual side of Artemis in our church spires. Near my house in New England a "peace pagoda" rests Artemislike on the top of a hill, surrounded by trees and accessible only by a lane into the woods.

During my years of university teaching I found that academic life had many Artemis qualities. The "ivory tower" of academe, like the goddess, prefers to look at life from a distance and to set a border around its campus, separating itself from the vulgarity of the world. A *campus* is a field or pasture—a typical Artemis setting. I was even once advised by an administrator not to get too involved in interdisciplinary studies because it was important to preserve the integrity of the traditional departments; apparently the commingling of disciplines looked promiscuous. And certainly any sign of intercourse between ordinary or personal life and pure study was met with the same "moral" dismay as any sexual misdeed.

Just because Artemis is pure doesn't mean she isn't sexual. Priests, nuns, rabbis, ministers, nurses, teachers—all people who engage in noble, spiritual professions—can be attractive to others precisely because of their purity. Sexual fantasy rises of its own accord in the presence of purity: not in compensation, but inspired by the special eroticism associated with Artemis.

We might reflect on some sexual difficulties as the symptomatology of Artemis. Sexual coldness and distance of a destructive kind could indicate a failure to respect Artemis necessities. If our sexual lives do not allow a sufficient degree of integrity, individuality, and self-containment, Artemis will complain, and she often complains with considerable ferocity. If our sexuality is a subtle mixture of desire and withholding, intimacy and distance, or surrender and self-possession, these paradoxical qualities may signal the soulful presence of Artemis spirits, which complicate sexuality in the most productive manner by heightening erotic tension.

In this way the cultivation of purity in life can enrich one's sexuality. It may not be mere prudishness or resistance to sex if a person is offended by off-color jokes or sexy magazines. Artemis retreats in the presence of casual sexuality, and yet she has a great deal of sexual pleasure to offer. Her retreat from life could be seen, too, as a way of drawing sex away from its literal expressions and into the realms of art—the Daphne theme—or into natural beauty. In her the more subtle forms of sexual pleasure find a home.

Imagination in Sexual Failure

To GET to the soul of sex we have to take it as it is, to accept its power both to attract and to disturb, and temper the various means we employ to protect ourselves from it. I'm not saying we need to act out any and all sexual fantasies that present themselves. Far from it: such acting out is also a way of avoiding soul. The person who knows only the compulsions of sex has never experienced its soul.

What if we expanded our hearts wide enough to contain the many emotions that form an aureole around sex? What if we embraced its anxiety along with its pleasure? I suspect that the anxiety around sex is of the same order as the apprehension we feel in the presence of anything that still has the breath of God in it, that has not been flattened out with conscious intentions and explanations. Fortunately, sex resists our strenuous efforts to bridle it and stuff it into acceptable forms. Not to run away from our anxiety about it may be a way of feeling the full presence of its mystery.

In ancient Rome people believed that Priapus, the god of sexual vigor and vitality, was also the god who visited in impotence. These two sides of sex—vitality and impotence—have equal legitimacy and importance, and both are divinely sanctioned. If we try to achieve one by defending ourselves against the other, we will never know the fullness of sexual pleasure. Not only the attractions and withholdings, but also the failures of sex can be given their place, if we are to draw close enough to sex so that it feeds the soul.

In our culture we automatically judge each and every failure negatively, and then we go to extreme lengths to find an immediate remedy. Any sex therapy that rushes to cure without listening to and honoring failure—dysfunction—plays into our unconscious values of nonstop success, performance, and good functioning. From the viewpoint of soul, failure to function is meaningful, worthy of our intense interest and study. Soul speaks through the chink created by dysfunction, corrects our Herculean willfulness, and occasions nourishing reflection. If everything were going well, there would be no need to stop and reflect on what we're doing.

From the soul point of view, sex can be even more revealing in times of dysfunction and mess than in moments of well-being. We become desperate to examine our sexual lives, to consider past experiences and present attitudes, to wonder about what is happening. This is all food for the soul. Sexual difficulty may also ask that we stretch the imagination to consider changes the soul is asking of us. We may need a different sexual philosophy, new attitudes toward men and women, or to consider whether we're living out power problems in a relationship through sex. The possibilities are infinite.

The anxiety, guilt, confusion, remorse, and apprehension we may feel about sex can be seen as part of sexual life rather than as literal failure of it. This more profound reading of the Priapus paradox suggests that one gift of sex is a dissolution of the complacency, egotism, and heroics that can rigidify all of life, not just sexual experiences. Sex may then become a way to soul, rather than a confirmation of the status quo.

Sex is involved in every relationship and in every aspect of a relationship. When I am working in therapy with a couple having sexual difficulties, I do not automatically focus on the mechanics of sex or on obvious sexual issues, even if the couple insists that their problem is physical. Rather, I try to see what the soul is presenting in life in general, in the understanding that sex is always related to other aspects of life.

A man complained to me that he and his wife had lost interest in sex. I noticed that he kept blaming his wife for their problem. "She was brought up in a puritanical home. She's too uptight. She's too wrapped up in being a mother." He never ran out of reasons why his wife was the culprit in their sexual "dysfunction."

This kind of blaming may be a sign of avoidance of something within oneself. I asked this man about his own feelings and especially his dream life. The dreams he was having had no specific sexual themes in them, but they did reveal a significant conflict. In one dream he was getting dressed for a formal dinner when his little boy ran by him, smearing chocolate ice cream on his jacket. The father, suddenly very upset, was concerned not to let anyone see this blotch on his coat.

I was interested in the dreamer's worry about having an image of cleanliness and formality that was spoiled by the child. The dream showed an interesting pattern—concern for image, a childlike smearing of that image, and anxiety about being seen in a messy condition. We talked at some length about a division within the man: wanting to appear adult and proper and yet feeling some childish undoing from within himself.

I was not surprised just two weeks after this conversation to hear that things had changed in his sexual relations with his wife. At least for the moment, they had taken a strong turn for the better. To the surprise of some people, a sexual difficulty can improve without any new understanding of the nature of the problem—simply touching, bringing to light, or stirring up the part of the soul that is involved can be enough.

Something in this man needed to be smeared by the child's own food, ice cream. Sex asks that we live joyously outside the perimeters of adult containment. We may feel soiled by the mess of this undisciplined world, which is sometimes that of the child, and yet it is healing. Ficino went so far as to say that all healing requires a movement into soul, which will be felt as outside the familiar structures of serious life.

If we define sex too narrowly, we may never reach the deeper and wider sources of sexual difficulty. A man and wife are in a sexual relationship all day long, every day: what happens in bed cannot be separated from what happens in life. It's no accident that the word *intercourse* means both physical lovemaking and intimate conversation.

The marriage bed is truly an altar on which many gods and goddesses are given reverence and ritual. Not all sex is Aphrodite, and even if her spirit is dominant, the rest of life is still profoundly affected by the devotion shown her in her special rituals of the bed. Conversely, because sex is not just about the physical expression of love, but is an aspect of one's entire life, lovemaking can be affected for better or worse by other issues.

Sex, Aggression, and Eros

ANOTHER WAY to describe the emotional range of sex mythologically is to take note of the pairings we find in the stories. Venus has a special relationship to Mars, for instance, which is depicted intriguingly in Botticelli's famous painting of Mars and Venus. Edgar Wind, in his profound study of Renaissance imagery, *Pagan Mysteries in the Renaissance*, traces the literary history of this tandem, the idea being that life is made up of the contraries beauty and discord. Marsian strife is softened, put to sleep in Botticelli's version, by the sweet but powerful spells of Venus. The seductress proves stronger than the soldier.

Modern psychological literature discusses this particular association in different language and tone, noting the importance for good sexual functioning of an aggressive spirit. There is no need, of course, to use the language of mythology. When a person complains to me about sexual problems, I may not think immediately of Botticelli, but I look for his or her particular tandems to sex. What are this person's fantasies in relation to sex, to relationship, power, self-expression, and so on, I wonder. In the case of the dreamer I just discussed, apparently the figure of the "smearing child" was important in his soul, and therefore in his sex life. Discussing sex, Patricia Berry says that married people usually lose the polymorphous quality of childhood sexuality, and therefore suffer from an excessively adult notion of sex. My ice cream man apparently needed a sweet, sticky, soiling brush with the child in order to recover his sexual capacities. His sexual feelings needed to be "contaminated" by childhood.

Another fascinating mythological partner to Venus is the god

Eros. In the ancient tale of Eros and Psyche, Eros is depicted as Aphrodite's son, although the story lingers on a long passionate kiss between them, suggesting that they are lovers too. It may seem redundant to say that an erotic life has something to do with sex, but it is still helpful to explore just how profound and far-reaching the implications of that connection can be.

Eros means "desire" and "longing." Most of us live our lives motivated by obligation rather than by desire and longing. Often, when a person comes to me complaining about some difficulty, I ask not "What is wrong?" but "Where is your desire?" I want to know about the condition of eros in this life, because the soul is affected much more by our treatment of eros than it is by the failure to do everything properly.

In *Eros the Bittersweet*, Anne Carson's thoughtful, precise exploration of eros based on classical texts in counterpoint with modern literature and philosophy, she summarizes her discussion of erotic longing with the conundrum, "All human desire is poised on an axis of paradox, absence and presence its poles, love and hate its motive energies."[4] Eros is a mystery because it is never fully satisfied, and yet it is always finding satisfactions; it seems to be identical with love, and yet it has an essential relationship with hate. If we identify desire only in relation to what we want, then we overlook the fact that when we struggle amid feelings of hatred, there may also be an erotic element involved.

In his excellent book on Dionysus, Karl Kerényi, the historian of Greek religion, brings up another paradox: eros is the affirmation of life, and yet it has a close relation to death. Kerényi describes eros as a "guide of souls,"[5] and in particular a guide of the soul to death. James Hillman long ago pointed out that this death does not have to be taken literally, but rather as the movement out of life as we literally live it and understand it, into a deeper perspective where the eternal issues of the soul are involved. In other words, eros leads us further into soulfulness, or in Hillman's language, "I discover that *wherever* eros goes, something psychological is happening, and that wherever psyche lives, eros will inevitably constellate."[6]

In classical art, Eros has wings. He flies as the spirit flies, and he touches us as the spirit does. He may take us to places quite extraordinary. Any of us may be seized by a desire that is impossible to resist and yet moves in a direction that makes no sense or even counters our established values and ideals. But whenever life becomes erotic, the soul is involved.

When we feel stuck in life or in a relationship, we might look closely at the place of desire in our lives, even those places where it seems neurotic. Do I find myself fantasizing a trip abroad? Do my fantasies move in the direction of anonymous sex? Am I preoccupied with food or alcohol or some other drug? Am I reading compulsively? These are all signs of desire, and they can be read perceptively in order to find both where the soul is settling and where it is hiding.

Another way to include desire in our care for the soul is to allow it to have a principal place in the shaping of life. It is important not to overlook longings or dismiss them for practical reasons, and not to rely exclusively in our decision-making on reason or common sense, thereby excluding the more mysterious turns of eros. An erotic life is not at all the same as a rational one. Living erotically, we understand that desires are central to the soul's unfolding and should not be dismissed before giving them careful attention.

Kerényi offers an interesting image for the way in which Eros serves as a soul guide. He mentions a vase in the Naples museum on which is painted a puzzling scene. A winged young man throws a colorful embroidered ball to a hesitant woman. On the vase is an inscription: THEY HAVE THROWN ME THE BALL. Kerényi interprets this as an invitation to the world of the dead. Eros is the messenger, the go-between. In Hillman's reading of this general theme, the woman is being enticed into soul through eros.

A woman once told me a dream in which a child tossed out a bright-colored ball that was covered with painted stars and other celestial bodies. The ball bounced along, leading the dreamer first to a house in which there lived an old, dominating woman, then to another house that was empty. The dreamer felt that she was supposed to enter this second house, but hesitated because she didn't want to trespass. Finally, as the dream ended, she went in.

There is a great mystery in this dream, made all the more interesting by the classical images Kerényi gives us. The bouncing ball, he tells us, can be an image for the seductions of eros. The dreamer's ball is also clearly cosmic—a sphere covered with stars—and in the early Greek Orphic religion, Eros himself was honored as a creator of the world, a demiurge.

Like a bouncing ball, there is often something playful about erotic experience. Invitations into deeper soulfulness often come to us in light, almost insignificant forms. This is an insight worth pondering: we are led profoundly into our soulfulness through the playful turns of life, and not necessarily or only in weighty matters. Heraclitus says, "Time is a child moving counters in a board game." How different this is from the fantasy that life is governed by a stern, weighty old man! In fact, Eros is usually pictured as an unruly adolescent, a young man wildly dashing from place to place, or as a child, always unpredictable and uncivilized.

I suspected that the woman's dream was extremely fateful, even though, or maybe because, it appeared so slight. In an essay on fairy tales Jung mentions the "pathfinding ball" that, serving as a magical talisman, sets the soul in motion. Joseph Campbell commented often on the tale of the Frog Prince, which begins with a little girl losing a ball that bounces into a pond. Campbell sees this slight occurrence as an example of a mythic "call to adventure." "The adventure may begin," he writes, "as a mere blunder, as did that of the princess of the fairy tale; or still again, one may be only casually strolling, when some passing phenomenon catches the wandering eye and lures one away from the frequented paths."[7] Again, one finds seduction an important theme in the soul's progress.

To live an erotic life is to follow the bouncing ball, to allow oneself to be distracted and enticed by something playful and childlike, or, to be more precise, by life itself in its playful mode. Our habitual seriousness can prevent us from seeing, and certainly appreciating, the erotic lures that come our way every day. Our medically minded seriousness about sex can also prevent us from glimpsing the cure of our sexual maladies and opportunities for expanding our sexuality. We may take it all too seriously, with too much adult knowledge and sophistication. Sex can sometimes be an invitation to the soul to come out and play.

Sex and Morality

SEX AND EROS are very closely allied, so that if the desire for a better sex life comes upon us, we might consider living more erotically in general. Of course, many people would find this suggestion objectionable, because we were brought up to believe that desire by its very nature is suspect and dangerous. It's better, we were told, to do what is right than to have what we want.

Although putting moral fences around sex is understandable, given its power and the strength of its shadow, the soulful aspect of sex can be deeply wounded by the wrong kind of moral sensitivity. If we place sex and morality in opposition to each other, then our morality will be defensive in nature, protecting us from the powerful lures of sex. But defensive morality is not the genuine article—it's self-protective and narcissistic, shallow and stagnant. We need a deep-seated, imaginative, constantly deepening moral sensitivity; defensive moralism not only thwarts the soul's thirst for pleasure, it also precludes a truly guiding morality founded in wisdom. What if we didn't oppose sex and morality so stringently? What if we thought that the more sexual we are and the more erotically we live, the *more* moral our lives would be?

Let me give an example of what I'm talking about. A woman I worked with in therapy had been married for fifteen years to a man she truly loved. But she also loved another man. Let's call him Timothy. Early in her marriage she had had an affair with Timothy. She loved being with Timothy, but she also felt guilty about it. She had three children, and she couldn't stand the thought of betraying her husband and her family just so that she could selfishly have moments here and there of real sexual fulfillment. So she ended the affair.

A few years later, however, she realized that her marriage felt wooden and in decay. She had set aside her strong desire for Timothy with the idea that her marriage would be better for it, but in fact her marriage continued to get worse. She didn't want to get a divorce, she didn't want to live an empty marriage, and she didn't want to give in to her desire for Timothy. Understandably, she felt there was no way to resolve her situation.

Eventually, her desire won out and she started up the affair once again. She knew her heart craved the comforts of her relationship with Timothy, yet she still didn't want to leave her family for him. She loved her family and didn't want to lose it. This time, however, she talked to her husband openly about her feelings, and even though he tried every way he could to make her feel bad about what she was doing, in order to pressure her to stop and give him emotional relief, she remained in the complexity of her emotions. She knew from past experience that if she resigned herself once again to giving up her desire in favor of an emotionally and sexually empty marriage, she'd "go crazy," as she put it.

Both she and her husband were forced to look closely at their marriage and at themselves as individuals. As long as they tried to find a moral solution or an intellectual answer, they got nowhere. But when they began to talk without pressing for a solution, something happened that shocked them. They began to enjoy making love with each other more than in all the years of their married life.

This time the affair ended without resentment or regret. Of course, the woman had strong feelings of loss and some concern about how lasting the change in her marriage would be, but she also felt peace about her decision. Something strong and loyal in her wanted to preserve the marriage. Her husband, for his part, discovered some of the ways in which he had been keeping intimacy out of their relationship. Over a long period of time, he gradually stopped blaming his wife for all their troubles. He could even glimpse, though not really accept, the idea that the woodenness of the marriage drove his wife outside of it. Meanwhile, by refusing to compromise her deep need for erotic intimacy, the wife not only stayed faithful to her own soul but helped return soul to the marriage.

The currents of eros make their own claims. This woman didn't simply turn blindly to a new passing flirtation. She lived for a long while in the painful complexities of conscience and in the entanglements of her desires. Out of that cauldron she found a new way of being married, and although neither she nor her husband could explain all that had happened, they felt a genuine renewal of their love.

I don't mean to suggest that because the outcome was an intensification of marriage, the situation was therefore moral. Had she decided to go with Timothy, she still would have preserved her moral sensibility. What was central was her faithfulness to the competing demands of her soul. Many times during the process both she and her husband would have loved to find a solution, but they both knew the importance of remaining in the confusion until *it* revealed a way. This attitude represents a morality close to the soul, deeply embedded in life, fate, and emotion.

Soulful morality is almost always subtle, complicated, paradoxical, individual, and gradual in its unfolding. It takes a long time in some areas to discover what is right and wrong, how one should live one's life, and which values take priority over others. Those who live by moralism, as opposed to soulful morality, believe they know all the answers. They can make quick judgments about the affairs of others. Even intelligent, sophisticated people who don't consider themselves moralistic often become drawn into moralism in areas where they are emotionally vulnerable.

Moral reflection that respects the unexpected movements of eros can foster intimacy and sexual fulfillment. But moral positions that are chronically suspicious of eros actually breed sexual acting out, by repressing its important role in the dynamics of the soul. They create the very moral confusion they are trying to counter.

When moral sensitivity and respect for eros merge, the two are so close the result might be called "erotic morality." This is a finely tuned ethical sense that recognizes the fact that soul is frequently set in movement by desires that may be initially confusing, but later may prove to be all-important in shaping life for the better. This kind of morality is life-affirming rather than prohibiting, and respectful of eros rather than suspicious. It trusts desire, and therefore, paradoxically, it doesn't breed compulsion.

From the erotic point of view, especially if we see eros as a "guide of the soul," our culture's fear of sex and our anxious controls on sex are at bottom due to a mistrust of the soul. Soul is a generator of life, spilling imagination into a world that tries to keep itself stable and secure. Sex is always making new connections, filling fantasy with new possibilities for intimacy, unfamiliar and exciting emotions and sensations, and new ways of experiencing life. Our literalistic attitudes and our reductionistic, narrow readings of sex try to bridle it, attempting to halt its threat to the status quo by squelching it at the physical level.

This narrow view of sex can also turn marriage into an uninteresting arrangement, giving the illusion that being married carries with it the demand to repress the exogamous tendency of sex toward further connections. With a soulful, erotic approach to sex, marriage can be a perfect setting in which all aspects of sex come into play. A person can be chaste, lewd, Dionysian, childlike, maternal, Priapic, experimental, Daphnic, and even philandering (erotically loving many people) without acting out these wonderfully life-creating ways among actual people. It takes a robust imagination to invite eros into marriage, and it takes a poetic response to our own sexuality to make it soulful.

Morality can be a powerful force in living a soulful life, and it can help us sustain our loyalties and fidelities in relationship, provided it does not act as the enemy of desire and pleasure. As a promoter of eros, a strong moral sensitivity helps cultivate eros as a humane dimension of everyday life, and not as the destroyer of culture. Eros invigorates the forms by which we live, and in turn it takes on effective human shape and dimension. Morality might be defined in these terms as the imagination for channeling eros into workable human forms. Above all, it is a positive force, not a negative one.

Pornography and Relationship

*I*N DISCUSSIONS I have led on the theme of soul and intimacy, participants have frequently brought up the topic of pornography as a problem in their relationships. Obviously, it is an important issue, especially considering the role of the imagination in erotic life.[8]

It sometimes happens that one person in a relationship shows an interest in pornography, while the other is offended or at least disturbed by it. A person might think that if her husband is turning to pornography for sexual stimulation, there must be something lacking in her. A woman tells me, "I wish my husband would find whatever he is looking for in sex in our relationship, not in a magazine or a video." A man says, "I guess I'm not what my wife is looking for in a man. She's interested in other men's bodies."

It's difficult to sort out issues surrounding pornography because in our culture response to pornography often divides into two extremes—compulsion and moral indignation. This split suggests that for us pornography is a problem, rather than an element integrated into everyday life. When we respond to *anything* with compulsion and moralism, we can assume that we haven't yet found the soul in it. We have yet to imagine it deeply enough to be free of either its compulsive lure or its frightening or repulsive aspect. In the case of pornography, we could look closely at our own repulsions and fascinations and ask with sincerity, "What is this thing doing in life?"

The fact that dreams are often sexually explicit suggests that the soul itself takes pleasure in pornographic images, that pornography is not just a personal problem, and that it may serve some significant purpose. Dreams are not fabrications of a neurotic mind; in fact, they seem so deep in our own natures, so primitive, that they show more directly than anything else, if sometimes obscurely, what the soul is made of. Jung once said in a lecture that dreams reflect certain tendencies "whose meaning embraces our whole life, or those which are momentarily of most importance." He went on to add a qualification that is important, especially in relation to pornographic dreams: "The dream presents an objective statement of these tendencies, a statement unconcerned with our conscious wishes and beliefs."[9]

Extremely fastidious people, proper in every outward respect, have told me dreams that are filled with sexual experimentation, impersonal or improper liaisons, and graphic lascivious situations, all often accompanied by almost preternatural degrees of pleasure. If we follow the idea that dreams indicate movements or conditions of the soul, then we might ask what it is that interests the soul in pornographic images. What is the point of the pornographic imagination?

Dreams are an art form created by the soul for our own edification. We must read them poetically, as we would any kind of art. When a person dreams, as many people often do, that a tornado is approaching, he doesn't necessarily have to build a storm shelter in response. It's fairly easy to see that this tornado may be an image of some threatening "weather"—emotional, fateful, relational—that could cause havoc. In the same way, a sexual dream doesn't have to be seen only in relation to physical sex. More broadly, it may present us with specific images of desire, attraction, pleasure, connection, self-expression, or a whole range of other possibilities.

When we ourselves or someone close to us suddenly becomes fascinated with pornography, we might keep an open mind, and keep that mind poetic, in order to "read" what is going on. A person who has repressed his own desires and lived mainly from obligation might well spend his nights in rich sexual extravagance. I don't want to suggest that dreams are always a compensation or are opposite the stance we take in life, for the soul may also be taking a turn, becoming interested in another direction in life, which might be embodied in sexual fascination.

An interest in pornography—books, movies, music, shows— clearly shows the desire for some kind of increase in erotic life, and in particular for an intensification and broadening of the sexual imagination. When we find this interest blooming in ourselves or in someone close to us, perhaps uncharacteristically and surprisingly, rather than move quickly into judgment, we might ask what it is doing there. Could this sexual interest be serving some purpose? Renaissance medical books described Venus as one of the most moist spheres of life; following this hint, we might inquire into our dryness. Could this appearance of erotic fascination be a response to dryness of thought and living? The pornographic imagination doesn't have to be justified, but it might ease our minds if we could find a context for it.

Our culture in general has difficulty with Eros and Venus, desire and sex. Our reactions as a society are often moralistic and repressive, an indication that we have yet to find ways to incorporate these powerful forces into our ordinary habits of life and thought. As individuals we are affected by the culture's impasse in this area, so that sometimes what may appear to be a personal problem may in fact simply reflect a larger struggle taking place in society. In order to deal with these things at the personal level, we may have to go against the prevailing sentiments of society, at least to some extent.

As long as we think of sex in a limited way, as a biological function or even as only a means of communication or intimacy, we will be mystified by its unexpected turns. It would be better to recognize from the beginning that sex is a profound, far-reaching aspect of the soul, bringing together body, emotion, and imagination in an intense experience that can touch every branch of feeling and meaning, yet one we may never fully understand. It is by nature mysterious. For ourselves, when we are seized by a fascination with pornography, we may have no choice but to follow the compulsion, while observing it carefully. When it's our partner who is so charmed, either we may have to tolerate the compulsion, and help with conversations about its possible direction, or we may be so repulsed that we may have to find ways to protect ourselves, at least temporarily. This kind of compulsion can be a beast, as necessary as it may be in the life of the individual soul.

The Greek word *porne* (literally "harlot") was used as an epithet for the great goddess Aphrodite. This striking bit of linguistic history suggests that pornography is not only normal, it must have something valuable to give to the soul. We might think about positive ways to cultivate an appreciation for erotic imagery, and we might also recognize that our resistances to it could be either an important natural mitigation of the compulsion or a fearful defensiveness toward a piece of soulfulness that asks us to become more complicated and flexible in our moral sensitivities. In our difficulties with pornography, both of these dynamics may play a role, and it may take considerable time for reflection and self-examination to sort them out. In any case, the goal would be a deeper appreciation of the erotic imagination, so that neither compulsion nor defensiveness would be the characteristic quality of our response.

Sex and Intimacy

THINKING ABOUT sex, we sometimes take either the position that it is entirely physiological or the one that it is primarily interpersonal. In either of these viewpoints, the soul of sex can be overlooked. Its soul is to be found in the imagination through which we experience sex, whether individually, interpersonally, or even societally. Each of us has a sexual history, stories, persons who figure prominently for good or ill, places, and events—some of them pulsing with emotion. We may also have strong sexual hopes and longings. We might regard all these images poetically, as creations of the soul aware that each may resonate on many levels. The memory of a pleasurable experience may carry longings about pleasure in life itself, or a painful memory may epitomize a more general disillusionment and hopelessness about joy, pleasure, and intimacy. The image of oneself as a lover, as beautiful or capable, may be wrapped up in these memories. Deeper still may lie fears of exposure, the old dynamics of family relationships, or even the difficult task of simply living a bodily existence.

The intimacy in sex, while always attached to the body, is never only physical. Sex always evokes pieces of stories and fragments of characters, and so the desire and willingness to be sexually transparent is truly an exposure of the soul. In sex we may discover who we are in ways otherwise unavailable to us, and at the same time we allow our partner to see and know that individual. As we unveil our bodies, we also disclose our persons.

It makes sense that such vulnerability requires inhibitions of all kinds. Part of sexual intimacy is protection of the other's inhibition, for that reserve is as much an expression of soul as is the apparent willingness to be exposed. It makes no difference whether the inhibition seems neurotic or even psychotic: it must be honored if soulful intimacy is to be maintained. It is not "abnormal" for a person to feel unusually reticent about physical and emotional exposure. Nor is it "abnormal" for a person to enjoy the exhibition of their sexuality. Exhibitionism and frigidity are states of soul. In the context of a relatively puritanical society, all robust sex may appear quite abnormal anyway.

Sexual intimacy begins with acknowledgment of and respect for the mystery and madness of the other's sexuality, for it is only in mystery and madness that soul is revealed. I'm referring to platonic madness, of course—the soul's natural expression that almost always appears deviant to normal society. At times we may have to protect ourselves from another's sexual confusion and acting out, but if we want an intimate relationship, we will have to find it in ourselves to create a place for the other's sexual fantasy. In extreme instances we may decide that we can't tolerate a particular erotic world, or we may realize that some sexual thoughts are dangerous for us. In most cases, though, we may want to try to stretch our imaginations and sensitivities, acknowledging that the soul shows itself in each of us differently, and particularly in the precise directions of sexual fantasy.

To find sexual intimacy we may also have to acknowledge that sex is often wounded. Our great stories often give us images of sexual wounds—Odysseus's scarred thigh, the lanced thigh of the Fisher King of the Parsifal story, Lady Chatterley's impotent husband, Emma Bovary's obsessions. Soul pours forth from our wounds in general; and the soul of sexuality in particular often enters through an opening made by sexual wounding. We can learn to see that the places of our sexual punctures and violations are areas of potential intimacy between us and those we love, even though on the surface they may seem to be precisely the areas of mistrust. In this it is terribly important to resist the modern tendency to champion health and wholeness. All of us have sexual wounds. It does no good either to wallow in them or to deny them, but it may be good for the soul of a relationship to give them a place—protecting them, not trying to figure them out and solve them, giving them the privacy they demand, and yet also inviting them into our most vulnerable conversations.

Current talk of sexual woundedness often turns to cause and effect. We want to know *why* we experience certain difficulties, and we would like to find someone to blame for the problem. Another, more soulful approach is to resist the temptation to stroll down the road of causality, which never leads to soul, and instead open ourselves to the thoughts, feelings, memories, and longings that are baked into sexual fear and regret. Sex then becomes a means of soul-making, a channel to the erotic caverns of the heart.

A few lines from a poem by Mary Mackey point to the difference between the soul's intimacy in sex—intimacy defined as "the most within," which happens to take the longest—and the quicksilver spirit of a passing sexual encounter:

> love comes from years
> of breathing
> skin to skin
> tangled in each other's dreams
> until each night
> weaves another thread
> in the same web
> of blood and sleep
>
> and I have only
> passed through you quickly
> like light

and you have only
surrounded me suddenly
like flame[10]

This is not to say that there can be no soul in a casual, quick sexual meeting, but that one way sex weaves people into soul is through the repetition, the mere sleeping and dreaming, and the years of breathing skin to skin. These are part of sex, and they are what give the soul its invisible threads of intimacy. Often, the poet says, we focus only on the light and the flame, wishing for the exceptional, overwhelming "experience," whereas the soul's need for sex may ask for a slender spider's web of connection and the steady weaving together of hearts and skin.

Sex has long roots that reach deep into the body's quick and far into the feelings of the heart. While sex is therefore tender and sensitive to invasion, it is also profoundly involved with the soul. Sex is the soul's limpid mirror, its litmus, and its gesture. Sex takes much of its emotional power from the vast amount of soul in its fantasies and in its touches. We can exploit sex, manipulate others with it, use it with fierce aggression, hide from it, misread it, and indulge excessively in it—these are merely means of struggling with its potential soulfulness. The soul of sex has the power to evoke relationship, to sustain it, and to make it worthwhile. As with all things of soul, we are asked to stand out of the way and be affected by its power to quicken life and to transform us from practical survivors into erotic poets of our own lives.

SHADOWS OF

INTIMACY

We are not very much to blame for our bad marriages. . . . In the worst-assorted connections there is ever some mixture of true marriage.

RALPH WALDO EMERSON

Chapter Nine

ENDINGS

THE ENDING of a relationship is as mysterious as its beginning. In the origins of a relationship fate often plays a dominant role, and as time goes on fate continues to give a relationship its twists and turns. Yet when a marriage or romance breaks up or when a friendship fades, we tend to look for rational causes and to blame one of the parties for committing the crime of ending. Fate and its important relationship to the soul are forgotten, and we take for ourselves both authorship and blame for developments that are clearly the work of the soul.

If we are going to honor the soul of a relationship, we will have to do so all the way, even, if necessary, through its ending. If we see soul seep into a relationship at the beginning through fate, we might watch it slip out fatefully at its end. Blaming the other party for the ending of a relationship is understandable as a way of avoiding the pain caused by the inexorable, sometimes heartless demands of fate, but by avoiding that pain we may condemn ourselves to years of being haunted by the very emotions and images we are attempting to escape.

A man once complained to me bitterly that his former wife was utterly selfish when she divorced him in order to be with someone else. He lived in his bitterness for years, as though waiting for his wife one day to admit her fault. It's especially easy to dodge fate when the partner has done something that has the slightest shadow in it. Yet after some conversation, it became clear that he, too, had felt the marriage to be an impossible burden. I asked him why he hadn't made any moves to leave a relationship that was obviously soulless and lifeless. "I kept hoping," he said, "that one day it would change." Fate demands receptivity of us, and yet receptivity is not the same as passivity. It takes courage to read the signals of fate asking for change, asking us to acquiesce to the bitter truths that are revealed slowly and painfully. An ending may be part of the special logic of relationship, an expression of its *logos*, its deeply inherent nature and its own laws and requirements.

The soul in a relationship is not only contained in each individual, it is also contained in the relationship itself. Blaming the other for the end of a relationship overlooks the soulfulness that has been crafted out of the original impulse of love. The bitterness surrounding the ending of a relationship may emerge from a great struggle of ego against fate, of personal will against impersonal factors. We may think that we want more than anything for a relationship to last, but the relationship itself usually signals its limitations, as the signs of old age signal death.

Part of the pain we feel at the close of a relationship is that it evokes memories of other endings, or the theme of ending itself. Understandably, we may be hesitant to enter those profound feelings that remind us of death in all its varieties. This is another way in which difficulty in a relationship can be only a particular instance of a problem that also appears in other aspects of life. I gave an example previously of a young doctor whose extreme jealousy made his marriage impossible, although there were strong signs that his jealousy was just one way in which a more fundamental failure of spirit made his whole life difficult, including his profession. In times of ending, it may be useful to consider one's own stories of ending in many areas of life, and see how this great challenge and mystery may be playing out in the relationship.

It isn't unusual for only one of the partners to see that a relationship is over. She may then go through terrifying struggle and aching decision-making to force a change that she would never have willed. The other may find it extremely difficult to acknowledge the same signs, or perhaps to bear the fatefulness, and a way out seems to be to blame the person who is causing the ending for being heartless and unfeeling.

"He isn't taking responsibility for his actions," a distraught woman told me once when her husband left her for another woman. It could appear that when a person sees fateful signs that a relationship simply isn't working out and moves toward a new life, this person is avoiding responsibility and is not showing any care for the partner. The issue is subtle: What is the difference between being responsible to the soul and being responsible to the relationship?

As we have seen earlier, our very idea of responsibility needs to be deepened. Etymologically, the word echoes ancient traditional rituals in which libations were poured in honor of a god or goddess. A common custom during special rituals or simply at dinner was to take a cup of good wine and spill it slowly onto the ground, to honor the god or spirit who was present. Imagine performing that ritual in our own personal ways, letting go of some of the emotion and desire we so cherish, in order to honor the spirit present in the ending.

In the deepest sense, to be responsible is to honor the mystery that lies at the very heart of every situation. Honoring the mystery may bring dishonor to the externals of a relationship and it may elicit the charge of irresponsibility, yet at a deeper level the action may be entirely responsible. This is so much the case that, as a therapist, whenever I hear someone complain about another's irresponsibility, I look for the mystery that is presenting itself as a frightening challenge to the offended one.

As with actual death, other kinds of endings may seem to come out of the blue and contradict all that we hold valuable and true. Death confounds us with its timing and its apparent disregard of human plans and hopes; the ending of a relationship may similarly throw us into endless wonder about its meaning. Plato said that a philosopher prepares for death by freeing the soul to contemplate eternal ideas. Perhaps we could prepare ourselves for fateful turns in a relationship, including its ending, by having a vision of it that is not limited to personal needs and concerns. Honoring the mystery in a relationship allows our willfulness about its shape and timing to be placed in a greater context, and we can give over some of our anxiety and effort.

It may happen that each person plays out a different side of a death in ending: one feels the call to move on, the other feels loss and abandonment. This is a condition that archetypal psychology calls a "split archetype": the reality has two sides, but instead of each person experiencing both, the two are divided between them. Unfortunately, soul disappears in this split arrangement, because then neither person feels the genuine tension that life has introduced. In fact, the split serves as a protection against feeling the necessities of fate and a greater will. In such a situation, it is useful to consider which piece of the mystery one has lost or has given over to the other. Taking on the whole is a way of regaining soul.

The most obvious sign of this kind of split is the habit one person may have of analyzing the other for signs of fault. One man I worked with, a psychiatrist, was convinced that the problems in his marriage stemmed from his wife's harsh, demanding, and emotionally cold father. He would begin telling me about his own feelings of depression, and then he would fade into the old familiar story of the father-in-law. His wife, according to this story, was oppressed from childhood, and he himself was depressed because his wife couldn't offer him a happy marriage. As long as he told this story, it seemed to me, he could overlook his own participation in the marriage, his own stories and emotions, his own role in the difficulties, and the opportunity for him to make some move out of the blockage.

There are many other ways, too, to maintain a divided relationship. For example, a son who considers his father too authoritarian may take up a life of total irresponsibility, thus keeping himself from a soulful life that would reflect the complexity of both responsibility and abandon. A daughter who hates her mother's interference in her life might go out of her way to be distant from her mother, and end up living her own life in utter detachment from other people. In times of endings, these old splits and longstanding open wounds often move to the forefront, accounting for painful and drawn-out separations and divorces, and rage and rancor for a long time after. The best advice for people who can't seem to end an unsatisfying relationship might be to stop waiting for something from the other person. Probably whatever it is will never come, and the dynamic of focusing attention on the other may be a way of keeping the soul at bay. It is not the other person that should be our focus, but the soul itself, with all its mysteries and initiatives.

We often assume that once two people have come together, they should never part; yet relationships are always ending, and people drift apart as naturally as they turn toward new connections. I'm not suggesting that we should simply be realistic and acknowledge the bitter truth that relationships end; the sense that they will go on forever is always a part of making new connections. But when they do end, we may have to face the dark and demanding will of the gods, which often goes against all human desire. We can take that lesson home and lodge it in our hearts— life is a constant interchange between human will and divine providence. We need both the courage to plan and create a life, and piety of the most profound kind in relation to the mysteries that undergird it. Each of us is asked to be at the same time existentialist and pious, responsible and responsive, practical and immensely imaginative.

A friend who has been close to me since childhood lost her husband to cancer several years ago. For a long while she was angry, and would tell me so in no uncertain terms, but over time she gradually fought her way into intimacy with providence. Struggling with the mysterious ways of fate may be the only path toward discovering that life is not a creation of our own will, but rather the crafting of a much greater will. There could be too much masochism in simply surrendering to fate, while in a fierce emotional struggle against it, a more loving acknowledgment of the divine may be achieved. Religion in the deepest sense takes shape as we learn through pain and loss that the creativity we exercise over our lives is finite, a mere participation in a greater creative act.

Loss of love and intimacy can be a profound form of initiation. Paradoxically, *initiation* means beginning, and yet the most powerful initiations always involve some sort of death. The renowned historian of religion Mircea Eliade describes the death experienced in rites of passage and initiation in this way:

> [D]eath signifies the surpassing of the profane, non-sanctified condition, the condition of the "natural man," ignorant of religion and blind to the spiritual. The mystery of initiation discloses to the neophyte, little by little, the true dimensions of existence; by introducing him to the sacred, the mystery obliges him to assume the responsibilities of a man. [1]

The idea that a relationship's ending is a form of initiation is not merely metaphorical. The pain in the breakup of a relationship is the pain of the neophyte being initiated into a new awareness. It is an arduous movement out of a pragmatic, self-reliant attitude and toward a religious sensibility, an awareness of ultimate dependence, and truly responsible living. One discovers again and again in such pain that responsibility is not a purely subjective, active position; it includes an acknowledgment of the mysterious factors that influence and structure life daily. Through these initiations, we move away from "natural" living, as Eliade would say, toward a sensitivity to the sacred. Through experiencing them fully, our very posture toward life can shift from secular ego-centeredness to a genuinely religious way of life.

I realize that friends and professionals sometimes urge those who suffer an ending in relationship to hold the other responsible, or tell them that they should move on in life, happy to be rid of such an irresponsible partner, but that hero's way of conquering the death of a relationship defends against the initiation that is offered. Eliade is more soulful because he addresses the theme of death in life from the point of view of religion. To sustain an ending—a soul death—without the defenses of blame, explanation, or resolution allows the soul to achieve the new level of existence that only initiation offers. In outer life, that achievement may even look like defeat, but to the soul, death experiences like these are the only way toward true beginnings.

Eliade's description of initiation is remarkable, suggesting that all endings are potential beginnings and that all beginnings carry the potential seeds of ending. The willful approach to life feels ending as a contradiction, but the soulful imagination, constructed out of many little initiations, looks from a different sense of time, recognizing that beginnings and endings enfold into one another in a mysterious way that can only be appreciated with a sensitivity to the sacred dimension of ordinary life.

Sometimes at the end of a relationship a person will think, "There is something wrong with me. I can't have a lasting relationship. Other people are happy together, while I'm doomed to loneliness." Certainly the feelings of depression and disillusionment that accompany an ending are appropriate, and if they are not taken personally and literally, there is even an element of truth in these reactions. The feeling of being inadequate may be a response to an awareness of new levels of relating and being, and there are times when we may need to feel inadequate. But to sink literally into those feelings could interfere with the initiation that is offered. Rather than say "I" am not able to be intimate—a narcissistic sentiment that goes nowhere—we might say, "My soul is asking more from me in relationship. I have the opportunity now to be close to another in a more profound way."

The only effective way to be initiated is to join the procession of initiates and to take on the costume of the dead. We have to enter the events, images, and feelings that make up the experience of ending. To resist those feelings is to excuse oneself from the rite. As religious traditions demonstrate, the soul benefits from an examination of conscience. There is nothing wrong with asking where I've gone wrong in a "failed" relationship. Trouble appears only when that examination is not honest or does not go deep enough. Then the examination turns into chronic self-pity and narcissistic self-judgment. The examination of conscience, a rite associated with initiation, has nothing to do with masochistic self-judgment; it is the soul's honest exploration of itself.

Endings are painful, and yet at the same time they may offer an indispensable way toward new levels of feeling and new areas of imagination. Renewal does not mean starting over where we were before: it is the discovery of a new beginning. Not only must we not split the one who effects an ending from the one who feels victim to that ending, we must also be careful not to split ending from beginning, and beginning from ending. The two go hand in hand, not only causally—we need an end in order to have a beginning—but paradoxically and emotionally: the pain of ending is of a piece with the exhilaration of beginning.

Going back to Eliade's observations on initiation, we can see that the ending of a relationship doesn't have to be read as literal failure, but can be seen vertically, as a means toward a new *level* of experience. That is the meaning of initiation, and that is why initiation rites around the world employ funereal imagery. We can only arrive at a new level of experience by means of a painful death in the soul, and what is more painful to the soul than the ending of a relationship?

If we resist the pain of ending, we skirt the opportunity for initiation. If we embrace the pain, not only do we find a beginning that is not simply a repetition of the experience we had in the former relationship, we may also find the consolation of knowing that in a mysterious way, effected by fate and not by human intention, the relationship has been fulfilled. In life it is a failure, but to the soul it has been brought to term successfully.

The word *divorce* doesn't mean "to end" or "terminate"; it means to turn away, to separate, or to be turned in different directions. *Divorce* and *diversion* are closely related, both coming from the Latin *divertere*. This etymology suggests that divorce is not a failure of the parties to maintain their commitments, but rather evidence of the tendency of fate to spin us in different directions. When our thoughts about endings are based on moralistic judgment, we create a culture filled with guilt, fantasies of impossible perfection, and the wrong kind of responsibility. When we are loaded with guilt, it is impossible to be truly responsible. If, on the other hand, our thoughts of ending were colored by genuine piety and an acknowledgment of life's centrifugal forces, then without overlooking the pain we might also see the wisdom in a relationship's ending.

Divorce is a word filled with opprobrium, while *diversion* is light to the point of irresponsibility. I recall a woman who once came to me filled with the desire for a divorce. The wife of a successful, wealthy corporate executive, she was tired of living as an adjunct to his professional life, and tired of his poor treatment of her. But even though she was driven by her desire for separation, her narrow sense of responsibility forbade her to take her strong feelings seriously. To her, wanting a divorce seemed like a mere diversion on her part. In comparison to her weighty marriage vows, her desire, in her own estimation, was light. In her conversations with me she seemed to be looking for a reason to separate that would give her feelings adequate weight.

Most of us have the tendency to look outside our own souls for the weightiness that might justify our feelings. The trouble is, the reasons we use to justify our actions keep soul out. If we could feel the seriousness of our own imagination, we wouldn't need rationalizations in order to make life decisions without guilt, and our decisions wouldn't feel so incomplete if we made them soulfully, granting authority to the intuitions and expressions that come to us from within.

The Future of Former Relationships

To OUTWARD APPEARANCES, endings are a structural matter—now there is a relationship, now there is no relationship. From the soul point of view, ending is a different experience of the relationship. Ending is not literal at all, but is rather a radical shift in imagination.

For example, a woman's father dies. In her soul the relationship may now intensify and may become the dominant myth shaping her other relationships, her career, and every other aspect of her life. Memories of her father may now become more vivid than ever, and new feelings may surface. He may be more influential in her life now than he was when he was alive.

A man divorces his wife, thinking that now his thoughts will turn toward a new life. Completely unexpectedly, he has dreams of her seducing him, suggesting that in some way "she" now has renewed desire for him. With the struggle of decision and separation now passed, feelings formerly nudged out of awareness come to the fore. Years later, he says what many people say: "I didn't have to go through that divorce. If I had known then what I know now . . ." Apparently there is something in every relationship that is eternal, that goes on forever, that wants to be exempted from the life decision to cut ties.

Obviously our relationships are not as simple or as limited in scope as we sometimes like to think them. There are only so many people we come to know in a lifetime, and an even smaller number with whom we live intimately. These relationships are all-important to the soul, whatever decisions we may make about them in the world. They initiate us into ourselves. They shape our lives, not only the story line of our biographies, but also the character of our souls. In life, change and forgetfulness may give the impression that relationships are temporary and conditioned by the events of time, but to the soul, remembrance and eternal connectedness are more important. The ending of a relationship may give the soul added emotion and attachment, not less. If we are going to live soulfully we have to respect these special preferences that lie deep in the heart.

In this respect it is important to honor the dead, especially those with whom we have had a close relationship. The soul is not limited in its experience to the confinements of life. Death doesn't erase a relationship, it simply places it in a different context. Fostering our relationships to the dead gives the soul its nourishment of eternity, melancholy, mystery, and the kind of relatedness that is not literally of this world. Many, many stories of the soul tell that it is not fully at home in this life and that it is always trying to break the bonds of this world's limitations. We can honor the soul by nurturing our relationships with the dead, whether by visiting and decorating their graves, by praying for them when their memories drift into mind, by naming our children after them, by preserving and using objects they've left behind, or by telling their stories and keeping photographs and paintings of them within sight.

Our ancestors give us something irreplaceable and precious in their relationship to us. They are truly our links with the eternal, and it is no wonder that many religions place emphasis on honoring them. We can learn from these rituals and practices to honor our own ancestors and our departed relatives and friends.

In one of the first therapy sessions I ever had as a patient, the therapist apparently suspected I had a father complex of some kind and began asking me about my father. Immediately my imagination went to my father's father, who died saving my life when I was four years old. As my memory of the accident grew clear, I felt overwhelmed with a profound sense of gratitude. For the first time I felt some of the weight and implications of my relationship with my grandfather. Tears flooded my eyes. The therapist was annoyed at my reaction because he was interested in a father complex. He told me to ignore the feelings I was having and get on to more important issues. Yet even today, when I remember that moment of awareness, strong feelings of gratitude rise again. I have an ongoing intimate relationship with my grandfather, feeling his life-breath in my own body and keeping a vivid memory of his gift of life to me.

One radical difference between care of the soul and a great deal of modern psychological work is that the former offers a profound appreciation for the personalities who are important in our lives, even if they are flawed people and even if the relationship is not perfect. Psychology prefers to analyze with the goal of increased understanding, yet understanding does little for the soul. Imagine telling stories of the dead, not for insight into ourselves, but simply to establish a deep, continuing relationship with them. The soul is given eternity in that exchange, while understanding offers it little more than another fragment of logic that has nothing to do with establishing a home for the infinite within our finite lives.

It isn't a question, anyway, of deciding whether we should or should not give attention to the dead. They present themselves to us in unsought memories, in dreams, and in momentary visitations during the day or night. They may appear in an event that hearkens back to a felt experience, or they may even inhabit our bodies: I see a piece of my grandfather in my daughter's face at certain moments, especially when she is finding some humor in a situation. I place my head on the pillow some nights, and a dear aunt fills my awareness, or my mother's parents. Whatever your metaphysics or theology, whatever your beliefs and expectations, such moments of visitation can be received by the heart without any need for mental interference.

The great mystery of death and what is beyond life also offers a constant challenge to our wish for understanding. While both science and some spiritual practices attempt to undo mystery, it is possible and utterly fruitful to give mystery a significant place in our lives. Who knows what kind of relationship with the dead is effective? Remaining in ignorance about the way these things work, still we can do much to cultivate that relationship. In our individual lives deep religious sensibility could arise from simple ways of remembering departed relatives and friends. Once again we can see relationship in service to the soul, rather than the other way around.

A modern way of making sense of former relationships is to learn from them not to make the same mistakes again, but this utilitarian approach has little soul in it, and in any case most of our own histories prove that we will continue to make similar mistakes. The point is not to learn from our supposed failures, but to be initiated into soul through them. By embracing the feelings that come at times of ending, as well as the thoughts and feelings that linger for a very long time afterward, we become renewed persons. The soul never learns, but it does metamorphose,

SoulMates

like worm to butterfly, to use Emerson's image. The soul makes these "ascensions of state," undergoes its initiations by means of life experiences, including relationships and their endings.

For many people, anger over the ending of a relationship becomes a barrier to initiation and renewal. They feel victimized by the other, and cannot find their way past that position. Many therapists encourage such clients to feel and express their anger and outrage. Modern psychology often deals with emotions in this way, emphasizing the experience and the expression of feelings as ends in themselves; but there may not be much soul in such simple self-expression.

Expression of anger may keep us in the realm of an interpersonal power play: set things right, don't be victimized, don't let the other person have the upper hand. Yet if we don't express anger, we seem to have no alternative but to repress it, and everyone knows that repressed anger is a dangerous commodity. A way out of this dilemma comes again from our ancestors in the Renaissance, who didn't talk about anger as such. They used the mythological image of Mars, the god of war and strife, as a great, transpersonal figure to give anger a much larger context. It's an axiom of the soul that material, whether it be emotion, thought, or fantasy, usually appears first in an unrefined condition. Our task is to cook this rawness, sometimes over a period of years, by means of reflection, experience, and experimentation to the point where it is sufficiently subtle to become an integral part of our personality and life. In itself, anger is not necessarily soulfully creative. We can use it like a commodity to protect our ignorance. But as raw material it can be the starting point, the seed, for an essential ingredient of soulful living imagined poetically as the Marsian spirit.

Renaissance philosophers taught that anger can be an invitation to Mars to constellate in one's soul. Tradition teaches that the presence of Mars can accomplish many things: whatever it touches it heats up, toughens and steels, and intensifies. Anger

can be expressed either purely as a reaction to events, or as a man-
ifestation of Mars who now has taken a home in the personality.
There is considerable difference in quality between these two
ways of expressing anger. The first is an explosion of emotion that
has no imagination in it, while the second is an expression of
Marsian qualities—firmness, forcefulness, intensity, clarity, and
focus.

The anger we feel in a relationship can be treated this way, neither defensively repressed nor simplistically expressed. Anger
may provide an opportunity to establish firmness and strength in
one's own character, and in that way, at least, prepare for a relationship that will be well grounded. Taking anger deep within,
making its qualities of strength and intensity a constant element
of character, a steeling of one's heart, constitutes a significant initiation of the soul, one that is necessary for an intimate relationship with another.

When relationships end, not only anger but other strong feelings may stir. At a deep level, our hopes for the future, our confidence in ourselves as persons, and our efforts to make a successful
life are shaken. We may feel overwhelmed with grief and despair.
The more difficult, soulful way to meet these feelings might be to
realize that our optimistic thoughts about the future and our own
self-confidence can "grow" only by being subjected to such on-
slaughts, and that these qualities in any case may not be as
grounded as we think. They may need deepening through the re-
consideration occasioned by failure. And we may need to acknowledge that the experience of grief and mourning is an essential part of the soul's life.

I would like to return to the idea explored earlier in this chapter, that the ending of a relationship can be recognized and experienced as a difficult rite of passage for the soul. In one ritual
that Mircea Eliade describes, a twelve-year-old boy is taken into
the bush and covered with blood. Later his skin is pierced and he
is given a new name. Then the boy is mourned by his clan as if he

had died. In the night forest he hears the sacred songs, while the next day his eyes are bandaged and his ears plugged. Whenever he walks, he is guided by an adult.

Eliade says of the young man undergoing this initiation, "He dies to childhood—that is, to ignorance and irresponsibility. That is why his family lament and weep for him: when he comes back from the forest he will be another; he will no longer be the child he was. As we have just seen, he will have undergone a series of initiatory ordeals which compel him to confront fear, suffering and torture, but which compel him above all to assume a new mode of being, that which is proper to an adult." [2]

Just as all initiations require an ending, all endings are an initiation. Just when we thought we were on the brink of a brilliant success, we may find ourselves in the uncultivated forest. We may sense loss and regression and may believe that time has been lost, that we are back where we started, behind others whose lives appear to be successful. We may feel blinded and deaf and may reach out to friends to comfort us and give us the least bit of guidance. We may feel drenched in the blood of emotion and raw feeling—tender, flayed, and pummeled.

I'm not suggesting that since our relationship has ended we must be childish and incapable. The most sophisticated and the most soulful person will be subjected to endings. No one ever reaches a point where he or she is immune to further movements of soul; the soul's capacity for richness is infinite. There is no end to the raw material that life and personality can provide.

It is important to realize that it is not the self that is initiated, but the soul. It is not really "I" who needs to grow up and hear the sacred songs that hold the secrets of adult life. My precious theories about relationship and certainty about my own capacity, my cockiness about being a worthy mate for someone, the control I may want to have over my own future, my ideas of what is or is not a healthy relationship—these and many other thoughts and fantasies may themselves need to be subjected to rites of passage before they can serve adult life and take their part in the sacred mysteries of intimacy. Eliade says that the neophyte is subjected to "revelations of the sacred, of death and of sexuality." An ending can be the opportunity to encounter life in its most elemental and awesome forms, including death and sexuality.

Seeing the ending of a relationship as an initiation of the soul has implications for psychotherapy. Frequently people enter therapy because of an impending breakup, or else in the wake of a divorce; often people consult a therapist in a futile attempt to prevent a relationship's ending. In each case, therapy could be re-envisioned as a way of helping a person experience the soul's initiation. In Eliade's account, the elders of the clan set up the rites and guide the young person through them, and they're careful to ensure that the neophyte experiences all the fear and trembling that come with it, knowing that the initiation can't be effective without such strong, "negative" emotions. A therapist could do something quite similar, helping a person stay within the emotions and images that accompany the ending of a relationship. Not only would the experience then be of great value to the soul, but the decision about what to do with the relationship or with the detritus of ending would be solidly founded in the soul. In the end, soul-work is much more effective for enriching our lives than the common "helpful" responses we make to endings—saving people from the pain, keeping a relationship alive at all costs, not falling victim to another person, understanding why it all happened, and so on.

I don't mean to suggest that we should just let endings happen because they're good for us. Obviously, that would be using another person for our own purposes. A true ending, not just a defensive withdrawal, comes about not only through decisions, but also with the spinning of fate and the turning of time. When deep attachment is set in place in a marriage, family, friendship, or community, it should not be let go of easily. We can rage against the ending and still enter its initiation. The words of Ficino on this point are strong, and as relevant today as in his time:

> Pythagoras asks that we not let a friend go lightly, for whatever reason. Instead, we should stay with a friend as long as we can, until we're compelled to abandon him completely against our will. It's a serious thing to toss away money, but to cast aside a person is even more serious. Nothing in human life is more rarely found, nothing more dearly possessed. No loss is more chilling or more dangerous than that of a friend.

The ending of a relationship is a time of difficult emotion, challenging fantasy, and vulnerability of the most "dangerous" kind, to use Ficino's word. It is also a crucial moment for the soul, an opportunity for either a new level of openness or a retreat into rigidity. If we could think of the soul, and not just of personalities or our own emotional protection, we might find that an ending is a door opening into an unknown and promising world. We could also discover that it is possible in an ending to dance with the rhythms and the lead of fate and not only survive, but enter an unknown world of unsurpassed vitality.

Chapter Ten

PATHOLOGIES OF LOVE

PATHOS IS one of those great words—like *logos, eros, dharma, tao,* and *esse*—that cannot be defined, pointing, like them, toward mysteries of infinite range and profundity. The ancient Greeks used the word *pathos* to denote emotion, felt experience, simply being affected, and even the impact of the divine upon human life. We find pathos in art, especially in music, as in Beethoven's soul-stirring sonata, the "Pathétique," and in Tchaikovsky's Symphony "Pathétique." It's a good idea to have these uses in mind when we consider a more recent, less aesthetic use of the word in medicine and in psychology: *pathology*.

Dictionaries define *pathos* as "suffering," but that definition is both limiting and misleading. When we feel the impact of life, as when someone close to us dies, when a powerful love strikes unexpectedly, or when a significant change occurs in our lives, we may call the impact of that experience "suffering," because it jolts us, disorients us, and causes the pain of not knowing what the future will bring. But from a less subjective point of view, pathos is the visitation of something angelic, fateful, or preternatural. It is both less personal and more constructive than the word *suffering* suggests.

If we were to take into account the ancient religious use of the word, we would have to describe a psychological *pathologist* as one who is concerned with disturbances of the soul owing to divine intrusion or philosophical trauma. In examining the pathologies that frequently accompany love, we might think of them as tremors associated with profound shifts of fate and reorderings of life and personality.

Pathologies of all kinds are usually disruptive and painful, but we have seen that they can also be viewed as opportunities for significant movements of soul. Even illness brings something of value to the soul and always, in spite of our efforts to find a cause in the temporal order, presents us with mysteries to contemplate and to face emotionally. Going to a hospital or to a doctor and seeing X-rays and watching blood drawn, one finds imagination going off in many directions, often with strong emotion. These experiences of pathos bring up memories from childhood and hopes and fears for the future. Of course, serious illness shakes the soul even more, offering it unusually fertile material for its rumination.

In a journal entry of 1975, Mircea Eliade connects the initiatory aspect of illness to the spiritual career of the shaman:

> [P]roblems linked to illness, such as psychic crises, but also pains of a physiological nature (fever, migraines, rheumatic pains) can be assumed to be just so many initiatory trials. Uncovering the religious significance of illness and physical pain constitutes in effect shamanism's essential contribution to the history of the spirit.[1]

Eliade's comments are both important and fertile. If the shaman is superior, it is because he or she has found a way to live profoundly in the sacred imagination, but the shaman can be seen as a model for each of us, who in our own small ways enter more deeply into the realm of soul through our illnesses. Further evidence of the connection between illness and the movement of the soul is also visible in the biographies of many of the medieval women Christian mystics, who often experienced strong physical symptoms, sometimes lasting for years, before entering an experience of divine love. (St. Teresa of Avila and Hildegard of Bingen are two of the best known of these women.)

It isn't difficult to make the move from physical illness to the maladies of love, and see that they, too, are an initiation into a spiritual condition that nourishes the soul. Tradition teaches that love is a daimon, a spirit, an angel, a trickster, an illness, or a madness, so it is not surprising that we often experience love pathologically. Love and attachment can breed such painful feelings as melancholy, jealousy, fear of separation, a special kind of loneliness, heartache, disillusionment, loss of affection, rage, insecurity, loss of identity, a sense of being smothered—the list goes on. The only surprise is that we are often surprised when love's dark edges come into view and that love rarely fits snugly into a calm and ordered life.

Insecurity

ONE OF the feelings that sometimes arrives with the establishment of intimacy is an unexpected emotional insecurity. I've known several people who have told a similar story. Once upon a time, when they were living alone as individuals, they were happy and carefree. They felt confident, content, independent, and secure. Then they fell in love, and suddenly security slipped away, to be replaced by an unfamiliar state of anxiety.

The insecurity accompanying intimacy may show itself in a morbid interest in the former relationships of the new partner. A physician once told me of his intense jealous thoughts concerning his wife, who apparently had had many intimate relationships before the marriage. He was acutely sensitive to any object in the house that might have something to do with a former lover. Masochistically he would ask her questions about these men, at some level delighting to find any new evidence of their intimacy, while at another level feeling excruciating pain at the thought. If she ever received mail or telephone calls from people he didn't know, immediately his thoughts turned to suspicion. In dreams, his wife would be in compromising situations with other men and his stomach would turn with jealousy.

In a different kind of dream he had one night, he noticed that his fly was open, and he zipped it up. Then a cousin of his, a timid man, came to talk to him. During the conversation he saw in a mirror that his fly was still open. His cousin told him that their grandfather had just died. "How sad," the dreamer said, "that he had to die without his wife being with him."

This brief dream, full of mysteries, led us to a conversation about mirrors, reflection, and self-consciousness. The physician was especially shaken by the idea that he couldn't do anything effective about his vulnerability—the open fly. I was concerned about the death of the grandfather, a signal, perhaps, of the loss of a deep source of fathering in his life, coupled with difficulty getting grandfather and grandmother together. All these themes, some of them suggesting that this issue had been around for a long time, suggested the need for a great deal of soul-work. I wondered in particular if he had to find a way other than narcissistic reflection (the mirror) in order to really see how exposed and vulnerable he was.

To me, the relentlessness of his thoughts and dreams suggested that the insecurity the man associated with his marriage had much deeper roots and broader implications, a more fundamental insecurity that would show itself in other areas of life as well. And in fact, though he was a successful young man, he was tentative and unsure about his position at the hospital where he worked. At times he felt overwhelmed by the responsibility he had for his patients, to the point that he considered giving up his profession. He told me that he had fantasies sometimes of driving a cab, a job that would have no worries or excessive responsibilities attached to it.

It seemed to me that an intense love had awakened and brought focus to this man's fundamental masochism and insecurity. He took his jealous thoughts and emotions literally, at face value— he believed he had made a mistake marrying a woman short on virtue—but other dreams he had of being attacked, wounded, and beaten, and other stories of his life characterized by diffidence and timidity, revealed that his obsession was more a matter of his soul's condition than his wife's prior history. His recent marriage was only amplifying a condition that already affected every aspect of his life.

One of the advantages of working with the soul rather than only attempting to find a "resolution" for the painful concerns of life is the opportunity it offers to get to the heart of matters, seeing through the issue as defined by the intellect. If the physician and I had focused only on his relationship with his wife, we might never have touched upon the deeper levels of his insecurity. Focusing on the literal details of his jealousy distracted and defended him against the deeper and broader issues. Going deeper, we were able to examine older and more basic patterns in which he lost his confidence and looked for easy ways out—becoming a cab driver was a myth he had lived out in many different ways, and in fact that very idea had occurred to him in other situations.

Intense feelings of love can bring the soul to the foreground, where, in the drama of marriage and separation, old patterns reveal themselves. In such circumstances, it is most helpful to remember that the soul always embraces more than immediate actual life, and covers a range of time exceeding the here and now of a disturbing problem. I imagine the soul as akin to Dante's tiered realm, where there are many levels of joy and suffering. A life problem, however acute it seems, may be giving us only a glimpse of a soul struggle. It's up to us then to use our imaginations in order to perceive further levels, and to care for the soul in its turmoil at a place where it counts. This is yet another way of applying Rilke's soulful and personally applicable cosmology: "All the worlds of the universe are plunging into the invisible as into their next-deepest reality." Dreams take the events of our lives into their next-deepest reality, and by stouthearted use of imagination we can do the same with our waking insecurities. We might remember in all of this that love is not only about the relationship between two people, it is an affair of the soul that embraces everything of importance to the soul, some of which may have nothing directly to do with the relationship.

I might also comment in passing on this man's acute sensitivity to things that stimulated his jealousy. His insecurity, as we narrowly call it, intensified his imagination so that the world itself came alive. It wouldn't be going too far to say that the world of objects became soulful through his jealous thoughts. They carried strong emotional tones and immediately gave rise to many stories and scenarios. I thought that this wakening of his fantasy life was important, because, at root, the man's insecurity was not a lack of confidence as much as a weakness of imagination. He didn't have the heart to enter the world with courage, because he couldn't imagine himself equal to it. He seemed to prefer hobbling along in life, giving most of his energy to self-analysis that always seemed arid and ineffective. The first step in our work together was to arrive at a point where we could both have a vivid sense of his paralysis, without letting it fade into stagnant analysis and despairing self-pity.

Love serves the soul, even in its jealousy, by making us crazy in one way or another. This craziness is simply the breakdown of our usual defenses. The physician I am describing sought a place of hiding in every aspect of his life, including his profession and his marriage. His jealousy, disruptive as it was, invited him to live in a larger world where he didn't have to be so suspicious and so afraid. Gradually, as he explored the deeper places in his own past and present where a failure in courage and in imagination was apparent, he found ways to open his heart. In living more fully in other areas of life, he also gained confidence in relation to his wife. His jealous thoughts were raw pieces of his own lost vibrancy. They only needed to be brought home and taken to heart, so that he could discover a more open, more transparent way of living. In so doing he began to risk more in all areas of his life, and in the face of this courage, over a considerable length of time, the jealousy disappeared.

When it is allowed to affect us to the point where we are changed, jealousy can give way to courage. The self-pity that often lies at the heart of jealousy involves a strong resistance against feeling one's own true inadequacies and failures. Once these are accepted as part of a fully rounded human life, courage, which can be kept out by adopting a false persona of strength, now has room to enter. Jealous people often engage in displays of rage and violence that betray their deep uncertainty. Through the initiation of jealousy, they may find an opportunity to develop an undefensive and grounded strength of character. In this regard, we might see the man's difficulty zipping his fly both as his symptom—the way he felt vulnerable was a painful issue he could not address effectively—and a clue to the soulful quality of vulnerability he needed in order to face his insecurity. One has to be unself-consciously exposed and vulnerable, transparent and "unzipped" in certain ways, before one can find genuine courage.

Issues of Power

A NOTHER KIND of pathology that can develop in an intimate relationship centers around issues of power. Slowly, quietly, and unintentionally, one person may take on authority while the other habitually submits to that authority, or in some cases, power is tossed back and forth between the people but is so polarized that one person is always dominant and the other submissive.

Every human relationship and interaction involves an exercise of power in which one person has some control over the other. We could make a microscopic analysis of a conversation between two people and graph the shifts in power. This power may be demonstrated as authority, strength of personality, emotion, articulateness, manipulation, guidance, knowledge, position—the possibilities are endless. The degree of dominance and submission also varies widely, so that in some interactions the imbalance may be very slight, while in others it is extreme.

In marriages, families, and friendships—wherever intimacy develops—we find that the fortunes of power are often difficult to detect and to deal with effectively. In my therapy practice I have heard many people describe themselves as a victim of someone else's power; yet after just a few conversations, sometimes after only a few sentences, it becomes apparent that the supposed victim is also flexing muscles of will and control. On the surface of a relationship it may seem clear who holds the power, but just beneath the surface may lie an inversion of that pattern. The more masochistic a person feels and behaves, the more hidden and therefore more destructive may be their sadism.

In an earlier book, *Dark Eros*, I have investigated sadomasochistic power relationships at length.[2] Here I will offer only a few recommendations for dealing with power. First, perhaps the most difficult lesson: know that problems with power are full of paradoxes. For instance, the person who feels victimized and powerless is likely to be the very person who needs to learn how to be vulnerable, open, and receptive to power without being literally destroyed. Getting stuck in one's powerlessness is a way of avoiding having power. In a person identifying with victimization, power doesn't go away; it is present instead in a raw form that appears as plain emotionalism or displays of anger and aggression, empty threats, scorn, curses, and so on.

The most ineffective reaction to problems of power imbalance is attempting a surface compensation. People who identify with the victim role may feel justified in responding with extreme manifestations of anger and aggression. Since these expressions show no sign of having been worked through in the soul and have little if any effect in the world, they simply make the situation worse. The person feels more and more powerless as his or her explosions of anger prove to be essentially impotent.

The remedy is difficult and paradoxical. People who feel victimized don't want to have anything to do with being vulnerable. They're afraid that they would be setting themselves up to be even more hurt. Yet the only solution is to enter more fully into soul and deepen both the feelings of vulnerability and those of power. Contrary to what may appear to be common sense, expressions of raw anger simply keep the situation divided. I would never recommend that a person express whatever anger they feel. Raw emotion has almost no access to soul. On the other hand, emotion *is* the raw material for grounded feeling. A person's anger is important—as important as plain food is to the body before it is broken down for assimilation. But anger, too, needs to be assimilated, as do all the emotions of victimization.

We have considered the problem of anger earlier, in the context of ending a relationship; but since it is such an important part of relationship in general, it seems useful to explore it further here, as a form of pathology. We have seen that when anger is broken down into more subtle feelings and fantasies, it can be assimilated in a number of ways: as firmness, strength, certainty, authority, self-knowledge, confidence, vision, and grounding. These refined versions of anger do have impact in life, and are drawn into the soul as elements of character—not momentary flashes of expression, but available resources. They connect to other aspects of soul: thought, imagination, values, and purpose.

Soulful anger is important for self-protection and for being effective in the world. James Hillman makes the point that anger lets us know what's wrong, and that if we repress it or ignore it, the world around us may in fact arrange itself in genuine opposition. In a more general way, this kind of anger, as tradition teaches, gives us an edge in all that we do. It provides forcefulness and vibrancy, the Marsian thrust of life placing us squarely and effectively in the world.

Like raw anger, feelings of victimization—so often split off from rage—also need cultivation and refinement, in the alchemical sense of ripening and becoming more sophisticated. The wish no longer to be victimized is as valuable a sentiment as plain anger. It points us in a necessary direction, but it would be a mistake to take that indication literally and identify oneself as a victim. Psychoanalysis recognizes identification as a form of defense, in this case defense against one's own Mars spirit. The plain feeling of being victimized has to be brought home, taken to heart, and transmuted into its more subtle forms of vulnerability, receptivity, and the capacity to be affected.

It takes courage and patience to perform the alchemy I am describing. It may seem easier simply to indulge in the plain emotions of justified rage or sympathy-getting victimization. We may have to discover that it's possible to be open to another person, to admit to our own mistakes and blindness, and to be dependent on others—all without loss of personal power and a feeling of strong identity. We may have to realize also that we can be forceful, individualistic, intense, single-minded, and even in some ways intolerant without loss of sensitivity.

In the best of circumstances and when the alchemy is obviously well along, it will be difficult to distinguish personal openness from personal confidence and strength. Each quality clearly allows and supports the other. Anger doesn't have to be reactionary, and being open to influence doesn't have to be associated with passivity and victimization.

Traditional societies that rely on images rather than concepts for their understanding of emotions have many advantages over us. Whether they refer to life's intensity as Mars, Hera, Kali, or as some other poetic figure, they have the means of embracing in their imagination the contradictions and paradoxes that are always present when such an important dimension of life is not split in two. We can learn from these traditions to do the same: to be more subtle in our ways of imagining feeling, to not divide life moralistically into various dualistic patterns, and to live everyday life with the wisdom that sees deeply into these matters, instead of translating them always into rationalistic categories. Our very ways of imagining anger and victimhood are both the problem and the remedy.

Obsessive Love

THE SOUL may hunger for attachment and love, but for one reason or another this longing may not be for something situated in ordinary life and therefore cannot be satisfied by ordinary relationships. As a result, people often become obsessed with a love that has an invisible object, or one that can't readily be brought into actual life. The soul's intense desire can find no place in life for adequate expression.

I once worked with a man who liked to call a telephone hot-line for counseling. He had fallen in love with the person he talked to regularly for a short time. For weeks she was constantly on his mind, and he talked about her at every opportunity. The rules of her counseling organization forbade her from seeing one of her clients in the flesh, but, given the mutual telephone attraction, the two decided to meet anyway. They quickly discovered that their telephone conversations were much more intoxicating than the dates they went on, and after a few weeks, the "relationship" ended.

I knew a woman who was an executive for a large corporation in the East. One day a man came along to apply for a job and swept her off her feet. They had a wonderful time together for two days, and then he went back home to the West Coast. They wrote to each other almost every day, and they piled up expensive long distance telephone bills. After about six months of intense passion at a distance, they came together once more. This time she visited him at his home, and by the end of the first day she was asking herself what she had seen in this man.

A third case: A therapist was deeply disturbed because she was insanely in love with a patient. When he first appeared in her office, she mentally labeled him psychopathic. He was a dark character, easily capable of physical abuse, completely uninterested in all the values she held dear; and yet she imagined herself running off into an exciting life with him. She couldn't talk to him about her feelings, because of their professional relationship, so whenever he showed up for an appointment, she kept her boiling emotions to herself.

One hears various responses to these kinds of erotic obsessions. It's easy for a friend or relative to become moralistic and warn the person about all the dangers and pitfalls in the situation, and usually, of course, a person is painfully aware of the danger in any case. But that awareness doesn't diminish the attraction.

Another response, a psychological one, would say that what you are really in love with is not the person, but qualities represented by the person. Take those qualities to yourself, this approach would say, and the obsession will be relieved. This is a version of what is known in therapeutic circles as "withdrawing projections." According to this theory, projection is an error in perception that can be corrected with the proper kind of insight.

What if we were to take obsessive attractions not as aberrations, but as pathos in the old sense: a passionate piece of life trying to break in? The fact that in the obsessive state we overlook "realistic" aspects of the object of desire and focus on sheer delight suggests that the loving eye sees something to which the cold eye of reality is blind. The improbable loved one is not simply a screen on which projections are cast; rather, the affected person has been nudged out of the circle of reason sufficiently to see an angel or demon embodied by the loved one. Soul, of course, is drawn to both.

From the soul point of view, it is disastrous to "withdraw the projection," since obviously the soul has a great hunger for the particular *mundus imaginalis*, the imaginal world, evoked by the loved figure. The soul needs to be united, not separated, in relation to that world, and this union can't be achieved simply by reducing a mysterious visitation of emotion and fantasy to certain abstract qualities. Human life doesn't operate on such simple principles. What, then, do we do, if we don't want to indulge or wallow in the overpowering emotions on the one hand, or extricate ourselves willfully from them on the other?

One possibility might be to live within the tension of the two extremes of indulgence and withdrawal. The movement toward indulgence keeps us within the dangerous waters of the soul's desire, while the movement away from them keeps us from acting out those desires literally and without imagination. Remaining in that tension, we might also bring imagination to bear by telling the story of the obsession over and over, allowing memories to be shaken loose, as well as ideas, images, and many other desires. The very quality of obsession suggests that the soul is doing what is needed to overcome frailty of imagination, and so our task is to bring imagination precisely where a static fantasy shows it to be missing.

The young man with the telephone romance could reflect for a long time on voices, for example, on the voice of his beloved, on the benefits of enjoying intimacy at a distance, on other figures of his imagination that stir his desire. He could view his attraction as reflecting a positive need of the soul, and not judge it negatively. It could be that what is finally achieved in this telephone romance is a deliteralizing of the man's imagination.

The woman who fell in love at first sight and continued the involvement through letters could reflect positively on the curious way her soul came to life. Relationship at a distance can do things for the heart that a closer, day-to-day companionship cannot. For one thing, as we have seen in some detail, letters offer an unusually fertile means for revealing one's deepest thoughts and feelings, articulating them with a degree of style and precision that conversation may not be able to achieve. This woman might also have had the opportunity to see how she had created ideal images of a lover cherished by her soul but not found in actual life. These images could hint at certain values important in her life that would otherwise be hidden and obscure.

Obsessive relationships take many forms, but in general they demonstrate once again how powerful are the stirrings and movements of the soul. When the soul comes to life, the ordinary wisdom of rational life goes into eclipse. In response, we may be tempted to force a rational conclusion, containment, or control, but none of these is effective in the end. Further repression simply increases the soul's pressure as it relentlessly nudges itself into life.

Faithfulness to the soul is the only approach that ultimately saves us from the oblivion of either a soulless existence or insanity. Our strongest emotions contain the pressure of the soul, as it asks us to wrestle with values that contradict reason but reflect the soul's evolution. Still, a soulful life is also full of pleasure and meaningfulness, although it may require of us a measure of unaccustomed eccentricity and irrationality as the price for a peaceful heart. And even a person who has made every accommodation to soulfulness can fall into these obsessions, because no one can predict the requirements of soul or limit his or her destiny. Some seem called to a life of intense struggle with their daimon—the confronting face of the soul—while others get by with relative serenity, each according to his or her fate.

Love's Retreat

THE WITHDRAWAL or absence of love is experienced deep within one's heart or life as a bitterly painful love malady. A person may feel unlovable, or may not have enough friends, or may be lonely, without desire, or impotent. Love gives life so much vitality, meaningfulness, and purpose that when it wanes, even if only temporarily, life can feel unbearably empty, and a person may be tempted to go to extreme measures to fill the resulting void.

We all feel the varying rhythms of sexual desire and the seasons in which we sense a need for companionship or a longing for solitude. It is tempting to ascribe these rhythms to physical causes, and explain sexual disinterest away as due to fatigue or illness. An alternative response is to follow an axiom of archetypal psychology: Stay with the symptom. If we feel variations in desire, then maybe the soul is simply displaying its own rhythms. When we experience these rhythms as problems—that is, when we're worried about being sexually inert or emotionally distant—we may need to enter more fully into these very states. Loss of desire need not be interpreted as a failure of ego or character, but rather as a removal of eros that from some mysterious soul point of view has its own purpose and value.

Most of us could learn to live more rhythmically. Medieval medicine drew a parallel between musical rhythms, the timing of the seasons, and the tonal variations of the soul. The soul has its own music that includes rhythms and tempos inherent in it and not to be explained by means of external causes. To continue the music analogy, there are also times of rest, like the metrical rests, the fermatas, and the pauses in music. When we feel a lessening of love, we could enter that feeling and perhaps discover the rhythms of our own soul—a worthy goal in itself. This may be a time when the soul necessarily quiets down in the areas of romance, desire, and sexuality in order to accomplish some other project for itself.

Even if there is something "wrong" during a period when love seems empty or absent, still the thing to do might be to enter the silence. In archetypal psychology we go with the symptom because it shows us exactly how the soul is expressing itself at the moment. Any other move comes from some clever place in the mind that would like to outsmart the soul and return life to a condition we judge "healthy." The *only* possible way that is in tune with the soul is in the direction of the symptom.

Loss of desire is part of the rhythm of desire, and failure in love is one of the ways we experience love. If we protect ourselves from the difficult emotions that accompany the retreat of love, we are shielding ourselves from the soul. Yet people often do just that: they hide from their painful feelings, not realizing that by doing so they disengage themselves from the soul; and then they find they have entered a circle that goes round and round, maybe even for years. When they feel the absence of love, they protect themselves by clutching at any handy substitute, and then they feel the loss even more poignantly. The process is painful and discouraging.

I have found as a therapist trying to be respectful of the soul that often the only thing I can do is speak on behalf of what is being presented at the moment. A person comes to me and says, "I can't stand it any longer. All my friends are married. They can all go to dinner together or go away for a weekend. I'm always alone. Help me find someone." If I see my role as fulfilling the stated wish of the client, then I would have to get on the crazed, spinning wheel of desperation with him or her. Instead, I typically stay away from the desperate moves and try to feel what it's like to be where the soul is: "I have no one in my life. I'm alone. I can't have the pleasures of living the married life. What is the lesson here? What do I have to discover before I can be relieved of my desperation?" This is the kind of reflection on feelings that helps create a sympathetic attitude toward them.

Running away from something is no way to find what is needed. To put it another way, defending against loneliness is no way to establish a relationship. We may have to befriend our loneliness and even our loveless life. Any other move goes contrary to what the soul is presenting. Besides, the "poor me" attitude in these expressions of lovelessness suggests a certain kind of narcissism, a whining for one's own wishes, while what is required in soul-work is a widening of heart and mind and an opening to fate. Narcissism is always a hint that we're not loving the soul in some essential way. It may be that we don't like the yin and yang of love and loss, and so we narcissistically moan and complain. But what the soul asks of us is a vision of human life sufficiently grand and profound as to embrace these contraries and appreciate their wisdom.

Numbness and Distance in Relationship

ONE DISTURBING experience that often overcomes people in relationship is the arrival not of searing emotional pain, obsession, or burning conflict, but of coldness, disinterest, distance, and a gradual numbing to feeling and connectedness. We have just seen how an individual might feel love draining out of his life. In a similar way people in families, marriages, and friendships sometimes experience an unexpected cooling, or a distance in the relationship itself that had never been there before. For all the emptiness that characterizes the onset of numbing, still this experience has its god—an archetypal, necessary, even productive source in the heart. The heart is not all warm and flowing; it has its frigid currents and its areas of ice.

One may never know why numbness comes over a relationship. If a relationship begins hot, we might expect it to remain at least warm, and it's tempting to ask what's wrong with our partner or with ourselves. But the problem may really be a mystery, an unfathomable shift in the soul that resists our understanding.

Whenever we imagine a relationship sentimentally as being good only when it is warm, we do a disservice to that element in the soul that wants coolness. For many centuries, medicine and philosophy placed faith in the doctrine of the four humors, one of which, the phlegmatic, was believed to be cold and moist by nature. We might learn from this ancient wisdom to give a place to the cool emotions and to cycles of coldness that visit a person or a relationship. We could understand the arrival of a cool emotional temperature as a phlegmatic phase in the relationship, and we could "ride" that emotion to wherever it is going to take us for whatever period of time.

A sometimes difficult yet important part of caring for the soul involves distinguishing carefully what is going on. It may take time, reflection, conversation, or even some form of therapy to discriminate the feelings and fantasies that are part of a cycle. Sometimes the emotion may be connected not only to the soul's own movement, but also to our reactions to that movement. A cold and distant air, different from the soul's own temperature, may develop as a quality of our relationship to the soul.

It is possible, for instance, to sedate the soul by strongly resisting its movement. Sometimes it appears that there is a standoff between us and the soul as it tries to offer us new possibilities that feel like too much of a challenge. This resistance to soul may be the work of one of the individuals in a relationship, or it could be a condition in the relationship itself. Couples, families, and communities may resist, as long as they can, some development in history, society, or their own interactions. A city neighborhood, for example, may have gone years without having to face the struggles of racial integration or a change in economic structures. The temptation might be to put off the challenge, to fear it internally without making any adjustments in life, or simply to bear anger at this intrusion into normal life. This standoff with fate may make life flat and spiritless.

Working against the soul in one area may numb our entire relationship to it, for the soul presents itself in particulars and yet the whole is present in each part. If our mate has suddenly decided to embark on a new career, we may be challenged to reimagine the entire relationship through that change, and resisting it may invite a general numbness and distance.

Living the soulful life is a constant challenge because life outside is always on the move, always shifting and changing, and internally, too, moods, fantasies, and thoughts are ever moving in new directions. We may prefer the family, the company, the marriage, or the children to remain as they always have been, but that preference has little to do with the mobile nature of the soul. It might be better to expect developments of all kinds, not just forward movements, but regressions and setbacks as well. If we don't enter the dance with the soul, we will likely feel the resulting alienation from our own deep source as a numbing to life and a flatness of experience.

Another way of imagining numbing in a relationship is to remember that as the soul moves in its cycles, we may sense the transition periods as empty and arid. For the moment there may be no focus and no clear theme. Relationships have their cycles, too, and their transitions may be difficult to live through because they feel cool.

When the cooling of feelings seems to be part of the natural soul rhythms, we could honor them and even take their lead as we cultivate our lives. For example, we could learn something about ourselves and about our partners and families by entertaining the thoughts and images that arise out of our cool moods. We could notice where the feelings take us in memory, thought, and fantasy. We could trust that these images contain insight into our situation and might help give us grounding in a time of confusion.

Couples who sense flat and cool moods descending on them might ask each other not why this is happening, but what it is asking of them. Entering into the numbness, they may find truths about their marriage and about themselves in marriage that cannot be seen from an active, enthusiastic life together. Numbness is a path, a rather perverse way toward a deeper and possibly more honest participation in life. And paradoxically, there is a special kind of fertility available in places that are allowed to be exquisitely emptied of former growth and productivity.

The arrival of a flat tonality in life can perform an important service to soul. By frustrating our attempts to live life as we imagine it best, the soul, so much more vast in perspective and potentiality, has a chance to insert itself. A flat mood, like a flattened piece of land, is something that can be built upon.

The pathologies of love do not necessarily work against relationship. They have a meaningful place, a job to do, and a color to add. They offer some of the most soulful moments in a relationship, as when marriage partners talk with real concern about the apparent cooling of their relationship, or when a family gathers together to reclaim a lost member, or when people turn to therapy for help in sorting through problems. If we could see our relationship problems as signs that the soul is trying to move, we might give them more positive attention, leaving behind attitudes of repair and mending, and our whole feeling about the relationship may remain loyal and attached, even when it seems to be in trouble.

Pathology is the voice of a god or goddess trying to get our attention. The Greek dictionary says that *pathos* means the opposite of "do"; it means "to have something done to you," and it is also the passive form of *poiein* or poetry. We are made poetry by our pathologies. Our lives are made into stories, and the most soulful moments may well feel unusually dramatic. Soul *is* the poetry of our lives, most strongly felt when the god is asking to be admitted. We are the stuff on which the soul's themes are imprinted. If our thinking is largely secular, we will think of love's pathologies as problems and assume that we're doing something wrong; but if we have a sense of the sacredness of relationship, then we might see the pathological moments as an opportunity for soul, as a visitation from eternity where relationship is seeded and at least in part crafted. Dealing with pathology in relationship requires enormous faith in ourselves, in the processes of soul, and in the person we love. We can be initiated and educated by moments of torment, if only we place a flower at its shrine, or spill some wine to honor that very place in our intimacy that has been painfully opened for our contemplation and attention.

PLEASURES OF
SOUL MATES

She loved nothing in the world except this woman's son, wanted him alive more than anybody, but hadn't the least bit of control over the predator that lived inside her. Totally taken over by her anaconda love, she had no self left, no fears, no wants, no intelligence that was her own.

TONI MORRISON

Chapter Eleven

THE SOULFUL RELATIONSHIP

BOTH IN TRADITIONAL teachings and in Jungian and archetypal psychology, certain qualities are regularly associated with
soulfulness. Soul is individual, vernacular, cyclic, eternal, partly
concerned with literal life and partly involved in its own inner
mysteries, concerned with poetics and nuances instead of explanation, and often raw and in need of an alchemy of refinement.
Considering these qualities one at a time, we can see how a relationship can be crafted into being soulful.

Individuality

WHILE SOUL is what allows us to make intimate connections and so create community—even a global and uni-
versal sense of shared life—it is also responsible for our most profound sense of individuality and uniqueness. These two—
community and individuality—go together. You can't have a
genuine community unless it consists of true individuals, and

you can't be an individual unless you are deeply involved in community.

As Heraclitus pointed out in an often quoted statement, because soul is so profound, its limits can never be fathomed. One ancient image of the soul—the night sky filled with planets and stars—portrays our subjectivity and interiority infinitely more accurately than all our twentieth-century images of the human being as a complex machine, an object of conditioning, or an ingenious arrangement of chemicals.

If we imagine ourselves as being every bit as huge, deep, mysterious, and awe-inspiring as the night sky, we might begin to appreciate how complicated we are as individuals, and how much of who we are is unknown not only to others but to ourselves. Our natures will always be largely uninterpretable. If we were only to stop interfering with this vast potentiality of soul, there would be no telling what we could achieve or how much life would flow through us.

Being an individual means allowing our innate soulfulness to find its way into our lives. Cicero, the first century B.C.E. Roman orator, said that you know a person best when you know the driving spirit that shapes the person's life. I would extend that observation to include not only the driving spirit, but also all the many manifestations of soul—moods, fantasies, memories, longings, passions, emotions, and fears. When you glimpse a person's soul, you see that person in ways they might not even know themselves.

The kind of individuality that soul generates is deeply rooted. It isn't the kind that is manufactured as a life project. It isn't the existentialist self made of choices or the psychologist's self fashioned by family influences. It isn't willed into existence, and it isn't shaped and sustained intentionally and consciously. It is a mysterious emergence that is seeded in eternity and is truly limitless. The power of this individuality is not forced but emanates from its own depth and inherent veracity.

When we give attention to our fantasies and longings, considering them seriously even when they contradict our conscious plans and preferences, and allowing them to influence the way we live, we are being creative in the soul sense of the word. We are allowing self-moving soul to generate our individuality and sculpt our lives. The identity that comes to light in this way resonates with the mysterious depths of ourselves that we will never fully fathom.

Our problem in relationships is how to have an ongoing, intimate life with another person at the same time as we invite this completely unpredictable depth to have a significant place in our lives. It isn't easy to live with the power and mystery of another's soulful personality. For one thing, you can't depend on what the person promises, since soul isn't willing to be chained to intentions or even to commitments. If the individual doesn't understand everything going on in the soul, how one can who is close, whose life is seriously wrapped up in the other, have even the remotest understanding?

The only solution to this problem I know is for both parties to respect soul, to acknowledge the mystery that is inescapably contained in the soulful life, and to come to treasure that very unpredictability. This may entail a radical shift in values. Ordinarily, without thinking about it, we honor commitments, promises, fidelities, and reliable habits. When these values are trespassed against, we become indignant and complain about a failure in relationship. If, on the other hand, we had a larger picture in mind and honored the tendency of the soul to move in mysterious ways, we might see that the unpredicted developments that come from the soul can have a positive effect on a relationship. They demand a great deal of adjustment and allowance, but they also offer continuous deepening of the connection and a grounding of the attachment in soul rather than in any one person's will. Besides, individual willfulness is usually laced with fear and manipulation, and is hardly solid ground for the building of intimacy.

Another aspect of a soulful relationship is the uniqueness of the relationship itself. Each relationship has its own soul which bestows upon the mutual connection many qualities of soul, including individuality. It doesn't tend to follow rules and expectations. It will have its own ups and downs, its own dangerous leanings toward dissolution, and its own bases for holding together. Isn't it shocking to see instances in which fate draws two entirely incompatible people together? Would you ever predict that certain couples could share a life? Isn't it surprising how seemingly incompatible people in a business or a project can argue and fight, and still produce outstanding results?

It's a simple thought: each relationship is unique. Yet to take this idea seriously could radically alter the way a person handles family, marriage, children, and friendship. We would toss away all generalizations and ideals, all expectations and comparisons. We could allow the other—parent, child, spouse, friend, neighbor, or lover—truly to be an individual, different from ourselves, and in that difference we could give our gift of intimacy. When we honor individuality, we are preparing a nest for the soul, an entryway. Norms, conventions, and traditional expectations serve some other interest and are foreign to soul's unique experiments. Soulfulness and individuality go together, one fortifying the other.

Vernacular Values

VERNACULAR means native, domestic, or indigenous. When I say that soul is always vernacular, I mean that it is located in some place—in one person's life, in a neighborhood or a region, in a specific culture or community. To say that the soul is vernacular is a variation on Hillman's statement that the soul is always connected to actual life, and to Jung's view that anima, or soul, is the archetype of life, or, as he says, it is "earth, nature, fertility, everything that flourishes under the damp light of the moon."[1] This "damp light of the moon" is in contrast to the dry light of the sun, or reason and classification.

According to Jung, a sense of meaning is a different archetype

altogether from the archetype of life. There is something important in us that craves meaning and order, change and transcendence. This work of finding meaning is not merely an act of conscious will and desire, but is profoundly rooted in the psyche. In
fact, to a great extent it is unconscious and self-directed. Sometimes Jung equates this love of meaning with the image of the
Old Wise Man, but there are many other ways of picturing this
archetype—Mercury's quick mind, Athena's wisdom, and Lao
Tzu's insightful meditations come to mind. For all the benefits of
the archetypal quest for meaning, the humid, lunar details of individual life are baked out of this path that favors the dry knowledge that is purposely extracted from experienced life.

Life as we find it is moist, in the sense that in itself it has no inherent dry meaningfulness. In the sixth century B.C.E. Heraclitus said that the soul takes pleasure in becoming moist. In the fifteenth century Ficino sorted the astrological planets according to
dry and moist, and named the most "wet" possibility the con-
junction of the moon and Venus. The moon is the "planet" closest
to earth, traditionally the channel through which all the others
pour their contributions. While not identical with earthly life—
it is a somewhat removed sublimation—yet it is a constant echo
of actual life as lived. And Venus, as Botticelli portrays her in the
Primavera, is the moist, florid, green lusciousness of life on earth.

To care for the soul's vernacular tastes in a relationship is first of
all to avoid making the person or the relationship abstract. Soul
doesn't retreat from the way things are, it inhabits these bodies
we have. Tracking the movements of the moon in his mystical
poem *"A Vision,"* W. B. Yeats says:

> All thought becomes an image and the soul
> Becomes a body.

We cultivate soulfulness in a relationship by honoring its vernacular life. We deal with the given relationship and forgo the indulgence of imagining something better or different. We respect

its style and its unfolding qualities. These vernacular qualities of family, marriage, or friendship may not appear in a flash, but may take years to be revealed. Only through time and experience do we discover the nature and styles of actual people.

Some people, of course, don't have the patience to get to know another over time. They want satisfaction immediately, and if they don't get it their thoughts are always off in the future or in an idealized world. One extremely creative man, an actor, once told me that he loved the woman he was living with, but in spite of his willingness to settle into that relationship, he found his imagination constantly conjuring up someone else. He seemed always to have one foot in an actual relationship and another in an idealized union, and he felt positively maddened by this unwanted split in his affections.

It's tempting in a case like this to become moralistic and try to convince the person to be realistic and grounded, but if we try to see value in both sides, we have to inquire into the desire of the soul for the person who is not present. In this particular case, my suspicion was that the split in affections had little to do with the relationship and everything to do with the man's approach to his own life. His imagination was not letting him settle down; it kept presenting him with new possibilities. His pain focused on a movement in his soul that went against his will: he willed settling, but his soul kept moving on. Eventually he found some measure of peace by taking more serious note of the signs he was seeing. He gave up, at least for the moment, his efforts to live a settled life, and instead cultivated a life of movement and change. He arranged his time so that he could travel to places he had always wanted to visit, and he told the woman he loved of his decision not to settle down, not to get married, and not to have a family. All of this rearranging was painful, and yet afterward he had the feeling of being more in tune with his heart.

While a relationship has its own unique culture, it may also have qualities that come from the vernacular in the more usual sense of the word. We might evoke soul by appreciating the traditional cultural elements people bring to each other. Obviously there may be difficulties in understanding among people of different religious, racial, and national heritage, but these differences also provide an extraordinary opportunity for soul. The union in a marriage or a friendship is not simply the togetherness of two people, it is also the mixing of their background qualities. People bring many valuable cultural gifts to a relationship: traditional rituals, old stories, ethnic food, icons, paintings, lace, and furniture.

Soul is not terribly moved by people living out ideals and principles. Even a healthy relationship is not necessarily a soulful one, but a relationship that cherishes the food of generations and of different cultural traditions may have an abundance of soul. If I were designing a weekend of renewal for couples, I would give much more importance to the concrete cultural, vernacular aspects of the relationship, including food and traditions, than to ideals and effective ways of loving.

At a family dinner the soul may be as hungry as the body. On a particular day in a particular place the soul may crave the vernacular tastes and colors of Italian pasta, or Indian curry, or a plain American hamburger. While the body takes in the foodstuff, the soul feeds on the cultural fantasies surrounding food. Some of that culture may be ethnic, while some of it may be connected to the styles, memories, and tastes of relationship.

As odd as it may sound, a relationship may find its soul more in attention to such things as the way we eat together or paint our bedroom ceiling than in mutual introspection. Soul is not necessarily nourished by what satisfies the mind. We have to give the soul what it needs, and those needs are generally vernacular. In my writing and speaking, when I borrow from poets and thinkers I make a point to emphasize American writers, and more specifically writers who have a relationship to my own neighborhood. I pass Emily Dickinson's house almost every day after dropping our children off at school. Emerson lectured in the towns around where I live, on similar subjects, and with the same problems of a self-employed, poetic-minded, independent scholar who was also a former cleric.

My good friends Alice O. Howell and Walter Andersen live in a cozy home in the Berkshires of western Massachusetts. Much of the color in their richly hued life comes from their affection for and attachment to Scotland. In their home you can listen to Celtic music not easily available, and hear traditional stories and personal anecdotes from their many travels in Scotland. Alice's books get much of their soulfulness from being set in Scotland and by unabashedly picturing the romance between her and her husband, who is in his eighties. All of this is exquisitely vernacular and is a lesson in crafting a relationship and a life work by honoring and appreciating the locales, personalities, and histories that fate has placed in our hands.

Here we see another example of how soul is *made*—recall John Keats's phrase "soul-making"—and doesn't grow on trees. A soulful relationship is not a simple gift; it asks for concentrated cultivation. Anyone can find vernacular sources of soul in the familiar world around them, but there is a spirit in our time that goes against the vernacular. It prefers the abstract, the general, and the numerically insignificant. This abstracting spirit trickles down to our relationships and shrinks the space necessary for soul. It is a philosophy that finds comfort in knowing what the majority feels and thinks. It's also a moralism that tells us, based on majority opinion, how to be in relationship. But to live a vernacular life and find vernacular intimacy, one has to go against the tide and cherish the things that call out to us in particular, whether or not they are valued by the culture around us.

A vernacular life is one that is intimate by nature: it is close to home, to the natural habitat, to family, and to one's own heart. It fosters the love and attachment the soul needs by presenting us with a world of particulars. If we're interested in living a life of attachment and desire, it helps to have bodies around, and the vernacular life is an embodied one. In the words of the philosopher Edward Casey, the soul's best habitat is not spatial, but "platial." Soul is not easy to find in infinite space, but it can always be discovered in a particular place.

Soul Cycles

YEARS AGO I received a birthday card that pictured in the style of Toulouse-Lautrec a beautiful and colorful bicycle. Across the bicycle was splashed the word CYCLES. To me the unusual card echoed images from India of the two great cycles of life, the eternal and the temporal—both suggested by the two wheels of the everyday, common-variety bicycle.

Sometimes we try to get along on a unicycle. Most people, I presume, choose the wheel of *samsara*—the spin of everyday life. Others choose the wheel of eternity and focus their attention on matters of the highest spirituality, sometimes not paying enough attention to daily life. It is best, perhaps, to recognize that life is a bicycle, a bi-cycle, the two wheels of temporality and eternity turning around endlessly, supporting us, keeping us in motion and upright.

A relationship, too, has its daily routines and its eternal cycles. When it is lived soulfully, both wheels are given value and honored. This is one good reason not to neglect the simple rituals that mark the most obvious cycles in a relationship—anniversaries, birthdays, and other revolving dates. Naturally, the cycles of the soul rotate also on less predictable timetables. There may be certain moods that come and go, or rhythms of closeness and distance. When we attend to the soul, we're aware that it doesn't move in a straight line. In discussions about their relationships, couples often bring up familiar themes, some of them going back years. These themes are signs of the relationship's soulfulness and may not indicate, as we sometimes think, unfinished business or unresolved issues. We may confuse the tendency of the soul toward "eternal return" with the failure to erase a theme by resolving a problem.

The eternal and cyclic nature of the soul also appears in the fantasies, memories, and emotional themes people bring to a relationship. They may have dreams, fears, and other feelings that are so deeply rooted in them that they talk about them as originating in childhood or even in their genes. These themes, which may come out in stories, memories, or strong emotional reactions, can be imagined as the particular motifs of an individual soul. In a relationship we can respect these themes as the stuff of the other's soul, and understand that they may appear with some regularity, under unwholesome guises at times, and that they will always need room for expression.

One such theme for me is an attraction to the countryside. I love farm lands and rolling hills and green woods. Once I took a friend through some of my favorite landscape in upstate New York, thinking that he would be as thrilled as I was. We were both living in Texas at the time, and I missed the special undulating contours and the particular hues of green that I knew in New York State. His reaction was disgust. For him the cultivated farms were a ravaging of primordial nature. He preferred the dry, red, rugged shapes of untouched Southwestern desert land. He couldn't wait to get away from the genteel farms of the north. I discovered on that journey how individual my most passionate loves could be, and how difficult to defend and to share.

My mother once said something in passing that rang out loudly and stuck with me. "It's that time you spent on the farm," she said. "That's why you like to live in the country." She was referring to the summers of my childhood when I lived for weeks and sometimes months on a farm with an aunt and uncles. As obvious as it was, I hadn't thought about those particular childhood experiences still affecting my desires and longings. On the other hand, memories of childhood are usually images of the soul's deeper yearnings. If that early experience remains strong in my heart, it must correspond somehow to a bucolic shading in my soul. Platonic memories go back beyond personal history.

In a marriage, one person may have to learn through close attention to the other's stories and emotional responses how important these ever-present longings and fantasies may be. To care for the soul, it may be necessary to make life decisions more on behalf of its cyclic patterns than for practical reasons, appreciating how much life they generate and what profound values they seed. In a friendship one may also have to respect differences in the other that are profoundly rooted in the soul, even though the friendship may seem to rest more on congruities and compatibilities. Focusing exclusively on life, we may give too much value to compatibility. Differences between people may give more to a friendship than what is held in common, precisely because the soul is so unique.

The soul's perspective on eternity is different from the spirit's. Spiritually we might imagine eternity as an infinite time. Or we might imagine a spiritual state in which time itself is transcended, such as the state of bliss in the Christian heaven, or of absorption in meditation in the East. The soul's eternity is closer to home. It is a way of being in the present, knowing that timeless issues, matters not directly caused and affected by temporal events, are in play. My relationship to farmland is eternal for me, and not fully explicable in temporal terms. It's full of mystery, and so it can only be honored, not understood; and yet it is clearly a significant part of my own life and personality.

Honoring the eternal elements in a relationship sets things in perspective. Arguments among people are often based on a personalization of the matters in dispute. Acknowledge their eternal dimensions, and it becomes apparent that taking everything personally is nothing more than a defense against mystery. On the positive side, when soul is given a place, the relationship receives a sacred grounding. We can relate to each other as persons even in the face of forces and issues that are difficult to deal with, maybe precisely because they come to us from outside.

I worked with a couple once whose marriage appeared to be on the verge of collapse. The woman had wakened one morning a couple of years earlier completely overwhelmed with the desire for a career in politics. She had shown no previous signs of wanting to enter such a demanding life, though she had been interested in local and national politics for years. Her husband reacted by judging her personally for the change that had come upon them.

"She feels no responsibility to the family, to our marriage," he said over and over again. "She just does what *she* wants. She knows this will destroy us, and yet she carries on. You can't reason with her."

What they both failed to face was the mysterious visitation of a powerful desire. The yearning for a public life is not something this woman invented. She didn't will it up from deep in her heart. In fact, as she told her husband many times, she didn't really want this new development, but she felt powerless to resist it. Many cultures other than ours have technologies and philosophies for dealing with such visitations, but we brand the arrival of these impersonal, eternal figures and spirits personal aberrations, and sometimes do all we can to get rid of them. Many of our psychological theories and medicines are apotropaic—designed to ward off perceived evil. We often judge incursions of the eternal too quickly, without giving them time to reveal their gifts and necessities.

A soulful relationship would approach the advent of a powerful spirit with respect. People in a marriage, or an entire family, could find ways to receive the spirit, at least for a period of time, so it could be discerned if the visitation were holy or unholy. Clearly, a receptive attitude would require significant adjustments on the part of those in the relationship, but that is exactly what a soulful connection asks—a sometimes extraordinary degree of adaptability and flexibility. It isn't easy, if it is possible at all, to banish an angel who has a mission. What we perceive as an intrusion into a comfortable phase of a relationship may be, from the angel's point of view, the opportunity for creative developments. Such turns and changes reveal the movement of life's cycles.

The Poetics of Intimacy

THE GREAT SIN of the age is literalism. People who profess religious belief in the surface, concrete meaning of a sacred text are called fundamentalists: they want nothing to do with nuances, multiple readings and interpretations, contexts, studies of texts, comparative studies, and other approaches that might distract them from the literal scripture. We find fundamentalism also in psychology, in theoretical systems that have only one explanation for human experience—whether genetic, conditioned, fated, traumatized, or determined by childhood or other factors. We can be literalistic in our relationships as well, and so I emphasize the importance of appreciating the poetics of our intimate connections and encounters.

In developing a poetic approach to relationship, we might first recognize that a person is a text of sorts, as are his or her stories, theories, ideas, memories, wishes, intentions—anything that a person expresses. Like any rich text, a person has many, many layers of meaning, most of them unknown even to himself. When a person expresses himself by saying "I love you" or "I hate you," we might realize, being sensitive to the personal poetry, that these and all other statements and professions of feeling are open to reflection, discussion, change, and emphasis. The poetics of a relationship are an aspect of its mystery: we never know fully the why's and wherefore's of our thoughts and emotions. Each relationship is so full of mystery that any discussion within it or about it must be provisional. We can always talk more next time, and we will inevitably find more in whatever it is we were talking about.

Sometimes people talk about parents and childhood as though this aspect of life alone could explain their adult behavior. The comparison of adult life to childhood can feed a poetic exploration of life richly, but it too often becomes a kind of fundamentalism. And while Jung can help us see archetypal and mythological themes in our lives, or his writings might lead us to a perception of the shadow qualities that are right under our nose, it would be antipoetic—fundamentalist—to lead a Jungian life.

One way to ensure a fully poetic appreciation for one's own life or that of another is never to exhaust the possible bases of comparison or the "causes" we imagine to be responsible for a person's character. For vivid and profound imagery we could turn to Shakespeare, Dante, Basho, Li Po, James Baldwin, Virginia Woolf, Joyce, Gertrude Stein, Stravinsky, Ingmar Bergman— the list is endless. We could find our life poetics in country music, jazz, Bach, rap, easy listening. By letting our imaginations be saturated with imagery that is moving, thought-provoking, instructive, and wise, we bring to our close relationships a mind and heart open to variety in human expression, individuality, eccentricity, pathos, joy, and the whole round of emotions.

Continuous exposure to the arts is one of the best ways to prepare ourselves for relationship, much better than relying entirely on the psychological in our approach to life. More important than the particular themes we find in the arts which may give us insight into relationship is the general education in poetic thinking and living that the arts provide. Through immersion in the arts, our reflection on life becomes larger, so that when we are confronted with the challenges of relationship we will have a rich imagination to bring to them and the ability to think poetically.

Alternatives to thinking poetically, besides fundamentalism, include: bias, prejudice, chauvinism, ethnocentricity, and a host of other dangerously limited points of view. If a man is having trouble with a woman and summarizes the problem by saying, "It's just like a woman," then the individual woman has been reduced to a category that is the object of prejudice. There is no imagination in such reductionistic moves that serve as defenses against the threat of individuality. But if we approach relationship with a fully engaged imagination, we will want to explore the contradictions and challenges of the individual.

Sometimes we limit relationship and lose the opportunity to quicken it with imagination by focusing excessively on personalities. Occasionally, when I am discussing ideas about soul with a group of people, someone will turn the conversation toward my personal life: "What do you believe, and how do you live your life?" a person will ask. I can appreciate an interest in individual experiences, but this kind of focus can take a discussion out of the fertile and complicated imagination of ideas and reduce it to the realm of personality.

When used as a power ploy, this reductionistic thinking is an example of the *ad hominem* argument, a logical fallacy described in classical philosophy. *Ad hominem* means that the discussion is directed "to the person" rather than to the ideas. I find this rule of logic violated frequently in discussions, as when a person will say, "You've never had the experience, so how can you talk about it?" or "You can only say that because you're a man." Sometimes when I'm talking about giving depression a place in life, a person will say, "Have you ever worked in the emergency room of a hospital?" There may be some truth in these questions, but their purpose is to win an argument, and so they turn the conversation away from an imaginative exploration of ideas.

Our culture puts a great deal of trust in facts, experiment, and experience, but all three of these can be dangerous to imagination if they are used one-dimensionally for their weight of proof rather than as a stimulus for discussion. One aspect of this cultural bias toward fact is our habit of treating relationships factually. As any marriage or family counselor will attest, discussions among people in intimate relationships often amount to little more than efforts to trump arguments with proofs or to win debates with logic. Relationships of all kinds suffer from this kind of intellectual combativeness, because the soul is nurtured and moved by poetics, not reason alone.

It might be better to treat a problem in a family as a poem than to deal with it as a psychological disorder. Family poetics might include stories told about parents and children, the roles each person plays in the dramas of the family, or certain expressions that have come to be identified with family members, such as "my talented daughter" and "my old-fashioned father." Once when I was teaching freshmen in college, I received a student's paper that began, "Meet my mother the mouth!" There was no lack of poetic resonance in that opening.

I was once in therapy with a woman who was not a "depth psychologist" but was extraordinarily good at seeing the poetry in the surfaces of life. One day as I followed her from her waiting room into her office I tripped on a rug, spilling awkwardly into the couch and ending up literally head over heels. Immediately she saw a major pattern in my way of living reflected in that single act of clumsiness. We talked for a long time about my tendency to follow someone too closely and become blind to my own way. I've never forgotten that good hour of therapy, another indication of its poetic substance.

We express ourselves poetically in our clothes, our language, our manner—in everything we do. If we gave more attention to these poetics in our relationships, allowing ourselves to discuss them with infinite patience, then the soul of the relationship would have a chance to appear more fully. That very appearance would enrich and ground the relationship, so much so that the sterile problem-solving that occupies so much time and attention might fade into the background. The soul is its own solution and its own reward. When we evoke soulfulness by thinking and living poetically, we are doing more for our intimate connections with people than any amount of analysis can achieve.

The Alchemy of Intimacy

O NE OF THE most fascinating aspects of the life of soul is that it starts out as raw material that can later be submitted to processes of refinement. We meet someone, start up a friendship, and then find ourselves in both the joys of intimacy and the morass of another person's soul stuff. The same is true of a job. On the first day, everything appears neat and bright. Prospects are high, the salary is all right, coworkers look ideal. Then, in a relatively short time, we may discover the swamp of the workplace. One person is moody, another bossy; affairs and enmities abound. Soul-work is usually a long process of taking the raw material life gives us, then making something out of it. The alchemists called the raw stuff *prima materia*. In one of Jung's books on alchemy he describes the rawness of the soul with graphic imagery:

> The prima materia is, as one can so aptly say in English, "tantalizing": it is cheap as dirt and can be had everywhere, only nobody knows it; it is as vague and evasive as the lapis that is to be produced from it; it has a "thousand names." And the worst thing is that without it the work cannot even be begun. . . . It is the most despised and rejected thing, "thrown out into the street," "cast on the dunghill," "found in filth."[2]

The phrases he quotes come from alchemical texts describing the *prima materia*. Raw soul is to be found everywhere—in the family that fate has given us, in friends new and old, in the first scintillating sign of attraction to another person. It's cheap, ubiquitous, and is often considered trite and insignificant. The truth is, the whole world and all of life are nothing but the raw materials for soul-making.

This idea has many implications for relationship. Intimacy doesn't appear ready-made, it must be refined into something truly valuable. We may have an intuition early in a friendship or romance that the possibilities are promising, but still what is given is rough and unshaped. The joy of life consists in taking its ubiquitous raw material and making sparkling gems and intricate tapestries out of it. We find this mystery in the story of the Cochiti girl who married Coyote. Her practice of making clothes is an image for the practice we can all engage in: cultivating the raw material life gives us in abundance, and making that cultivation part of our relationships. Since our daily work is one way to engage the opus of the soul, relationships we have on the job are particularly important. Family relationships are also obvious raw material, begging for refinement, even if it takes more than a lifetime to accomplish it. Many of us have to reach a certain age before we begin to see family with fresh eyes and find a new richness in that utterly fundamental relationship.

We might expect, too, that, because of all the raw material that is present, relationships are going to have some difficulties in the beginning. Emotions may be strong but aimless and confusing, separated from the fantasy and thought that would give them content. It might be especially difficult to be intimate in our youth, when we haven't had much experience in the refinement of soul, although of course there are many exceptions: young people—like John Keats—who are adept at discovering the secrets of the soul's alchemy, or elders who seem never to learn. The youthfulness that inhibits soulful refinement is archetypal, anyway—not tied to any literal age.

If we could understand this fundamental intuition about the soul, that it is given raw, then we might forgive ourselves and others for not being quick to handle relationships with grace. We might see that many problems are not due to one person's maliciousness but to the law that soul stuff is given in unrefined lumps and requires a long process of sorting, shaping, refining, and even transmuting—all operations of the tradition of alchemy. A relationship problem may be like the piece of marble Michelangelo confronted with his hammer and chisel: the inner figure waiting to be sculpted out is not easy to perceive and is certainly invisible except to a poetic eye.

In therapy I've talked more than once with intelligent people who can't lower themselves to own up to the kinds of situations and feelings that everyone gets stuck in. A highly educated woman told me that even though she felt victimized by her husband's affair, she constantly disowned that awareness by telling her friends, "I can handle it, everything's under control, I'm prepared for this." My sense was that her soul-work would remain stuck until she could take this common piece of "filth" home with her as her own given raw material. "I'm a feminist," she said. "I can't admit that I'm victimized by my husband's waywardness." We all have high moral positions that keep us from taking soul's *prima materia* into hand, getting dirtied by it, and eventually finding that it is sculptor's clay. One of the many paradoxes about soul-making is that its reward is the most valuable and unique a person could ever have, and yet its raw material is often the most despised and common.

Whether in family, friendship, or marriage, we would do well to remember these ancient secrets, for intimacy is an invitation to be drawn into the thick soup of soul—a familiar feeling to most who have ventured deeply into relationship. Soul is more likely to feel heavy, thick, gray, and pasty than light and airy. It may reveal no glimmer of meaning or direction. In a relationship we may feel soiled by the common thoughts, paltry emotions, and vulgar situations it conjures up, but it does no good to try to be above all this dirt, for this is the stuff of soul—our common humanity, in which hides the jewels of our individualities and our intimacies.

Soulful intimacy is not to be found in clean, well-structured, meaningful, unperturbed, ideal unions, if such a union even exists. Perfection may well appeal to the mind, or to the part of us that craves spiritual transcendence, but soul doesn't establish a home there. For some perverse reason, it prefers the colors of feeling, the tones of mood, the aberrations of fantasy, and the shades of disillusionment. Although these vagaries of the soulful life may be disturbing and painful, there may be some consolation in knowing that, like a compost heap, they are fertile and promise a rich future.

I wouldn't want to be misunderstood on this point: living a soulful life, staying with the "muck of it," as Samuel Beckett would say, is not a clever, paradoxical way to achieve the goals we have been pursuing in many other directions and with other methods. Soul usually thwarts the ego at every step. Its rewards may not coincide with the goals we intentionally choose. I am offering no step-by-step path to soulful relating: every relationship is unique, and we never know ahead of time the destined goal for any intimate tie. Living soulfully requires that we allow hope, faith, and love to be open-ended; we do not know what to hope for, may not believe in any particular thing, and will love whatever it is we receive. Soul also embraces the shadow sides of these "virtues," so that it is important to experience despair, to sink into doubt, and even to fight sometimes against the presentations of fate.

Perhaps the best solution is to embrace the paradox, to fight to the last, and at the same time to recognize and honor the divine providence that makes us mortal. The issue is similar to the one raised by W. B. Yeats where he confesses to a lifelong struggle with the very daimon that accounts for his creative output. Like death, this daimon is an adversary, whom no amount of effortful psychological "integrating" is going to subdue. Struggle is the nature of the relationship with such adversaries, and it could be that much of what we perceive as struggle in relationship is a distant echo of this profound, creative engagement with the other that takes place at the level of soul.

As sweet as it sometimes sounds, care of the soul is a radical departure from modern notions of living correctly and successfully—at all levels: moral, theological, psychological, social. The same could be said of soulful relationships: they are not necessarily the healthy ones, the successful ones, or the peaceful ones.

Soul, by reason of its vast dimensions and its mysteries, injects life and relationship with reasons and movements that go against much of what is felt to be good, intelligent, and prudent. On the other hand, the soulful relationship is not willfully perverse, either; it has qualities of the paradoxical and unexpected. And eventually we may perceive a subtle vein of wisdom and benevolent providence in all its twists and turns, it agonies and ecstasies, even while a satisfying rational understanding may well prove to be eternally elusive.

We are left with a different kind of participation: not a controlling one, not a reasoning one, not an idealizing one. Fate brings the soulful relationship into existence, then its profound implications unfold, as we watch, enter into it with imagination, and glimpse its unique spirit. Over five hundred years ago Nicholas Cusanus, a theologian and philosopher, asked us to look at all experience as a paradox of *implicatio* and *explicatio*, weaving and unweaving, enfolding and unfolding, or, like Penelope, weaving a shroud by day and unraveling it by night. It isn't enough to say, as some do, that as persons in relationship we are always caught in the dilemma of being coupled and uncoupled. Relationship has deeper ties. Life itself, like a loom's shuttle, is always moving back and forth. Strong feelings of dissolution in a relationship, or of dissatisfaction, thoughts of getting out, the sense that it's all over, may be distant hints of a far deeper pattern entering and going out of our lives.

Soulful intimacy asks that we imagine our family connections, our friendships, and our coupled loves as having cosmic proportions. This grand viewpoint takes nothing away from interpersonal value and emotion; in fact, it grounds these feelings and makes them even more solid. If a relationship were a defense against the mystery of life that lies at the core of each of us, against destiny and fate, then it wouldn't have much of a chance. If our commitments and expectations, or our anger and frustration, were means of trying to control the ever-moving soul of another person or group of persons, then these would not be sacred vows but rather narcissistic defenses.

In the final paradox, if we want to light the fires of intimacy we have to honor the soul of the other. A relationship demands not that we surrender to another person, but that we acknowledge a soul in which the parties are mingled and respect its unpredictable demands. All of these paradoxes keep the mind spinning and the heart superficially insecure yet deeply trusting. Our intimacies reach out and preserve the world around us, so that our interpersonal movements toward union, grounded as they are in deep threads of soul that reach far beyond human persons, keep the world itself from falling apart.

Relationship as Grace

WHEN WE shift our attention from the mechanics and structures of a relationship to its soul, a number of changes occur. We no longer have to carry the weight of guilt about not having done relationship properly, we can give ourselves a pardon for having engaged in folly in our younger days, we can feel the sting of endings without bearing a neurotic degree of responsibility, and we can enjoy the pleasures that a lifetime of relationships has given us. We can end the impossible quest for the perfect structure—the happy family, the completely satisfying marriage, the unbroken friendship. We can find some purpose in the failures, the intimacies that never got off the ground, the possibilities that never took flesh. The soul does not share the spirit's love of perfection and wholeness, but finds value in fragmentation, incompleteness, and unfulfilled promise.

I'm not saying that being soulful allows us to excuse ourselves, deny, avoid, dissemble, and exploit; following the lead of soul we become more responsive, not less, to those whom fate places in our lives. But when we forgo taking on exaggerated responsibility for mistakes in relating, we are able to feel those errors and misjudgments more fully, and to become people of wisdom, sensitivity, and perspicacity. Guilt blunts sensitivity, it doesn't sharpen it. Only by fully embracing the shadows of love and closeness can we be capable of any genuine union of souls.

Relationship is not a project, it is a grace. The difference between these two is infinite, and since our culture prefers to make everything in life a project, to be accomplished with effort and understanding, to be judged pure failure when it doesn't arrive at an expected conclusion, it is not easy for us to treat intimacy as a grace.

Though we try to be expert at life projects, we are not used to dealing artfully with grace. Responding to the grace of relationship, it is important to appreciate, to give thanks, to honor, to celebrate, to tend, and to observe. We can't complain absolutely when that grace is taken away. We feel the pain, but that is not the same as berating ourselves for failed opportunities. Berating is a way of avoiding pain and love's corresponding initiation.

The soul of relationship is not goal-minded, nor is it any one narrow, clearly defined entity. A friendship may not have to endure throughout life in order to leave its eternal mark on the soul. A marriage may not have to live up to its promises of lasting a lifetime in order to generate an eternal union. A family may be riddled with betrayal and misunderstanding, and still offer the soul the cradle it craves. A partnership in work or business may dissolve and yet continue to feed each of the members with gifts of remembrance.

The soul of a relationship doesn't ask for the "right" ways of acting; it wants something even more difficult—respect for its autonomy and mystery. The soulful relationship asks to be honored for what it is, not for what we wish it could be. It has little to do with our intentions, expectations, and moral requirements. It has the potential to lead us into the mysteries that expand our hearts and transform our thoughts, but it can't do that when our primary interest is in pursuing our cherished ideologies of love, family, marriage, and community. The point in a relationship is not to make us feel good, but to lead us into a profound alchemy of soul that reveals to us many of the pathways and openings that are the geography of our own destiny and potentiality.

Ultimately, relationship brings us to the brink of the ultimate family and the absolute lover, who is nameless and indescribable. We get a taste of this eternal love when we experience an ending and glimpse the deep darkness of death that lies in it. Personally, I know it in the mixed feelings that rush upon me in a moment with my daughter, when I'm feeling the bliss of her presence, and at the same moment and because of that bliss I fear for her safety and hope never to lose her.

Relationship is not only about the people who interact with each other. It is a vehicle as well to the absolute factors that shape human life fundamentally. Every relationship that touches the soul leads us into a dialogue with eternity, so that, even though we may think our strong emotions focus on the people around us, we are being set face to face with divinity itself, however we understand or speak that mystery. The Sufi woman poet Rabi'ah bent Ka'b says:

> Love
> an ocean
> with invisible
> shores,
>   with
> no shores.
> If you
> are wise
> you will
> not swim
> in it.[1]

Few have such prudence that they avoid love, and of course it is in our folly that we allow ourselves to be drawn into all kinds of loves, there to be transformed through the acids of love's chemistries into lovers. Love is an alchemical process in which we are the material to be transmuted. And all love invokes one or another divinity who gives love its fathomless depth.

A relationship to the divine is part, in fact the culminating piece, of this discussion of love and loss, friendship and loneliness. Relationship to the divine, hardly discussed in these days of personalism and secularism, satisfies the soul in ways that no substitute can touch. We may well be preoccupied with the theme of interpersonal relationship precisely because we are stuck in a shallow pool of love, unable to arrive at the mystic's view in which the divine is the only satisfying lover, the only true soul mate.

What is divinity? What is the nature of this ultimate relationship? He who speaks, the *Tao te Ching* says, does not know. It can't be spelled out in so many words. Many religions teach us that this ultimate intimacy is not separable or even distinct from our day-to-day relationships in family, marriage, community, and friendship. Yet it is a dimension that may be missing if we are closed off to its presence. We could turn to the religions of the world, a vast source of poetry, confession, prayer, and ritual, to be instructed in this dimension of relationship, but ultimately we will find this divine undercurrent in all our relationships in our own unique way. For some it may appear in a moment of ecstasy, for others in a time of torment. It may take the form of utterly satisfying community, or it may appear in a quiet moment of solitude when, with Emily Dickinson, we discover that the hills are our most true friends.

Knowing that relationship has this divine strain, we may be free to enjoy its human elements more fully. We won't be distracted by imperfections in our partners or families. We won't demand that relationship play itself out according to our expectations and ideologies. We won't have to control every inch of the way amid anxiety and judgment. We may even discover that by being kind to others we can learn to be kind to ourselves—a virtue lacking in a time of far-reaching psychological moralism.

Caring for the soul in our relationships, and through them, we can enjoy them both practically and mystically, and with genuine tolerance for individuality in others, in the relationship itself, and in ourselves. We can let unplanned developments happen, allow people to change, tolerate our own idiosyncratic needs and cravings, and enjoy and appreciate a community of individuals who may think differently than we do, live oddly, and express themselves none too rationally. For this is what relationship is about: the discovery of the multitude of ways soul is incarnated in this world.

Every relationship, from the intense closeness of parent and child or partners in marriage to the more distant connections with coworkers and business acquaintances or even the driver of the bus we take daily to work, is an entanglement of souls. The gift in this entanglement is not only intimacy between persons, but also a revelation of soul itself, along with the invitation to enter more deeply into its mysteries. What better expresses the point of human life than engagement with this soul—with its manifest and hidden qualities, its mysterious alchemies and transformative pieties? If we can find the whole world in a grain of sand, we can also find the soul itself at the small point in life where destinies cross and hearts intermingle.

Notes

CHAPTER ONE

1. Text of poem from Richard B. Sewall, *The Life of Emily Dickinson* (New York: Farrar, Straus & Giroux, 1974), p. 434.

2. All references to Samuel Beckett are from the biography *Samuel Beckett* by Deirdre Bair (New York: Harcourt Brace Jovanovich, 1978).

3. James Hillman, "Peaks and Vales." In *Puer Papers*, James Hillman, ed. (Irving, Tex.: Spring Publications, 1979), p. 66.

4. This distinction between soul and spirit is difficult to appreciate in our day, when spirit is usually given a religious meaning. Hillman uses the word the way medieval and Renaissance philosophers used it: as a dimension of human experience that is vertical, tending toward abstraction, development, evolution, and transcendence. Spirit and soul are absolutely necessary to human life, but they are

not identical. In our day it seems easier to honor spirit and more difficult to respect the soul.

5.   In my book on sadomasochism, *Dark Eros: The Imagination of Sadism* (Dallas: Spring Publications, 1991), I explore in some detail the connection between bonding and bondage. There I use the term *sadomasochism* not to refer to a clinical disorder but rather to the power issues that are at work in every human encounter. Rarely, if ever, is there a perfect balance of vulnerability and strength in our interactions. Almost always it is possible to detect some element of surrender or even wounding on one side, and an attempt to be victorious on the other.

   The idea of symptoms pointing in the direction of the soul's need I have taken from the general theories of James Hillman and from an article on the theme by Patricia Berry, "Defense and Telos in Dreams," *Spring: An Annual of Archetypal Psychology and Jungian Thought* (1975), pp. 115–127.

6.   Norman O. Brown, "Daphne, or Metamorphosis," in *Myths, Dreams, and Religion*, Joseph Campbell, ed. (New York: E. P. Dutton & Co. Inc., 1970), pp. 91–110.

7.   Teresa of Avila, *The Interior Castle*, trans. Kieran Kavanaugh, O.C.D., and Otilio Rodriguez, O.C.D. (New York: Paulist Press, 1979), p. 59.

8.   W. B. Yeats, *"Per Amica Silentia Lunae"* in *Mythologies* (New York: Collier Books, 1959), p. 335.

CHAPTER TWO

1.   C. G. Jung, "Marriage as a Psychological Relationship," trans. R. F. C. Hull, *Collected Works*, vol. 17, Bollingen Series XX (Princeton: Princeton University Press, 1954), § 330. One way to deal with this problem of assuming that everyone has the same psychological "structure" is to become more aware of individuality among people in general. Uniqueness is one of the signs of soul, and so the more we know about the soul, the more we will appreciate the uniqueness of the person with whom we are intimate.

2.   C. G. Jung, *Letters*, vol. 2, Gerhard Adler with Aniela Jaffé, eds.,

trans. R. F. C. Hull, Bollingen Series XCV:1 (Princeton: Princeton University Press, 1973), p. 27.

3. Paul Tillich, "You Are Accepted," in *The Shaking of the Foundations* (New York: Charles Scribner's Sons, 1948), pp. 158, 159, 161.

CHAPTER THREE

1. *American Indian Myths and Legends*, Richard Erdoes and Alfonso Ortiz, eds. (New York: Pantheon Books, 1984), pp. 308–312.

2. R. B. Onians, *The Origins of European Thought* (Cambridge: Cambridge University Press, 1988). Onians gives a great deal of information on ancient beliefs about the soul, genius, and daimon. For our purposes, we might note that although all three are closely related, each has a particular emphasis: daimon suggests mysterious guidance and help; genius is more the indwelling spirit giving personality and vitality—along with the important ingredient of procreation; soul is the receiver of these spiritual gifts.

CHAPTER FOUR

1. C. G. Jung, *The Structure and Dynamics of the Psyche*, trans. R. F. C. Hull, *Collected Works*, vol. 8, 2nd edition, Bollingen Series XX (Princeton: Princeton University Press, 1969), § 336.

2. Black Elk, *The Sacred Pipe*, Joseph Epes Brown, ed. (New York: Penguin Books, 1953), pp. 102–103.

3. Quoted in Raphael Patai, *The Hebrew Goddess* (New York: Avon Books, 1978), p. 145.

CHAPTER FIVE

1. Paul Oskar Kristeller, *The Philosophy of Marsilio Ficino*, trans. Virginia Conant (Gloucester, Mass.: Peter Smith, 1964). I take this description from Kristeller's authoritative work on Ficino.

2. Emily Dickinson, *Selected Letters* (Cambridge, Mass.: Harvard University Press, Belknap Press, 1986), p. 302.

3. Richard B. Sewall, *The Life of Emily Dickinson* (New York: Farrar, Straus & Giroux, 1980), p. 617. This whole passage from the Sewall biography is worth reading for its insight into the special phi-

losophy of friendship espoused by the reclusive and socially sensitive Emily Dickinson.

4. Angela Livingstone, *Salomé: Her Life and Work* (Mt. Kisco, N.Y.: Moyer Bell Limited, 1984), p. 121.

5. James Hillman, *On Paranoia* (Dallas: Spring Publications, 1988), p. 53.

6. Marsilio Ficino, *The Letters of Marsilio Ficino*, vol. 2, trans. Language Department of the School of Economic Science, London (London: Shepheard-Walwyn, 1978), pp. 51–52.

7. Ivan Illich, *Tools for Conviviality* (New York: Harper & Row, 1973). While I take the idea of conviviality from Ficino, Illich's analysis of culture in the light of conviviality is extremely useful and practical. He defines "conviviality" as "autonomous and creative intercourse among persons, and the intercourse of persons with their environment; and this in contrast with the conditioned response of persons to the demands made upon them by others, and by a man-made environment" (p. 11).

8. Ralph Waldo Emerson, "Self-Reliance," in *The Portable Emerson*, new edition, Carl Bode and Malcolm Cowley, eds. (New York: Penguin Books, 1981), p. 149.

CHAPTER SIX

1. Richard Ellmann, *Oscar Wilde* (New York: Alfred A. Knopf, 1988), p. 314.

2. *Emily Dickinson: Selected Letters*. Thomas H. Johnson, ed. (Cambridge: Harvard University Press, Belknap Press, 1986), p. 189.

3. J. Hillis Miller, "Thomas Hardy, Jacques Derrida, and the 'Dislocation of Souls,'" in *Taking Chances: Derrida, Psychoanalysis and Literature*, Joseph H. Smith and William Kerrigan, eds. (Baltimore: Johns Hopkins University Press, 1984), pp. 135–145. Miller makes a point about letters that is beautifully and intriguingly expressed: "Writing is a dislocation in the sense that it moves the soul itself of the writer, as well as of the recipient, beyond or outside of itself, over there, somewhere else. Far from being a form of communication, the writing of a letter dispossesses both the

writer and the receiver of themselves. Writing creates a new phantom written self and a phantom receiver of that writing. There is correspondence all right, but it is between two entirely phantasmagorical or fantastic persons, ghosts raised by the hand that writes" (p. 136).

4. Marsilio Ficino, *Letters*, vol. 2, p. 20.
5. Marsilio Ficino, *Letters*, vol. 1, p. 71.
6. Marcel Proust, *Selected Letters, 1880–1903*, Philip Kolb, ed., trans. Ralph Manheim (New York: Doubleday and Company, Inc., 1983), p. 272.
7. *Leave the Letters Till We're Dead: The Letters of Virginia Woolf*, vol. 6: 1936–1941, Nigel Nicholson and Joanne Trautmann, eds. (London: The Hogarth Press, 1980), p. 163.
8. Johnson, *op. cit.*, p. 330.

CHAPTER SEVEN

1. Marsilio Ficino, *Commentary on Plato's Symposium on Love*, trans. Sears Jayne (Dallas: Spring Publications, 1985), p. 54.
2. David L. Miller, *Gods and Games: Toward a Theology of Play* (New York: Harper & Row, 1973), p. 168.
3. David L. Miller, *Three Faces of God: Traces of the Trinity in Literature and Life* (Philadelphia: Fortress Press, 1986), p. 44.
4. Arthur Rimbaud, *Illuminations and Other Prose Poems*, trans. Louise Varèse, revised edition (New York: New Directions, 1957), p. 75.

CHAPTER EIGHT

1. A renowned scholar of Greek religion, Walter Burkert, makes a comment that shows how sometimes very small reactions to life in our day echo rituals of the past: "We have the word of Diodorus that Priapos Ithyphallos played a role in nearly all the mysteries, though it was 'with laughter and a playful mood' that he was introduced." Burkert, *Ancient Mystery Cults* (Cambridge, Mass.: Harvard University Press, 1987), p. 104.
2. Wallace Stevens, *Opus Posthumous*, revised edition, Milton J. Bates, ed. (New York: Alfred A. Knopf, 1989), p. 192.

3. Norman O. Brown, *Love's Body* (New York: Vintage Books, 1966), p. 252.

4. Anne Carson, *Eros the Bittersweet* (Princeton: Princeton University Press, 1986), p. 11.

5. Karl Kerényi, *Dionysos: Archetypal Image of Indestructible Life*, trans. Ralph Manheim, Bollingen Series LXV.2 (Princeton: Princeton University Press, 1976), pp. 365–366.

6. James Hillman, *The Myth of Analysis: Three Essays in Archetypal Psychology* (New York: Harper & Row, 1972), p. 91.

7. Joseph Campbell, *The Hero With a Thousand Faces*, Bollingen Series XVII (New York: Pantheon Books, 1949), p. 58.

8. I am considering pornography here as erotic imagery. Often it also involves violence, sadomasochism, scatology, and other generally offensive kinds of imagery. These darker areas I discuss as expressions of soul in my book *Dark Eros*.

9. C. G. Jung, *The Development of Personality*, trans. R. F. C. Hull, *Collected Works*, vol. 17, Bollingen Series XX (Princeton: Princeton University Press, 1954), § 123.

10. Mary Mackey, "The Kama Sutra of Kindness, Position No. 2," in *Deep Down: The New Sensual Writing by Women*, Laura Chester, ed. (Boston and London: Faber and Faber, 1989), p. 258.

CHAPTER NINE

1. Mircea Eliade, *Myths, Dreams, and Mysteries*, trans. Philip Mairet (New York: Harper & Row, 1960), p. 200.

2. *Ibid.*, p. 196.

CHAPTER TEN

1. Mircea Eliade, *Journal III 1970–1978*, trans. Teresa Lavender Fagan (Chicago: The University of Chicago Press, 1989), p. 211.

2. Thomas Moore, *Dark Eros*. Among other things, I point out the devastating shadow sides of innocence and victimization.

CHAPTER ELEVEN

1. C. G. Jung, *Mysterium Coniunctionis*, trans. R. F. C. Hull, *Collected*

Works, vol. 14, Bollingen Series XX (Princeton: Princeton University Press, 1963), § 646.

2. C. G. Jung, *Alchemical Studies*, trans. R. F. C. Hull, *Collected Works*, vol. 13, Bollingen Series XX (Princeton: Princeton University Press, 1967), § 209.

EPILOGUE

1. Rabi'ah bent Ka'b, "The Wild Horse," in *The Drunken Universe*, translated by Peter Lamborn Wilson and Nasrollah Pourjavady (Grand Rapids: Phanes Press, 1987), p. 64.